Willa Cather: Queering America

BETWEEN MEN ~ BETWEEN WOMEN
Lesbian and Gay Studies

Lillian Faderman and Larry Gross, Editors

Willa Cather   *Queering America*

Marilee Lindemann

COLUMBIA UNIVERSITY PRESS

NEW YORK

COLUMBIA UNIVERSITY PRESS
Publishers Since 1893
New York   Chichester, West Sussex

Library of Congress Cataloging-in-Publication Data
Lindemann, Marilee.
    Willa Cather: queering America / Marilee Lindemann.
      p. cm. — (Between men—between women)
    Includes bibliographical references (p.171) and index.
    ISBN 0–231–11324–2 (cloth : alk. paper). — ISBN 0–231–11325–0
(pbk. : alk. paper)
      1. Cather, Willa, 1873–1947—Criticism and interpretation.
    2. Homosexuality and literature—United States—History—20th century.
    3. Feminism and literature—United States—History—20th century.
    4. Women and literature—United States—History—20th century.
    5. Lesbians—United States—Intellectual life. 6. Love-letters—History and
criticism. I. Title. II. Series.
    PS3505.A87Z724 1999
    813'.52—dc21   98–29688

Casebound editions of Columbia University Press books are
printed on permanent and durable acid-free paper.
Printed in the United States of America
c 10 9 8 7 6 5 4 3 2 1
p 10 9 8 7 6 5 4 3 2 1

For Martha,
and in memory of my father

Where there is great love there are always miracles.
—Willa Cather, *Death Comes for the Archbishop*

One realizes that human relationships are the tragic necessity of human life; that they can never be wholly satisfactory, that every ego is half the time greedily seeking them, and half the time pulling away from them.
—Willa Cather, "Katherine Mansfield"

Contents

Note on Texts and List of Abbreviations

The University of Nebraska Press is currently producing a series of scholarly editions of the works of Willa Cather, but at this writing (1998) the most accessible (and yet generally reliable) texts are commercial paperbacks. In cases where multiple options are available, I have chosen versions whose editorial apparatuses make them particularly useful. Citations to Cather's letters are made in the endnotes.

Cather's Writings

AB   *Alexander's Bridge*. 1912; Oxford and New York: Oxford UP, 1997.

ALL   *A Lost Lady*. 1923; New York: Vintage, 1990.

CS   *Collected Stories*. New York: Vintage, 1992.

DCA   *Death Comes for the Archbishop*. 1927; New York: Vintage, 1990.

KA   *The Kingdom of Art: Willa Cather's First Principles and Critical Statements, 1893–1896*. Ed. Bernice Slote. Lincoln: U of Nebraska P, 1966.

LG   *Lucy Gayheart*. 1935; New York: Vintage, 1976.

MÁ   *My Ántonia*. 1918, rev. 1926; New York: Penguin, 1994.

MME   *My Mortal Enemy*. 1926; New York: Vintage, 1954.

NUF   *Not Under Forty*. New York: Knopf, 1936.

OO   *One of Ours*. 1922; New York: Vintage, 1971.

OP   *O Pioneers!* Boston: Houghton Mifflin, 1913.

OW   *Willa Cather on Writing*. 1949; Lincoln and London: U of Nebraska P, 1988.

PH   *The Professor's House*. 1925; New York: Vintage, 1990.

SL   *The Song of the Lark.* 1915, rev. 1932; Boston: Houghton Mifflin, 1983.

SSG   *Sapphira and the Slave Girl.* 1940; New York: Vintage, 1975.

WP   *The World and the Parish: Willa Cather's Articles and Reviews, 1893–1902.* 2 vols. Ed. William M. Curtin. Lincoln: U of Nebraska P, 1970.

Secondary Sources

CHAL   *The Cambridge History of American Literature.* 4 vols. Eds. William P. Trent, John Erskine, Stuart P. Sherman, and Carl Van Doren. New York: Putnam, 1917–21.

EV   Sharon O'Brien. *Willa Cather: The Emerging Voice.* New York: Oxford UP, 1987.

LL   James Woodress. *Willa Cather: A Literary Life.* Lincoln and London: U of Nebraska P, 1987.

SCAL   D. H. Lawrence. *Studies in Classic American Literature.* 1923; New York: Penguin, 1977.

SOJ   *The Best Stories of Sarah Orne Jewett.* Ed. Willa Cather. 2 vols. Boston: Houghton Mifflin, 1925.

Acknowledgments

"Blessed are they that teach," Jesus ought to have noted in the beatitudes, and I have been richly blessed in brilliant and generous teachers. My thanks go first and especially to Susan Gubar, who awakened me, and Catharine Stimpson, who civilized me, but also to Alice Crozier, Sandra Gilbert, Myra Jehlen, Alicia Ostriker, Barry Qualls, and Elaine Showalter. I feel a debt to that courageous, visionary first generation of feminist scholars that can never be repaid. I have also benefited immensely, though from a distance, from the ground-breaking and equally courageous work of scholars in the field(s) of lesbian/gay/queer studies, who have inspired, taught, and challenged me in recent years. Those debts are more specifically acknowledged in my endnotes.

For hands-on assistance with this project, among Cather scholars I am grateful to Sharon O'Brien, whose reading of a very early draft helped me figure out what it needed to become, and Ann Romines, who gave me an opportunity to test some of the ideas as they developed. Robert K. Martin's and Deborah Carlin's readings of the manuscript at a late stage bolstered my confidence in what the study had become and helped polish the final version. Ann Miller of Columbia University Press was enthusiastic, supportive, and quick when it counted. Thanks also to Alexander Thorp and Anne McCoy for squiring the manuscript through the process of publication with efficiency and patience and to Susan Heath for editing out my mistakes and laughing at my jokes. Of many valued colleagues and students at the University of Maryland, I should thank for individual gifts of friendship and intellectual exchange Linda Kauffman, Katie King, Sangeeta Ray, and Brian Richardson. Robert Levine has been wise, kind, and constructively critical. He worked mightily to make sure that my queer literary history was rigorous and fair.

Any remaining gratuitous slams at Hawthorne are my fault, not his. Special thanks are also due to the survivors of my graduate Cather seminar in the spring of 1997, who patiently bore with my obsessions and helped me to realize that Cather's "contesting" of "America" was in fact a "queering."

For research and travel support, I gratefully acknowledge grants or fellowships from the National Endowment for the Humanities, the American Association of University Women, the Woodrow Wilson National Fellowship Foundation, and the General Research Board at the University of Maryland. For allowing me to consult their holdings of Cather letters and memorabilia, I am indebted to the Willa Cather Historical Center, Red Cloud, Nebraska; the Clifton Waller Barrett Library, University of Virginia; the Houghton Library, Harvard University; the Lilly Library, Indiana University; the William R. Perkins Library, Duke University; and the Harry Ransom Humanities Research Center, University of Texas.

Thanks also to my extended cybernetic, telephonic, therapeutic support network, including Debra Burns, Lisa Honaker, William Malloy, Maria Merkling, my siblings, Margaret Beatty and the Takoma Park t'ai chi players, and Paula Schuster. I am also grateful to the girls in my 'hood, for their various gifts of reading, feeding, walking, community-building, laptop-sharing, and for sending me to the beach to write. They teach me daily that a queer world begins at home. My mother, Patricia Brown Lindemann, was my first English teacher. She taught me not to waste words and to embrace risk. I know, therefore, that she will find some way to explain and brag about my scholarly preoccupations to her friends. To my great sorrow, my father, Welman Louis Lindemann, did not live to see this book, but his faith in me helped to produce it. He also deserves credit for the recurring allusions to Julie Andrews.

Finally and always, my greatest debt is to Martha Nell Smith—partner, cowgirl, comrade-in-everything—whose good sense, easy laughter, and rugged love help me to know there's magic in the night.

Willa Cather: Queering America

Introduction

The Novelist, the Critic, and the "Queer"

We would do well to construct queer theory, then, less as the site of what we communally want than as the want of any communal site. Queer theory is no one's safe harbor for the holidays; it should offer no image of home. . . . What, then, can one say of queer theory to those who are gathered to attend to its state? Reinvent it. Resist it. Refuse it. Pursue it. Get over it. Just do it.

> —Lee Edelman, "Queer Theory"

This time, when Thea left Moonstone to go back to Chicago, she went alone. As the train pulled out, she looked back at her mother and father and Thor. They were calm and cheerful; they did not know, they did not understand. Something pulled in her—and broke. She cried all the way to Denver, and that night, in her berth, she kept sobbing and waking herself. But when the sun rose in the morning, she was far away. It was all behind her, and she knew that she would never cry like that again. People live through such pain only once; pain comes again, but it finds a tougher surface. Thea remembered how she had gone away the first time, with what confidence in everything, and what pitiful ignorance. Such a silly! She felt resentful toward that stupid, good-natured child. How much older she was now, and how much harder! She was going away to fight, and she was going away forever.

> —Willa Cather, *The Song of the Lark*

Willa Cather was not a Queer Nationalist, and neither am I. She might have been a Queer theorist, but I don't claim that lofty title for myself. Indeed, I didn't think I was even a Queer critic—merely a practicing lesbian whose work as a feminist critic occasionally attended to sex as well as gender—until I began searching for a way to frame a study of Willa Cather's entanglements in the social and literary histories of the United States in the first quarter of the twentieth century. Slowly but surely, certain ideas I had—about Cather's wranglings with sex and gender; race, ethnicity, and nationhood; literary nationalism and the culture wars of the 1920s—began to coalesce and converge in the image of her "queering" "America."

But what, really, do I mean by "queering" "America," and why do I wish to insist that Nebraska's first lady of letters—with her starched shirt-waists and her lifelong loyalty to the Republican party—participated in such a dubious-sounding venture? It would seem more logical and more, as it were, straightforward to enlist Cather's audacious contemporary Gertrude Stein into the cause of queering America. She, after all, wrote stories celebrating women who were "every day regularly gay" and has sel-dom been described as homophobic or misogynistic. And why, moreover, do I wish to affiliate Cather and myself with a contemporary critical and political project whose trendiness cannot mask its significant limitations and liabilities?[1] Part of the point in conjoining the terms "queer" and "America" as a way of rethinking Cather is cultural and historical: both terms achieved new salience and ideological power in the same moment, as historians of sexuality and U.S. culture have demonstrated, and that "moment"—from the 1890s to the 1920s—coincides with Cather's sexual and literary coming-of-age. During this period "queer" became a way of marking the differences between the still emerging categories of "homosexuality" and "heterosexuality," and the word acquired a sexual connotation it had lacked in nearly four hundred years of usage, according to the *OED*,[2] though its new meaning was a fluid one.

George Chauncey, for example, in his study of the gay male subcultures that developed in New York City between 1890 and 1940, reports that "queer" (as an adjective) was one of the terms "most commonly used by 'queer' and 'normal' people alike to refer to 'homosexuals' before World War II" (*Gay New York* 14).[3] Chauncey also notes that in the 1910s and 1920s, "queer" was not a derogatory term and that it was preferred, partic-ularly in the middle-class culture of Greenwich Village (where Cather lived from 1906 to 1927), by men who did not see their homosexuality as con-nected to any abnormality in their gender persona, which, in their minds, distinguished them from the effeminate "fairy" whose flamboyant style was so visible on the streets of New York. The "queers" were, according to Chauncey, the sexual assimilationists of an earlier era, eager to distinguish themselves from both "fairies" and "normal" men but also devoted to middle-class values of "privacy, self-restraint, and lack of self-disclosure" (99–106).[4] "Queer" was in some instances, however, a crossover term that applied to lesbians as well as male homosexuals and a term that to some clearly signified the kind of gender slippage Chauncey attributes to "fairies." A headline from a Broadway gossip sheet of 1932 shows the ambiguity of "queer" and also indicates the immense popularity of the drag balls of the 1920s and early 1930s: "6000 Crowd Huge Hall as Queer Men and Women Dance" (cited in Chauncey, *Gay New York* 310).[5] The expatriate writer Natalie Barney, in her unpublished autobiography, also offers evidence that some women of Cather's generation and inclination self-identified as queer. Barney, who was born in 1876, three years after Cather, writes of being pressured by a family friend who confronted her with rumors of scandalous sexual exploits that had reached her parents:

> When the family friend set out again, having fulfilled his "painful duty" and I found myself alone, I considered myself without shame: albinos aren't reproached for having pink eyes and whitish hair, why should they hold it against me for being a lesbian? It's a question of nature: *my queerness isn't a vice,* isn't "deliberate," and harms no one. What do I care, after all, if they vilify or judge me according to their prejudices?   (quoted in Chalon 47, emphasis added)[6]

As "queer" was sexualized, "America" was even more radically desta-bilized as the nation careered into the twentieth—often designated the "American"—century. The battle to authorize and claim custody of the word "America" was waged on many fronts and persisted for many years. Alan Trachtenberg examines the "controversy and struggle" that swirled around the word in light of the massive structural and economic trans-formations that occurred between the Civil War and World War I, a process of redistribution of wealth and reorganization of society that he terms "the incorporation of America." For Trachtenberg, the meaning of "America" is precisely what is at stake in arguments that raged between populists and elitists over the pace of industrialization, the rise of the robber barons and the financiers, and the increasing standardization and mechanization of American life. For Ann Douglas and Walter Benn Michaels, who focus on the later part of the period, "America" in the 1920s signals on the one hand "an intoxicating and irresistible identity windswept into coherence by the momentum of destiny" (Douglas 3) and on the other hand the nativist anxieties of a culture that, with the passage of restrictive immigration laws after World War I, defined itself largely through its difference from the foreign, the "un-American," transforming "Americanness" from an identity rooted in political allegiance to one connected instead to a racial and cultural inheritance, "from an achievement into a heritage" (Michaels 140–41, 35).

Both "queer" and "America" were, then, sites of contestation, up for grabs in the game of the nation's emergence as a modern industrial, imperial, and cultural power in the late nineteenth and early twentieth centuries. As has already been noted, though, part of my point in conjoining the two terms relates quite specifically to Cather, whose sexual coming-of-age as a woman who loved other women occurred in the midst of the transition from romantic friendship to sexual deviance and whose literary career is both a celebration and a fierce, fearful critique of the emerging nation. In a direct and personal sense, then, America "queered" Cather by labeling her erotic identity deviant, "unnatural," as she herself put it in a crucial letter of 1892. In a less obvious but very consistent way, though, she "queered" "America" by examining the axes of difference—psychosexual, racial/ethnic, economic, and literary—that made the nation a space of vast energy and profound instability.

Cather's "queering" of "America" is a process of making and unmaking, settling and unsettling that operates at times on the surfaces and at times on the deep structures of her fiction. It is a blend of or an uneasy movement between ecstatic optimism and a sometimes deadly anxiety, an often volatile mixture of utopian possibilities and dystopian dreads. It is inscribed upon the bodies of a range of characters and evident in the images of homes that leave them feeling homeless, alienated, othered— like Thea Kronborg in the passage I have used as an epigraph, sobbing in the train, made "tougher" and "harder" by her sense of estrangement from family and community and by her determination to go away in order to make herself the artist and person she is determined to become. It is manifest in the ethnic and cultural hybridity that so often marks Cather's fictional worlds, as immigrant characters and communities contend with the complexities of an unfamiliar and often hostile environment—such as the Norwegian Ivar, of *O Pioneers!*, who is pronounced "queer, certainly" (100), even by the sympathetic Alexandra, because he refuses to adopt American customs of dress and hygiene. It is apparent, too, I will argue, in the "disobedience" or the eccentricity of Cather's texts,[7] qualities that arise out of their revisionary engagement with prior texts as well as their refusal to conform to generic expectations, as they move instead between and among the categories readers of American fiction deploy in order to situate texts historically and aesthetically—categories such as, for example, "realism," "romanticism," "regionalism," and "modernism." Finally, Cather "queers" the reading experience by writing "novels" that are stubbornly antinovelistic in their deemphasis on heroic action, their insubstantial (Jim Burden) or unlikable (Sapphira Colbert) characters (who balk the reader's longing for sympathetic identification), and their flagrant lack of interest in the drama of heterosexual desire, the plot that had supplied the bourgeois novel with its raison d'être from *Clarissa* to *Ethan Frome*, the grim tale of adultery and punishment Edith Wharton published just a year before Cather published her first novel, *Alexander's Bridge*, in 1912. (*Alexander's Bridge* is also, I hasten to acknowledge, a grim tale of adultery and punishment, but it is unusual among Cather's twelve novels in being so driven by the plot of heterosexual love. More on this point later.)

Willa Cather: Queering "America" is not a biographical study, though I draw upon certain important facts of the writer's life—her lesbianism, her movement from Middle West to East, her background in journalism— in order to situate her more precisely within the dynamics of particular historical processes. I have examined and will make extensive use of the few letters that survived the search-and-destroy missions of Cather's later years, when she sought frantically to protect her privacy and her public (asexual) image. I do not, however, examine Cather's fiction as a reflection or transmutation of her life experiences or as a working through of personal anxieties and developmental issues. Cather studies has already been well served by two scrupulous biographers, Sharon O'Brien and James Woodress, and by a long tradition of biographically inflected criticism.[8]

O'Brien's *Willa Cather: The Emerging Voice* laid the groundwork for the kind of study undertaken here, particularly in the unapologetic case it makes for Cather's lesbianism, and I and all of Cather's feminist readers are indebted to O'Brien for helping to enlarge her contemporary audience and for finally putting to rest the image of the celibate writer who sacrificed her personal life for the sake of her art. My emphasis and approach, though, differ significantly from O'Brien's. In examining Cather's lengthy apprenticeship and creative emergence, O'Brien traces a progressive consolidation of her identities as lesbian, woman, and writer, a story that ends happily with the publication of *O Pioneers!* in 1913. With this book, dedicated to her mentor and precursor Sarah Orne Jewett, Cather discovers her own "distinctive voice," according to O'Brien, by claiming kinship with the women of her literary and personal past and recognizing at last "the narrative power of women's voices" (448). As the subject of biography, O'Brien's "Cather" is necessarily unified and coherent, and her shift from male to female identification is decisive and, one assumes, permanent. The "Cather" in Queering "America" is, by contrast, less stable and certain, though no less stubborn. (Indeed, Cather's stubbornness is part of what has always attracted me to her. She was, as the poet Ruth Stone has said of herself, "[her] own quick woman.") In this study she is a figure in and a producer of discourse, an agent and a subject of historical process, and her texts are interventions in such processes that outstrip and often contradict whatever conscious intentions or beliefs Cather the person might have held. My goal is not to map the trajectory of her self or her career but to examine a few nodal points on the far more devious path of her relationship to the various "regime[s] of the normal" (Warner xxvii) that operated in the U.S. between 1873 and 1947, the years in which she lived and wrote.

In a sense this study is a contribution to what Jennifer Terry terms "deviant historiography," for my assumption is that Cather's lesbianism predisposed her to occupy an oppositional subject position vis-à-vis the discourses of heteronormativity and of male and white supremacy, but I also recognize that her oppositionality is neither fixed nor simple, particularly on matters of race. Her fiction consistently subverts and resists such discourses, and "queer" is often the mark or the name of that resistance, the sign of differences that cannot be erased or repressed. However, Cather is not installed here as an exemplary, transhistorical "queer" whose fiction stands as a prolepsis of Stonewall, AIDS activism, the lesbian dildo debates, body-piercing, and the struggle for same-sex marriage. Terry is wise to point out that "a lesbian and gay history which hopes to find homosexuals totally free of the influences of pathologizing discourses would be an historiographic optical illusion," and she proposes instead that the task of deviant historiography is to "map the techniques by which homosexuality has been marked as different and pathological, and then locate subjective resistances to this homophobia" (58).

Cather's fiction is clearly and deeply marked by the medical and juridical discourses that pathologized nonprocreative sexualities; often, instead of being subverted or critiqued, those discourses are brutally enforced, even by those who are most oppressed by them. The most well-known example of the mechanism of internalized homophobia is the suicide of Paul in "Paul's Case" (1905), a carnation-sporting dandy with a narrow chest and eyes remarkable for "a certain hysterical brilliancy" who throws himself in front of a train, realizing "It was a losing game in the end, . . . this revolt against the homilies by which the world is run" (*CS* 170, 189).[9] My point, however, is not to chastise Cather for failing to imagine a political solution to Paul's dilemma but to investigate the complex interplay of oppositionality and anxiety about deviance that animates her fiction. The "Cather" of "Paul's Case" and of *Queering "America"* bears some resemblance to Edith Wharton, who said in regard to her dead heroine Lily Bart that "a frivolous society can acquire dramatic significance only through what its frivolity destroys" (*Backward Glance* 207) and some resemblance to Michel Foucault, whose analyses of the ubiquity of power have struck some critics as being so circular that they serve to justify "political quietism."[10] In replying to such charges, Keith Gandal says of Foucault something that might easily be said of Cather—or, for that matter, of Wharton:

> Those who come to Foucault's work looking for political solutions will be perpetually disappointed. Foucault's project—in both his politics and his histories—was not to lay out solutions, but rather to identify and characterize problems. . . . Identifying and sizing up a problem was the most determinate act of thought.   (quoted in Halperin 54)

Cather may have wished that her fiction would induce "political quietism" or at least offer an escape from rather than engagement with the problems of "industrial life" and "social injustice," as she groused in a defensive letter to *The Commonweal* in 1936 (*OW* 21–2), but in fact her texts constitute anything but escapism, for they lay bare the operations of an eroticized and racialized nationalism through a process of restless and ambivalent interrogation that I have termed "queering 'America.'" Paul may find rebellion "a losing game" and the story may seem deeply divided in its attitude toward him, but his "case" exposes the unfair nature of a game rigged to destroy children who don't know how to play it. Thea Kronborg, who "go[es] away to fight, and . . . go[es] away forever," is more equipped and prepared. If Paul is a queer agonistes, Thea is a queer triumphant, the one who subverts the game by mastering it through sheer force of will. She even winds up married, for heaven's sake, though her accession to institutionalized heterosexuality is easy to miss, tucked as it is into one fairly cryptic reference to "her husband" in the 1932 edition of the novel.[11] In my reading of Cather, Paul and Thea stand at opposite ends of a strategic spectrum, each enacting an assault on a system that seeks to control difference by policing the boundaries between the natural and the unnatural, male and female, white and nonwhite.

Cather's critical stock has risen significantly in recent years, reversing a process of decanonization that got underway in the 1930s and 1940s when a younger generation of writers and reviewers judged her to be out of step with the times.[12] Her status in contemporary popular culture is evident in the fact that both *O Pioneers!* and *My Ántonia* have been made into movies for television in the 1990s, featuring such high-powered stars as Jessica Lange and Jason Robards.[13] Her status in the academy is evident in the attention she has garnered lately from theorists and New Americanists who are not Cather specialists, including (such high-powered stars as) Eve Kosofsky Sedgwick, Judith Butler, and Walter Benn Michaels. *Queering "America"* builds upon this crucial work, extending their virtuosic analyses of individual texts into a full-scale reassessment of Cather's career and endeavoring also to bridge the current gap between the inquiries into sex and gender and the discussions of race, ethnicity, and nationality. Sedgwick and Butler do not, for example, pay much attention to race or ethnicity, though Butler at least remarks upon the ethnic as well as the sexual significations of the term "bohemian" in her discussion of *My Ántonia* (*Bodies* 149). Michaels, throughout *Our America*, insists that sexuality in modernist American writing is finally "about" race and that homoeroticism is merely a trope of the nativist desire for racial purity. Thus, for him, the all-male family comprised by Tom Outland, Roddy Blake, and Henry Atkins in *The Professor's House* is "the model for a puri-fied Americanism, which ... deploys homosexuality on behalf of nativism and, in so doing, legitimates the homosexual as the figure for a purified American identity" (49), while for Sedgwick the "gorgeous homosocial romance" between Tom and Roddy is a "cross-translation" of the lesbian love story that Cather could not write "as itself" ("Across Gender" 68–9). In my analysis, as in Gail Bederman's *Manliness & Civilization*, race and gender are not treated as discrete categories, and one is not given primacy over the other, as, I think, is the case in Michaels's formulation. Rather, in Cather's fiction as in the turn-of-the-century discourses of civilization examined by Bederman, race and gender (as well, I would add, as ethnic-ity and sexuality) "have been interwoven so tightly that they [are] impos-sible to disentangle" (239). Instead of trying to untie the Gordian knot, I will aim in this study to elucidate the logics of substitution and displacement that keep the knot securely in place.

If Cather was "queered" in the first place by the late-Victorian stigmatization of same-sex love, she has been re-"queered" in the last twenty years by a series of readings that, though less theory-driven than Sedgwick's and Butler's, have attended to the instabilities of gender and sexual identities in Cather's fiction and to the texts' massive resistance to compulsory heterosexuality as a social institution. From Larry Rubin's 1975 study of "the homosexual motif" in "Paul's Case" to Judith Fetterley's analysis of lesbianism and the point of view problem in *My Ántonia*, critics have combed the novels and short stories for signs of how sexuality is translated into textuality, for evidence of lesbianism masked in order to evade detection and censure.[14] This provocative body of work has been extremely productive in situating Cather within traditions of lesbian and gay American writing, but, as I have noted elsewhere, the psychologizing tendencies of these readings are limiting in several respects: they localize desire and the complex of issues associated with it in particular characters, symbols, or situations; they confuse to a greater or lesser degree Cather's life with her art; and they often flatten texts into case studies of, depending on the critic's point of view, the struggling homosexual, the lonely lesbian, the "strange" bisexual, the miserable heterosexual.[15] In my reading, Cather's notion of character is too slippery and antinovelistic to support the case-study approach, for she consistently foregrounds the processes by which people are turned into ever-proliferating *figures*—of speech, of memory, of desire—in the narratives of fiction and history. Thus, for example, I am not particularly interested in psychoanalyzing Ántonia's shift from adolescent bragging about her ability to "work like mans now" to her midlife paeans to marriage and prolific motherhood. More important for my purposes is to examine Jim's role as an agent of the border patrol, as it were—a policeman and gatekeeper who in his first-person narrative is constantly on the watch for signs of transgressions related to gender, sexuality, and ethnicity. From that standpoint, Ántonia's transformation matters not as a sign of Cather's determination to thwart the character's incipient lesbianism but for the clues it provides to the broader and deeper interrogation the complexly layered narrative offers of networks of surveillance and prohibition. All we know of her transformation is, after all, what we see through Jim's never neutral eyes.

Finally, a word or two about this thing called "queer theory": my engagement with Cather's fiction began in the early 1980s, at the dawn of the AIDS crisis and in the initial stages of feminism's installation as a critical movement inside the academy. Though feminism is still my primary interpretive and theoretical tool, it has changed much in the past fifteen years, through the processes of institutionalization, through its encounters with poststructuralism and critical race theory, and through the development of new fields—such as gender studies and lesbian and gay studies—that emerged out of feminism and challenged many of its basic assumptions. Queer theory and queer cultural studies are merely the youngest of feminism's critical progeny. Their boundaries are not yet determined, their futures not yet clear. Throughout this study, I invoke "the queer" not as a way of pledging allegiance to any particular political program or critical paradigm but, indeed, as a mark of my skepticism toward any kind of programmatic thinking.

This book is a work of criticism rather than theory, and my relationship to the myriad theoretical positions and possibilities currently but loosely gathered under the term "queer" is strictly pragmatic: I use what seems to work best on any given problem in any given text. I do, however, deploy "queer" to articulate both the antiassimilationist dream of liberation from heteronormativity as well as the rage experienced in communities of sexual minorities through the 1980s and 1990s as the dominant culture ignored (or homophobically exploited) AIDS and denied our civil rights. I use it as the editors of *GLQ: A Journal of Lesbian and Gay Studies* used it in their note to the first number of the journal, as a signal of my intention to revel in these pages in "the fractious, the disruptive, the irritable, the impatient, the unapologetic, the bitchy, the camp" (Dinshaw and Halperin iv). I use it as Michael Warner used it in his introduction to *Fear of a Queer Planet: Queer Politics and Social Theory*, as a rejection of "a minoritizing logic of toleration or simple political interest-representation in favor of a more thorough resistance to regimes of the normal" and as a way of "mess[ing] up the desexualized spaces of the academy" and "mak[ing] theory queer" rather than just having "a theory about queers" (xxvi). I use it as Lee Edelman used it in his elegant deconstruction of an invitation "to inquire into the state of queer studies." In cautioning against premature efforts to synthesize, systematize, and confer "state"hood upon queer studies, Edelman extolls the virtues of thinking other-wise, insisting that "queer theory can only become itself through the gesture whereby it refuses itself, resists itself, perceives that it is always somewhere else, operating as a force of displacement, of disappropriation: operating, in short, as a vector of desire." He concludes with the words I have used as an epigraph to this introduction, by exhorting his audience not merely to "attend to" the state of queer theory but to "Reinvent it. Resist it. Refuse it. Pursue it. Get over it. Just do it" (345–6).

If my insistence on maintaining a strategic multivalence in the term "queer" strikes some as evasive or conceptually mushy, I can reply only that I see instead a capaciousness and mobility that are productive, revealing, and necessary. My point is to suggest that queer bodies have had a crucial role to play in the constituting of official and unofficial sexualities, subjectivities, and literary histories in the U.S. throughout the twentieth century. Was Cather alone in "queering 'America' "? Obviously not. Was being a lesbian a necessary prerequisite to her participation in the project? Of course not, though members of sexual minorities had particularly charged relationships to discourses of the queer after the 1890s. Works by many of Cather's contemporaries are marked by signifying practices that similarly reveal the incoherent minglings of sex, gender, race, and ethnicity in U.S. culture. Edith Wharton again provides a concise, illuminating example. In *The Age of Innocence* (1920) Ellen Olenska, whose mother was American and who spent part of her childhood in New York, returns to the city after a disastrous marriage to a Polish nobleman with a determination "to become a complete American again" (64). She is thwarted in that effort because, despite her bloodlines (her father is a British banker), Ellen is figured in the text as a southern European immigrant who poses both a racial and a sexual threat to the settled world of old New York. When, following her parents' deaths, she and her aunt step off the boat from Europe, for example (an entrance that already underscores her immigrant status), Ellen is dressed in crimson merino and amber beads and is said to look "like a gipsy foundling" (59). Years later, Newland Archer is both drawn to and unsettled by what he perceives as her otherness. In his mind, she and everything attached to her are linked to "the southern races" (69), including her "swarthy foreign-looking maid" (68), who is Italian, and the "intimate, foreign" atmosphere of her house, suffused with a "vague pervading perfume . . . rather like the scent of some far-off bazaar, a smell made up of Turkish coffee and ambergris and dried roses" (70). Ellen's neighborhood "far down West Twenty-third Street" is described as a "strange quarter" of "small dress-makers, bird-stuffers, and 'people who wrote' " (66), a "Bohemian quarter" (103), and a "queer quarter for such a beauty to settle in," according to Newland's journalist friend Ned Winsett (121). This cluster of ethnic and sexual associations surrounding Ellen, her figurative (and actual) links to Italians, Turks, Poles, Bohemians, and queers, helps to situate *The Age of Innocence*, which is set in the 1870s, in relation to the

cultural politics of the 1920s, as Ellen's expulsion from the family/
city/nation may be compared to the closing of the gates that followed
World War I in response to what the nativist Lothrop Stoddard termed "the
rising tide of color" in the American population. Clearly, even the heterosexual, expatriate Wharton was anxiously and critically fascinated by the
process of "queering 'America.' "

Even as I embrace Edelman's challenge and move into the unstated
state of queer cultural work, I have to acknowledge that "queer" is not a
name I call myself, not because I have gotten over it but because, genera-
tionally, I never quite got to it, having arrived at lesbianism more or less
through feminism, as the women's movement of the 1970s evolved into
the women's studies movement of the 1980s. Personal preferences and
experiences aside, the Supreme Court of the United States has recently
named "gays and lesbians" as defining a class of "homosexual persons"
who cannot be denied the Constitution's guarantee of equal protection
(Romer v. Evans), so the name "lesbian" has a legal status and a sexual
specificity that "queer" currently lacks.[16] In certain contexts—i.e., the
context of the contemporary struggle for civil equality—I believe it
is important and even urgent to use names that insist upon what
Sedgwick has called the legal and "the epistemological distinctiveness of
gay identity and gay situation in our culture" (*Epistemology* 75). In terms
of the present study, however, what really matters is that "queer" *is* a name
Willa Cather called *her*self, and she did so in the only documents we have
that speak directly to her sexual self-identification, the letters of the 1890s
that are either to or about her college crush, Louise Pound. Beyond these
private, terrified acts of self-naming and -unnaming, the word "queer"
resonates throughout Cather's fiction with the snap, crackle, and pop
of acute anxiety and ideological work. It becomes, like the indolent,
receptive Thea in Panther Canyon, "a continuous repetition of sound, like
the cicadas" (*SL* 373).

Queering "America" attends to that continuous, extraordinary repetition as it echoes throughout Cather's career and presses into our own
moment. In Part 1 I track the queer as a figure in Cather's private and
public writings between 1892 and 1922, with particular emphasis on the
Pound letters and her first five novels (*Alexander's Bridge, O Pioneers!, The
Song of the Lark, My Ántonia,* and *One of Ours*). With the exception
of *Alexander's Bridge*, which is set in Boston and London (though the
protagonist did grow up in the West), each of the early books is more or
less a "prairie novel." (*The Song of the Lark* is set in Colorado, which isn't

quite the prairie, and *One of Ours* moves from Nebraska to Europe when Claude Wheeler goes off to fight in World War I.) In these books the prairie is the space where "America" is coming into being, and "the fear of a queer prairie" is a set of anxieties, which the texts at times interrogate and at times perpetuate, about the play of samenesses and differences within that space. By looking at eruptions and inscriptions of the "queer," I situate Cather within Progressive and World War I era discourses of the body and the body politic.

Part 2 takes a somewhat different tack, aiming to situate Cather within the cultural and literary politics of the 1920s, the decade in which she produced some of her finest fiction as well as some important critical and editorial work, including her essay "The Novel Démeublé" and her preparation for Houghton Mifflin of the two-volume *The Best Stories of Sarah Orne Jewett.* "Queering the 'Classics' " puts Cather in dialogue with D. H. Lawrence's influential critical volume of 1923, *Studies in Classic American Literature*, and with such crucial precursors as Jewett and Walt Whitman as a way of imagining what something called a "queer literary history" might look like. "Queer" in this instance signifies her affiliation with Jewett and Whitman and her efforts to subvert, problematize, and radically reconfigure the notion of the "classic" that was shaping the canon and the new field of American literary study. I focus especially on *The Professor's House* and *Death Comes for the Archbishop* as texts in which Cather's entanglements in matters of influence and literary and cultural history are particularly acute. Cather did not embrace the Jazz Age ethos and aesthetic of "terrible honesty"—the modern, thick-with-irony-and-alcohol mode of "accuracy, precision, and perfect pitch and timing" (Douglas 8)—but she was a forceful participant in the major debates of the period and, as has often been noted, an influence on writers as central to it as F. Scott Fitzgerald.[17]

My conclusion briefly examines Cather's work in the 1930s, a dark period in her career and in U.S. history, as a moment of dystopian un-writing. I look in particular at *Sapphira and the Slave Girl*, her last published novel, as a text in which anxieties about the body and/as the nation reerupt with singular fury. I also consider some questions about the future and the utility of queer critique, whose utopian dream of world building and knowledge changing I share and hope to advance with every word of this book.

Part I

Fear of a Queer Prairie

Figures of the Body and/as the Nation in the Letters and Early Novels

A love letter is anxious discourse, perhaps the most viscerally anxious of all discourses. To bare one's soul in writing to a beloved other, to speak desire, need, longing is to put oneself at risk, to leave oneself vulnerable to rejection, misreading, or an unbearable silence.[1] A novel may also be anxious discourse, as Priscilla Wald has suggested, particularly within the context of U.S. literature if it engages in "debates about the constituting of America and Americans" (3), if the story it tells is an attempt to articulate a cultural identity that would "legitimate the political entity of a United States nation" (2).[2] For Willa Cather, the anxieties of eros and of nation-building combine in immensely productive ways, in both the putatively private genre of the love letter and the public, fictional mode of the novel. This chapter begins with a discussion of the private documents as literary and rhetorical performances because they—painfully, aggressively—display Cather's queer stance, her occupation of a queer discursive space—a stance at odds with and a space some distance from the "normal." Over time the queerness of the apprentice writer struggling to articulate her "unnatural" love would be modulated considerably into the more subtle yet ambitious queering of "America" that is the project of Cather's novels. The bulk of this first part of my study will be devoted to examining the shape that project took between 1912 and 1922, the first decade of her career as a published novelist. First, though, we must attend to the queer voice of the letters, for in its artful yet unguarded emotionalism it clearly demonstrates that Cather's prairie functioned not as an emblem of the lost glories of America's pioneer past but as an unstable space of shame and terror, power and passion.

1

Driving One-Handed

The Law, the Letter, and the Unsanctioned Voice

Small ciphers though they are, quotation marks are critical in upholding the constitutional principles upon which American jurisprudence is based.
—Margreta de Grazia

A mong other things, Willa Cather didn't want you to know that in a series of letters she wrote between 1892 and 1897 she used the word "queer" six times in writing to or about Louise Pound, the multitalented scholar-athlete whom she met and fell in love with at the University of Nebraska in 1891.[1] The story of Cather's battle to keep such information—and, indeed, practically all personal material—out of public circulation is by now a familiar one. It bears repeating here, though, because of what it suggests about Cather's authority over the letter as a "writing technology"—i.e., as what Katie King terms one of many "cultural technologies for producing meaning in a very broad sense" (92)—and the ways in which the legal and ideological apparatus of the letter (in this case especially the laws of literary ownership and the institutional powers of the literary executor) have served to perpetuate that authority.

In her later years, so the story goes, feeling increasingly despairing about the state of the world and believing herself to be surrounded by enemies (from hostile reviewers to fellow Nebraskans who pretended to be friends), Cather sought to protect her reputation by destroying as many letters as she could lay her hands on, urging friends to destroy those she could not, and finally stipulating in her will, executed in 1943, that direct quotation from and republication of surviving letters be forbidden.[2] That stipulation, which is still dutifully enforced by Cather's estate and by the repositories that hold and control access to the letters,[3] has hampered Cather scholarship immeasurably, though it has by no means succeeded in keeping the author's "private" life and letters out of bounds. Cather's prohibition of the scholarly practice of direct quotation has imposed not silence but a condition of "translation and displacement" in discussions of her life and of her letters as texts, a condition that is, according to Judith Butler, "the very condition . . . of lesbianism as a refracted sexuality." The peculiar situation surrounding the letters serves to prove and extend Butler's claim that lesbian sexuality is "produced through the very historical vocabularies that seek to effect its erasure" and that this production-through-erasure is precisely what we see in Cather's fiction:

> The prohibition that is said to work effectively to quell the articulation of lesbian sexuality in Cather's fiction is, I would argue, precisely the occasion of its constitution and exchange. It is perhaps less that the legibility of lesbianism is perpetually endangered in Cather's text than that lesbian sexuality within the text is produced as a perpetual challenge to legibility. (*Bodies* 145)

Prohibition, in other words, is always doomed to fail, calling into being the very thing it wishes to outlaw and calling into question the security of its own foundations. But that doesn't mean prohibition isn't powerful in its ability to skew, to create illegibilities, a problem apparent throughout Cather studies by virtue of the continuing prohibitive power of the author's "will." The field suffers from the lack of an accessible, carefully edited collection of letters and from the tension and ambiguity that arise when biographies must struggle mightily but uneasily against their sources in the effort to achieve a paraphrase that is at once fair to the language of the letters and faithful to the rules of the game. Nevertheless, Cather's most recent biographers, Sharon O'Brien and James Woodress, have done a commendable job of circumventing Cather's will without obviously flouting the strictures it contains.

The letters have received little attention, however, as literary documents and rhetorical performances, though they are fascinating in their allusiveness and their sliding from one set of discursive possibilities to another, moving as they do from courtship tales to Bible stories, from the gothic to the pastoral, from Sappho to Henry James to Ella Wheeler Wilcox (1850–1919), the prolific sentimental poet who penned the lines, "Laugh, and the world laughs with you;/weep, and you weep alone."[4] The lack of critical attention is due in part to the problem of access, but it is also difficult to make a case for the qualities and strategies of a voice one is enjoined from quoting directly. Trust me, the scholar seems to be saying, in the unhappy compromise of paraphrase. Trust that Cather sounded this way, argued that way, used this word in this context—six times. The situation here is in some sense the reverse of what Margreta de Grazia describes in her discussion of the legal history of quotation marks as a means of "sanctioning voice" by protecting words as the property of the person who spoke them (289).[5] Cather, in denying me the right to mark her words as hers, ambiguates the question of property, making the voice that speaks here unsanctioned, the words in a profound way unauthor-ized—though the intentions of her will are of course to assert an absolute right to her words as private property. In what follows, however, I reluctantly join in the tradition of using a paraphrase so faithful that it is virtually indirect quotation and beg the reader's indulgence—and, yes, trust. I will, though, allow myself the luxury of indicating Cather's use of a few specific, crucial words, most notably "queer," making me in this discussion neither quite a ventriloquist nor exactly a thief.

O'Brien's argument that Cather was a lesbian rests largely—and correctly, in my judgment—on her reading of the letters to and about Pound, particularly those written in the summers of 1892 and 1893 when Cather was facing the prospect or reckoning with the pain of being separated from her friend during the university's summer recess. The raw, highly charged language of the letters proves the emotional intensity the relationship had for Cather during the two and a half years of the women's closest involvement. Moreover, Cather's self-conscious sense of the deviant nature of the relationship, even in the absence of certain proof that it was sexual, places it on the modern side of the line historians of sexuality have drawn between romantic friendship and lesbianism.[6] When Cather rails to Pound in the first of the surviving epistles that it is manifestly unfair that feminine friendships (a phrase she encloses in quotation marks) should be unnatural (her word, not mine), she acknowledges the gulf that stands between her passion for Louise and the supposedly idyllic, pre-Freudian "female world of love and ritual" that is now such a familiar part of discussions of intimate relationships in nineteenth-century America.[7] Her quotation marks underscore the fact that feminine friendship is both a social institution and a contested category, a term whose meaning is subject to dispute and radical change. She signals her position in that interpretive dispute, protesting the new medical model under which female same-sex affections had been marked as "unnatural" and finding an ally for her stance in Miss De Pue, a classmate with whom, she tells Pound, she agrees that far—i.e., in protesting the unfairness of feminine friendship having been labeled "unnatural."[8] Despite her brave dissent, she shows signs throughout this letter of being tormented by the pervasiveness and the logic of the opposing view, particularly by the assumption that she and Pound will outgrow their youthful attachment as they move into mature, "natural" heterosexuality. She concedes that time will inevitably alter their relationship and supposes that some day they will look back on it and laugh, as women do. But, she says, it makes her feel horribly to think of that possibility, for to mock the relationship would be worse than if they should come to hate each other.

Beyond its obvious biographical value, this first letter to Pound is important because the word "queer" keeps finding its way onto the page, appearing four times in the course of a letter that contains five paragraphs and a postscript and occurring in a range of contexts that suggests its polysemous character and its productive force. The letter demonstrates as well the tendency of deviant desires to confound or be confounded by "normal" systems of communication and representation, as the voice veers from one culturally powerful model of romance to another in the effort to overcome both Louise's and society's resistance to "unnatural" love. The letter is written over the signature of William, the masculine alter ego of Cather's adolescence and early years in college, when she sported a short haircut and often dressed in boys' clothes.[9] Heading home to Red Cloud for the summer, Cather pauses to write the letter in the midst of what she calls a nasty job of packing, because, she explains, she realizes she had neglected to give voice to her admiration for the new Worth gown Louise had worn at a party she had attended earlier that evening at the Pound home in Lincoln. In the first paragraph "William" adopts the pose of the Jamesian drawing-room observer, sketching out a flattering portrait of "her"[10] lady by musing upon the general effect created by Louise's costume, which, she says, struck her so hard that she was overcome and lost track of the incidentals. "William" is not unlike Ned Rosier encountering Isabel Archer (Osmond) framed in a gilded doorway in a black velvet gown. Where Isabel strikes Ned as "high and splendid, . . . the picture of a gracious lady" (James 309–10), "William" notes the very distinct impressions created by the neck, the train, the color of the gown, and what the whole affair set off, then steps back from the portrait and pronounces Louise handsome, though she supposes Louise will object to her saying so. The paragraph ends with an ambiguous remark about a man at the party who, "William" says, had the greenest envy she was able to generate. Whether the envy was generated by her in him or in her by him is unclear, but Cather's uncertainty in the relationship is palpable—both in her fear that Louise will object to her use of a lover's discourse of admiration and extravagant praise and in her pride (or anxiety) about eliciting (or experiencing) envy in the public setting of a party.

The second paragraph shifts from James to another touchstone of late-Victorian culture (and sexual ambiguity), an edition of Edward FitzGerald's translation of *The Rubaiyat of Omar Khayyam*, which Cather had bought as a parting gift for Louise. Feeling both emotionally and literarily self-conscious, "William" explains that she had chosen *The Rubaiyat* over a set of Ruskin because it was something she liked awfully herself, and so she hoped it would seem less formal, less like carting merchandise up to her house. She tells Louise she has been fond of *The Rubaiyat*—which she refers to at one point as that Persian poem whose name she has forgotten how to spell—, since she was a kid, and that she was particularly smitten with the illustrations.[11] They are so *queer*, she says, unlike anything else. Their swirls and whirling curves convey the horror and the mystery of the whole thing more powerfully than anything she knows of. She felt a right to inflict the book upon Louise because she loved it through and through, as much, the young writer hastens to add, as it is possible to love another person's work.

In the first instance, "queer" is offered as a positive aesthetic judgment and as a means of representing and circulating deviant desires. It connotes power, uniqueness, a visual force that captivates Cather both as a "kid" and as a young woman in love. Ruskin is merchandise, but a Persian poem with queer pictures is a gift, a sacred object loved through and through and offered to Louise as a kind of fetish, a substitute for Cather's soon to be absent body, or so she seems to hope. Anxious to position their relationship within an erotic economy of intimacy and abundance opposed to the commercial economy of mere "merchandise," "William" invokes her own affection for and pleasure in the text as a justification for offering it to Louise. FitzGerald's *Rubaiyat* is an ideal vehicle for the articulation of "unnatural" love because his translation obscures the gender of the beloved whose presence transforms the Wilderness into "Paradise enow" (l. 48) and because his passionate speaker argues forcefully for pleasure and the fulfillment of desire, even "under pain/Of Everlasting Penalties" (ll. 311–12).[12] As a gift, *The Rubaiyat* is a safe choice in that gift editions of FitzGerald's translation were enormously popular at the turn of the century, but it is also a risky, risqué invitation to revel in the Orientalist fantasy of the Orient as a space of "sexual promise (and threat), untiring sensuality, unlimited desire, deep generative energies" (Said 188).[13] The book's "queer" illustrations foreground the racial and sexual otherness that is endemic to Orientalism as a "style of thought" (Said 2), an otherness that "William" both acknowledges (in being drawn to the horror and the mystery conveyed by the poem and the pictures) and inhabits (in fearing that her gift is something she inflicts upon Louise). This letter stands, then, as an early, important example of the mingling of racial and sexual inflections in Cather's figuring of queerness and the queer and of the high degree of instability that characterizes the figure.

As the letter goes on, however, "queer" tends in the more negative direction indicated by Cather's concern that her gift may not be wholly welcome. It appears three times in the next paragraph, signaling in each case a sense of deviance or shame arising from the intensity of the feelings "William" experienced in leaving Lincoln and thus Louise for the summer. She claims to have been a bore at the party, the result of feeling strangely affected by the realization that she wouldn't see Louise again for some time, and says if she had known how queer it would make her feel she would not have gone up to the house at all. Noting that Louise probably didn't feel the same way, since she herself wasn't leaving and would still have a great many friends on deck (so that one gone won't make much difference), Cather says again and emphatically that she did feel queer and hadn't known it had gotten such a hold on her, though what "it" is is never specified. She shook herself after going away, but that hadn't altered the facts of the case any. She goes on to say she had wanted very much to ask Louise to go through a formal goodbye, but she thought that might disgust her a little so she had refrained. Clearly puzzled by her state and seeming to address herself as much as Louise, she avers that it was so queer that she should *want* to go through such a formality when three years ago she had never seen Louise, and she supposed in three years more—and a long dash surrounded by blank space in the sentence marks "William's" refusal to contemplate the difference three more years might make in their relationship. That refusal sets up the defense of "feminine friendships" that began this discussion. From there, the letter moves to a somewhat hasty conclusion, with Cather explaining that she hadn't congratulated Louise, presumably on her graduation from the university, because she cared more for what Pound would do than for what she had done. She then notes that this epistle is infinitely sillier than one she had written and torn up in March, but that she was sending it because she hadn't physical energy enough to tear it up. She asks Louise to pardon her frame of mind (another phrase enclosed in quotation marks) and says she must lay it all to the weather. The letter is signed, Yours, William. The postscript urges Pound not to let anyone look over her shoulder at the letter, as Cather supposed she would receive it in bed.

As reader and giver of *The Rubaiyat*, "William" values queerness as a source of aesthetic pleasure and power. As a young woman who imagines her pseudonymously written letter finding its way to her beloved's bed late at night, "William" is haunted by a fear of queerness as an aspect of her self and yet compelled to "give voice" to her feelings, to set out what she calls the facts of the case. In that compulsive exposure and, moreover, in her repeated projections of Louise's reactions and her anxious, excited conjuring of the reader-over-the-shoulder, "William" underscores the theatrical[14] nature of queer desires and the shame that so often accompanies their articulation. Eve Sedgwick's remarks on "shame-consciousness" and "shame-creativity" as a "structuring fact" of queer identity and expression have some bearing on "William's" acute self-consciousness in the letter and on the slippages apparent in the oft-reiterated "queer." Reflecting on the phenomenology of shame, Sedgwick observes, "shame effaces itself; shame points and projects; shame turns itself skin side outside; shame and pride, shame and self-display, shame and exhibitionism are different interlinings of the same glove: shame, it might finally be said, transformational shame, *is performance*" ("Queer Performativity" 5). "William," in her preoccupations with how her desires affect her—strangely, powerfully, bodily, prompting her to shake herself after leaving Louise at the party—and with how voicing them will likely affect the recipient of her letter—eliciting objections, disgust, derision—demonstrates the "experimental, creative, performative force" of shame (4). Her inability to shake herself free of her queer feelings suggests that for "William" the forms of shame are, as Sedgwick explains, not "distinct, 'toxic' parts of a group or individual identity that can be excised; they are instead integral to and residual in the processes by which identity itself is formed. They are available for the work of metamorphosis, reframing, refiguration, *trans*figuration, affective and symbolic loading and deformation; but unavailable for effecting the work of purgation and deontological closure" (13).

That Cather achieved neither purgation nor closure in her relation to shame is made clear in letters written the following summer, 1893, to Pound and to Cather's Lincoln friend and confidante, Mariel Gere. A year had apparently done little to diminish Cather's ardor, but a long, chaotically scribbled missive written in late June pleading with Louise to come visit her in Red Cloud indicates both how precarious her sense of the relationship was and the profound emotional investment she had in it. The word "queer" occurs only once in this letter, but it is tied directly to Cather's nearly desperate desire to see Pound and the hurt and anger arising from her friend's refusal to commit herself to a time for the visit. It is queer, she complains at one point, that just because I happen to *want* you, your coming is as impossible as the suspension of the law of gravity.[15] Here, "queer" marks the crisis of a desire that cannot reach its object, a desire indeed whose very force increases the likelihood of its not being satisfied, as if the law of desire were a law of equal and opposite reaction. As in one instance in the previous letter, "queer" and "want" are contiguous terms, the one seeming to produce and modify the other, and "want" is underlined. In naming herself as the subject and Louise as the object of such fierce desires and constructing the allusive passion play of "Willie and Willwese" (as the pair was called by one of Cather's younger sisters)[16], Cather anticipates Teresa de Lauretis's claim in *The Practice of Love* that "it takes two women, not one, to make a lesbian" (283). For de Lauretis, "the conscious presence of desire in one woman for another" is what defines and specifies lesbian sexuality (284), which explains the logic of the two making one.[17] For Cather, "queerness" is the instantiation of her obviously conscious desire for Louise, so this tormented letter is an important instrument in her practice of lesbian love. Its strange twists and turns—from sadness to light banter to sarcasm to complaint to threat to plea—resonate with the surprising tactical maneuvers that often crop up in Cather's fictional analyses of the dynamics of desire—the sudden drowning of one adulterer in *Alexander's Bridge*, the equally sudden murder of two others in *O Pioneers!*—which makes it worthy of particularly close examination.

The salutation on the letter is My Dear Louise, a proprietary gesture that Jim Burden will make to dramatic effect in the introduction to *My Ántonia* and that Cather as author will repeat in claiming the name he gives his narrative as the title of her novel. In this case, though, the claim is a tenuous one, undercut at every point by the writer's emotional fragility. Instead of "William," she signs herself "W. C." (and an angry postscript closes with a terse "W."), a cutting back of the (im)proper name that underscores the instability of her identity. Though "queer" is used but once, Cather refers throughout the letter to being caught in the grip of a debilitating "blueness," a depression clearly linked to her separation from Pound, despite her insistence that her condition has no apparent cause. She opens the letter by reporting she has not written sooner because she has been too horribly blue and disconsolate to inflict herself upon anyone. The next several paragraphs are devoted chiefly to literary matters, as the young writer preens before an interested, cultivated audience, showing off her knowledge, bragging of her accomplishments, and deploying the literary as a measure of her intimacy with and desire for Louise. Cather triumphantly announces she has finished a story she calls the tale of the tipsy prima donna and then invites Louise to come down and tell her whether it is good or bad. She describes the story as horribly unconventional and utterly different from anything she has tried to do before, though she preempts criticism by insisting she hadn't spent much time on it.

In the next paragraph Cather accuses Louise of answering a previous letter without having read it, because her reply seemed ignorant of Cather's allusions to a poem she had written in praise of actress Edna Erline Lindon and enclosed. It is sometimes wise to glance over my epistles since you answer them, Cather remarks, even if you risk finding excessively bad spelling and profanity. In reply to Louise's inquiry about where she got the word "bassoon" (an obscure reference, since it does not appear in the poem, "After-Glow," to which she has just referred), she cites as the best of all authority, page 29 of Ella Wheeler Wilcox's *Poems of Passion* (1883), "The Beautiful Blue Danube." Cather offers no further explanation of the allusion, an indication, perhaps, of how familiar the volume was to the two women, if primarily as an object of ridicule. In the poem, Wilcox's lovelorn speaker wonders "If the great bassoons that mutter,/If the clarinets that blow,/Were given a voice to utter/The secret things they know," would they include her—watching her lost love "drift down the hall" with another woman as "the strains of the 'Danube' rise"—among the lists of those who "find death in the music's swell" (29–31)? Wilcox is, of course, precisely the type of lady writer who would inspire Cather to wonder contemptuously in her newspaper reviews of the 1890s "why God ever trusts talent in the hands of women, they usually makes such an infernal mess of it" (*WP* 1:275–7), but in borrowing Wilcox's word and deferring to her, even sarcastically, as an authority,

Cather betrays her indebtedness to a tradition she deplored. Indeed, her "After-Glow" owes much to Wilcox's manner and method, deploying the same ballad meter and a similar fondness for the sentimental tropes of shimmering smiles and overheated atmospheres that cause the brain to reel, though it is significant that Cather's "effusions," as she describes them in the letter to Louise, are inspired by an actress and not by the male lovers who prompt Wilcox's woman artist to assert that "For love's sake, I can put the art away" ("Individuality" 18–20).

Despite her ambivalence toward the tradition exemplified by the author of *Poems of Passion* and her alienation from the idea of renouncing art for "My king, my master," Cather found in Wilcox something that was valuable to her ongoing erotic and literary in-queery, a vocabulary— "Love's Language," as one of Wilcox's poems calls it—for exploring the somatizations of desire, its effects on and in the body.[18] "How does Love speak?" Wilcox asks. "In the faint flush upon the telltale cheek," in "uneven heart-throbs, and the freak/Of bounding pulses that stand still and ache," she enumerates (9–11). For the blue and disconsolate Cather, the desiring body is a body that similarly signifies, and in this case it signifies lovesickness. Halfway through the letter Cather shifts abruptly to an analysis of her condition, invoking everything from gothic melodrama— with cryptic allusions to murders and attempted suicides going on in the neighborhood—to biblical parables in a frantic effort to persuade Louise to come and relieve her suffering. It seems that all the accumulated blueness of ages has hurled itself upon me, she complains, turning her whole mental atmosphere one dense submarine color. She has sought relief in both indolence and hard work, but neither has helped. She is not in fit shape to do anything. Her only hope for help at this point is the prospect of a visit from some other Lincoln friends, upon whom she intends to uncork all the enthusiasm and wine she had saved for Louise. She is determined to try to have a good time and be satisfied with second best, but she rebukes Louise, saying I was and am sick and in affliction and you visited me not. Later, Cather raises the stakes even higher, insisting that this concentrated sublimated essence of blueness is getting to be too much for her and noting that Louise would either disperse the feeling altogether or make it very much worse. You always do one or the other, she says, but she is so desperate she is willing to run the risk. Existence is not worth much of this sort of thing, she intones, and in the next paragraph she declares herself in a state of internal revolution. Come thou down and deliver my soul, she implores, and bring your pistol along and do me a kindly service.

The desiring body is a wounded body, one whose integrity is so precarious that the subject of that desire imagines being delivered from it only by a further, perhaps mortal, wounding by her pistol-packing cowgirl-lover. There is considerably more to Cather's plaints, however, than manipulative histrionics and evidence to support de Lauretis's claim that in lesbian fantasies the fetish is not a phallic symbol but "something which signifies at once the absence of the object of desire (the female body) and the subject's wish for it" (222). For the moment I am more interested in the biblical language and allusions noted in the preceding paragraph, in Cather's echoes of the story of the burning bush and Christ's parable of the talents, because they suggest that she has begun, even in the midst of great personal crisis, to transfigure the shame of deviant desires, to unleash their creative, transformative energies. To paraphrase Emily Dickinson, one might propose that "After great [shame] a formal feeling comes," and that for Cather such a formal feeling undergirds her appeals to Louise as well, perhaps, as much of her fiction. Through allusion, Cather allies herself analogically in her relationship with Louise with Moses, God, and Christ in ways that indicate she could, for strategic purposes, view the deviance of her desires as a form of righteous suffering that endowed the pariah figure of the lesbian with significant power. In pleading with Louise to come down and deliver her soul, for example, she mimics God speaking to Moses from the burning bush, when he explains that "I am come down to deliver [the children of Israel] out of the hand of the Egyptians, and to bring them up out of that land unto a good land and a large, unto a land flowing with milk and honey" (Exodus 3:8).

In transforming God's assurance into her own plea, she appropriates for herself both the magical powers of a god whose face is flaming and inflammable and the uncertainty of Moses, who, at this early stage, understands neither his mission nor this fiery leader. Her earlier charge that she was sick and in affliction and Louise visited her not borrows from Christ's interpretation of the parable of the talents and allies her with both Christ the scapegoat and Christ the judge. The full context of Christ's message to the unfortunate "goats" who sit on the left hand of his throne of glory suggests the raw, apocalyptic power she associated with marginality, as well as the high symbolic price Pound was expected to pay for toying with her affections: "Depart from me, ye cursed, into everlasting fire, prepared for the devil and his angels: for I was an hungred, and ye gave me no meat: I was thirsty, and ye gave me no drink: I was a stranger and ye took me not in: naked, and ye clothed me not: sick, and in prison, and ye visited me not" (Matt. 25:41–4). Cather's postscript to this letter, written after she has received a card from Louise indicating she will not come to Red Cloud, shows her declaring that matters between them will be *eternally* cut short, that if she fails to come, it is good-bye. Like Christ, she vows to cast out the infidel Louise and condemn her to the punishment of eternal separation. Taken together, these figures—the omnipotent, magical God, the dazed Moses, the afflicted Christ, and the triumphant, judging Christ— form the broad symbolic contours of Cather's early sense of deviance, suggesting that she recognized not only the pain of being subject to the law but reveled in the power and the imaginative possibilities of living outside or even above the law, or of being, like Christ, the author of a wholly new law. Driven to the margin by desires called "unnatural," she nevertheless claimed the right to name herself "William" and to imagine that, like the God of Moses, the face of the woman she loved might appear in a "Red Cloud" and deliver the soul of the captive lesbian.

O do come, my dear fellow, she pleads in her postscript, and her "fellow" relented late in July and finally came out for a visit. In an August letter to Mariel Gere, Cather reports exultantly on the women's activities. The letter is important, both for what it says and because it is a rare, exceedingly direct example of Cather commenting to a third party on her intimate relationship with another woman.[19] Pound's arrival supplied the hoped-for deliverance, transforming the parched prairie into a herland flowing with milk and honey and so restoring Cather's spirits that she could coyly confess to Gere that she was feeling pretty well now, save for sundry bruises received in driving a certain fair maiden over the country with one hand, sometimes, indeed, with no hand at all. But, Cather continues, the fair maiden didn't seem to mind her method of driving, even when they went off banks and over haystacks—and concludes with the teasing comment that she drives with one hand all night in her sleep.

Despite the buoyant tone, bucolic setting, and the presence of the fair maiden (who in absence was a "dear fellow"), the mingling of pastoral pleasures with real or imagined dangers (bruises, reckless crashes) marks this prairie as fundamentally similar to Cather's fictional sites of youthful eroticism. Here, as in *O Pioneers!* and *My Ántonia*, pastoral language evokes the fantasy of a space that is erotically charged but also precarious and vaguely threatening. One thinks in particular of the country romps and reveries of Jim Burden—of Lena Lingard's famous reaping-hook and his dreams of "Tony and I . . . out in the country, sliding down straw-stacks as we used to do; climbing up the yellow mountains over and over, and slipping down the smooth side into soft piles of chaff" (*MÁ* 172). Much more openly than in the novels, however, the force that "drives" the passage in the letter is the joyous/dangerous release of an energy that is palpably sexual—as sexual, say, as a pack of Lawrentian horses—and Cather seems intoxicated by the risks and the recklessness of such a release.

Further, the image of Cather as the one-handed or no-handed driver evinces a conscious and, in this instance, unashamed awareness on her part of the physical dimension of her desire for Pound, since her elision of the object of the verb "to drive" (in driving a certain fair maiden over the country) implies that she "drives" neither carriage nor wagon but the maiden herself. Both homoerotic and autoerotic (a possibility made explicit in the image of her driving alone, in sleep, with one hand), desire "drives" Cather to recreate the again-absent beloved first in a masturbatory fantasy and then in the bragging account to a third party of her chivalric exploits with the fair maiden. Desire gratified may also wound, but Cather's pride in the sundry bruises she eagerly displays to Gere transforms this pastoral interlude into a butch-femme drama of exploration of a dream "country," a topsy-turvy world in which "fellows" become "maidens," hands are constantly and methodically mobile, and a mark of pain or shame is offered as proof of erotic conquest. This prairie is queer indeed, but far from fearing it, Cather for the moment races happily across it, at once secure and reckless in the driver's seat, with the maidenly "Willwese" at her side, tacitly approving of her "method."

Cather's state of romantic intoxication seems, however, not to have lasted long. Less than a year after she succeeded in enticing Louise out to Red Cloud, a sudden and permanent rupture occurred in the relationship, a break that biographers attribute to Cather's cruel lampooning of Pound's brother Roscoe in a satire published in the *Hesperian*, a campus paper (*EV* 131, *LL* 86–7).[20] For my purposes the larger significance of the collapse of this college passion—a denouement that is in many respects wholly unremarkable—is that it seems to have engendered Cather's retreat from the overt sexual radicalism manifest in the prolonged drag show of "William Cather," a retreat whose consequences are felt throughout her fiction. Three additional letters to Mariel Gere, written between June 1894 and April 1897—a period that includes Cather's graduation from the university and her move to Pittsburgh to work on a women's magazine, *The Home Monthly*—document the loss and sketch out some of its consequences.[21] In the first, from the summer of 1894, Cather expresses gratitude to Gere for her support when Cather was in hard straits over the winter and spring. The thing I was living for and in was torn away from me, she says, and it left just an aching emptiness in me. I don't think the scar will ever heal. By 1896, though, the signs of a determined retreat are evident, as Cather, writing of the new life she was building for herself in Pittsburgh, reprimands Gere for accusing her of being Bohemian, pointing out that she could most effectually surprise her friends and pain her enemies by living a most conventional existence, and she intended to do precisely that. To prove the point, in the spring of 1897 she teases Gere with the prospect of marriage to a young doctor. She doesn't much care for him but supposes that doesn't really matter, noting that it would be an excellent match in every way. You see, she carefully explains to the friend who knew "William" so well, here I have neither short hair nor dramatic propensities nor any of the old things queer to me. It's like beginning a new life in broad daylight away from the old mistakes.

A scar that won't heal, the division of the world into friends and enemies, an emphatic renunciation of the queer—the rhetorical and ideological shift that occurs over the course of these four letters to Gere is breathtaking in its scope. From the celebration of fair maidens to the crucifixion of the short-haired mannish lesbian (an analogy justified by the resurrection trope Cather uses to describe her life in Pittsburgh), Cather aims to convince Gere that she has moved from a stance of resistance and subversion to one of apparent, public capitulation vis-à-vis the discourses of sex and gender normativity. "William" dies, and "Willa Sibert Cather," journalist, editor, and author of Cather's books from *April Twilights* (1903) through the first edition of *My Ántonia* (1918),[22] is installed in "her" place. If Pittsburgh is daylight, the prairie—once the site of desire, of daytime and nighttime revelries—is implicitly reconfigured as the negative darkness of shame. The prairie is still queer, but now Cather is in fearful flight from it.

Given the scantness of the epistolary record, one runs the risk in examining these documents of making too much of them—of fetishizing what is there and making generalizations without feeling constrained by what is not there. That, I imagine, is what some readers are already convinced I have done in this—admittedly, happily—perverse analysis. I need hardly point out that Cather herself, in her most well-known critical essay, "The Novel Démeublé" (1922), encourages readers to attend to "the inexplicable presence of the thing not named," which seems to invite speculating about what is "not there" on the basis of what "is there."

However, that is not what I have been up to in these pages. I am not, for example, offering generalizations or claiming clear, causal links in the movement from adolescent heartbreak to adult closet to adult fictions of the closet. Nor, let me be clear, am I presuming to judge Cather for trading in the lure and the look of the mannish lesbian for the no-nonsense style of the early twentieth-century career woman (anymore than I seriously regret my own sartorial switch from jeans and tee-shirts to tailored slacks and silk blouses). Even in the age of gender performativity, as Judith Butler has labored to clarify, gender is not "a construction that one puts on, as one puts on clothes in the morning" ("Critically Queer" 21), though Cather, in growing out her hair and declaring herself reborn, seems to have wished for such a voluntarist, radically fabricated notion of the gendered self. Regardless of how decisive the movement into the closet may have been in Cather's life (and the dearth of evidence about her subsequent relationships with Isabelle McClung and Edith Lewis makes judgments on this point highly speculative), my interest is in the fact that in her fiction, the word "queer" retains the multivalent, slippery character it has in these letters, and the prairie—particularly in the early novels—is even more elaborately figured as the staging ground for several impossible struggles: between immigrant and native-born, the illicitly sexual and the erotophobic, the effeminate male and the too-powerful female, the homewreckers and the nation-builders. Finally, it is to those struggles and the gorgeous fictions in which they are rendered that we will now turn our attention.

2

"Filling Out Nice"

Body-Building and Nation-Building in the Early Novels

The best world is the body's world
filled with creatures   filled with dread
misshapen so   yet the best we have
our raft among the abstract worlds
and how I longed to live on this earth
walking her boundaries   never counting the cost
—Adrienne Rich, "Contradictions: Tracking Poems"

In the letters to and about Louise Pound, Cather figures the queer body as marked and restless. It is bruised, wounded, shaking, driving. It subjects itself to regimes of indolence and hard work in a battle to discipline itself, to get into what Cather calls fit shape. In sleep, it touches (or "drives") itself. Awake, it ultimately refashions itself so as to appear neither queer nor Bohemian anymore. Long after Cather grew out her hair and claimed a place in the broad daylight of the un-queer, her fiction remained preoccupied with bodily matters of health and illness, vitality and weakness, hygiene and filth, naturalness and unnaturalness—and with the constellation of sexual, racial, and ethnic anxieties that undergirded such concerns in Progressive Era America. In short stories and novels, particularly in the period from *The Troll Garden* (1905) through *One of Ours* (1922), Cather rises to the challenge of "getting the body into writing," as Peter Brooks puts it in his illuminating study of the body in modern narrative (1). As in the Pound letters, the bodies in Cather's fiction are thoroughly semioticized, relentlessly scrutinized, and radically ambiguous—"queer" in some instances because they are signifiers of perverse desires, in some because they are markers of racial or ethnic difference (whether that difference is coded as superiority or abnormality), and in others because they are physically "extraordinary" (icons either of power and autonomy or of "bodily vulnerability").[1] From the nervous, "twanging" body of the young aesthete in "Paul's Case" (*CS* 173) to the "stalwart, brown" body of the nearly toothless, middle-aged Ántonia (331) to the powerfully elastic bodies of the singers Eden Bower and Thea Kronborg, Cather's bodies sizzle with contradictory significations, as she pushes representation to its limits in probing her own and her culture's eroticized and racialized nationalism. Her bodies both interrogate and aim to satisfy America's hunger for authoritative, appealing images of itself, and they assess the cost, to individuals and social groups, of deviating from these increasingly pervasive normative images. In writing the body, Cather's fears of the queer, which are always also an attraction to that loathsome, lovely figure, are writ large and in a specifically American mode.[2]

In the years just before and after the turn into the twentieth century, the pace of the process of national self-imaging accelerated greatly, spurred on by advances in the technologies of mass communication and the development of low-cost, high-quality popular magazines such as *McClure's*, which employed Willa Cather as a writer and editor from 1906 to 1915.[3] As "image-making" and "image-reading" grew to be major cultural activities, images of women came to dominate the marketplace and the cultural imagination, as Martha Banta has demonstrated in her sweeping analysis of the verbal and visual iconography of the period (xxviii). The American Girl—the complex, energetic figure made familiar through the fiction of Henry James, the illustrations of Charles Dana Gibson, and Frederic Bartholdi's Statue of Liberty, to name but a few of the most prominent examples—was "singled out as the visual and literary form to represent the values of the nation and codify the fears of its citizens" (Banta 2). She—a general type with a range of subclassifications—became the habitual means "for interpreting the nation's achievements and gauging its weaknesses," for displaying "American pride, American immensity, American morality, American material success" (Banta xxix, 505).

Cather enters into this emphatically gendered and highly contentious process of image production and consumption with the sharp eye of a journalist and the ironic distance of someone who had lived and worked in the rising media capital of the U.S. for years without ever seeming to relinquish her sense of being a Nebraskan rather than a New Yorker. Criticism has tended to describe Cather's entries, particularly from her early fiction, in the contest to image the nation as celebratory—unironic iterations of "the heroic myth of national destiny" (Carlin 7), revisionist and feminist only in that they (sometimes, sort of) place women at the center of pioneer stories as actors and not merely as passive emblems.[4] Cather herself did much to establish the climate of reception for her early works, helping to shape the categories, as Deborah Carlin calls them, by which some are read and others are less read. Her most aggressive and effective intervention into the building of interpretive paradigms and the history of the early part of her career is her effort to promote *O Pioneers!* as the better of her two "first novels" because, unlike her other (and actual) first novel, *Alexander's Bridge*, it was about a world she knew and loved rather than the "drawing-room" world that writers like "Henry James and Mrs. Wharton" had taught American readers to expect (*OW* 93). Cather builds her case against *Alexander's Bridge* and in favor of *O Pioneers!* on the grounds of quality (the former being conventional and imitative and the latter being authentic and spontaneous) and form (*O Pioneers!* representing her pioneering venture with "the novel of the soil" [*OW* 93]), but her biases persist in the "good girl/bad guy" dichotomy that shapes many contemporary analyses. Readings that emphasize Cather's brave revision of "America's story" (O'Brien, *EV* 74) privilege the "good girls" of the early novels—Alexandra, Thea, and Ántonia (as exemplars of a woman-centered, humane revision of the national myth)—and discount or problematize the "bad guys"—Bartley Alexander and Claude Wheeler (as suckers for or victims of an unreconstructed version of the myth of progress, conquest, and destiny).[5] My aim in what follows is to offer a less bifurcated view of the early fiction, using the notion of queer bodies and/as national bodies to explore Cather's ongoing entanglements in political and literary discourses of personhood, in "representation as both a political and a semiotic or literary system" (Sanchez-Eppler 5). My method will not be to explicate full texts, though I will linger for awhile over *O Pioneers!*, but to excavate salient images or moments from a range of texts and place them in dialogue with one another. In this way, I hope to explore some of the bumps in the "wild and beautiful" road (*SL* 68) cut by Cather's fiction.

"Immune from Evil Tidings"

Exemplary or abject, revelatory or duplicitous, the looked-at body in Cather's fiction is, I propose, a "queer" body because, as the object of a gaze that is either punitive or possessive, it is made ec-centric—off-centered in the sense of not fully belonging to the person who inhabits it. Queer bodies may be male or female and many shades of "white" or non-"white," for "America" is not always a Girl—nor a Great White Girl—in Cather's corporealizations of the nation. Such "queerness" may or may not be related to the sexualities of individual characters and may or may not be marked as "queer" in the text. Paul, for example, with his lifelong dread of "the shadowed corner" and his "champagne friendship" with a boy from Yale (*CS* 183, 186), has struck many readers as homosexual, but the word "queer" is never attached to him, though, as Claude Summers notes, "Paul's Case" deploys "diction suggestive of homosexuality" in its pervasive use of terms such as "*gay* (used four times), *fairy*, *faggot*, *fagged*, *queen*, *loitering*, *tormented*, *unnatural*, *haunted*, *different*, *perverted*, *secret love*, and so on" (" 'A Losing Game' " 109). On the other hand, Ivar, the Norwegian hammock-maker and religious mystic of *O Pioneers!*, is described by the narrator as "queerly shaped" and called "queer, certainly" by his protector, Alexandra (36, 100). His queerness is bodily but not explicitly sexual, an attribute arising from his "bandy legs" being "completely misfitted to his broad, thick body and heavy shoulders" (90), though important evidence associates Ivar with a shame that seems sexual: his obsessive cleanliness, his desire to live far from other people so as to be subjected to "fewer temptations" (34), and his going bare-footed as a means of allowing "for the indulgence of the body." As Ivar explains to one of Alexandra's maids, Signa:

> From my youth up I have had a strong, rebellious body, and have been subject to every kind of temptation. Even in age my temptations are prolonged. It was necessary to make some allowances; and the feet, as I understand it, are free members. There is no divine prohibition for them in the Ten Commandments. The hands, the tongue, the eyes, the heart, all the bodily desires we are commanded to subdue; but the feet are free members. I indulge them without harm to any one, even to trampling in filth when my desires are low. They are quickly cleaned again. (278)

Where Paul is a sensualist who becomes a thief in order to bankroll the indulgence of his rebellious body's every desire, Ivar is a sensualist who relentlessly polices his body for signs of vulnerability to temptation and scrutinizes the Ten Commandments in order to locate a zone of permissible indulgence. The narrative of *O Pioneers!* swerves and strains visibly in order to accommodate Ivar's explanation, but it is crucial to making sense of a text that seems disarmingly simple yet is in some ways deeply enigmatic. It comes near the end of the novel and at an unpropitious moment in the plot, as Signa "suddenly" asks Ivar about his bare feet when he is preparing to go search for the grief-stricken Alexandra, who has wandered off in nothing but a thin dress and is now out in a cold October storm. "All the time I lived here in the house I wanted to ask you," Signa says, and Ivar obligingly pauses in his preparations to satisfy her curiosity. His response is a brief but revealing developmental narrative, tracing his movement from "youth up" to "age" and framed entirely in terms of his relationship to subjectivating norms and constraints. Ivar's is a story of subjugation, prohibition, and limited resistance or subversion. Elsewhere in the text, Ivar is figured as an Old World rebel against New World conformity, whose difference is valued by Alexandra as a resistance to homogeneity and feared by others, who view Ivar as pathological and "disgraceful" (101). "Here, if a man is different in his feet or in his head, they put him in the asylum," Ivar explains to Alexandra (93), and she declares herself his ally, assuring him that "we will go on living as we think best" and vowing to "start an asylum for old-time people" (94–5). In the end, though, Ivar reveals that his "difference" stems from his brutal subjugation to the religio-juridical discourses of proper and improper bodies. Called queer and crazy by his neighbors and the narrator, Ivar is terrorized by the specter of the queerness within himself, driven to "trampl[e] in filth when my desires are low" and then compulsively clean his "free members" again.

How, though, does O Pioneers! finally assess the status of the "queer" and the problems of embodiment represented not only in Ivar but in the text's generalized fascination with bodily types, stories, and significations? Ivar's queerness—his bodily difference and his apparent deviation from socially constructed notions of the normal—clearly masks a deeper sameness—i.e., his self-loathing is fueled by the same rage for order and conformity that also fuels Lou's persecution of him—but to be queer in this instance means to be vulnerable to the medical and juridical authorities that have established themselves in the recently domesticated prairie town of Hanover. Lou, Alexandra's scheming, intolerant brother, presents Ivar's "symptoms" to the superintendent of the asylum in Hastings, who reportedly pronounces Ivar's "case" "one of the most dangerous kind" (99). When Lou suggests to Alexandra that neighbors could have Ivar committed by making a complaint against him, she replies that if such a thing should happen, "I'll have myself appointed Ivar's guardian and take the case to court, that's all" (101). Like Paul facing the punitive tribunal of his school teachers, who eventually expel him and judge his to be "a bad case" (*CS* 181), Ivar cannot adequately defend himself and must rely upon Alexandra to protect him from the authorities he fears,[6] which are different from the biblical authorities he reveres only in that they threaten him with imminent bodily confinement. Besieged from within by the dictates of conscience and from without by those who see his "spells" not as divinely inspired but as threats to their own bodies and property ("he's likely to set fire to the barn any night, or to take after you and the girls with an axe," claims Lou [100]), Ivar has in effect been to the asylum without ever actually going there, having internalized the disciplinary mechanisms Foucault associates with asylums—i.e., guilt organized into consciousness, a guilt that transforms the madman into "an object of punishment always vulnerable to himself and to the Other" (*Madness and Civilization* 247).

With his misfit, disorderly body, Ivar is the ideal servant of the order that holds him in thrall, greeting the abject Alexandra, when he finally finds her in the graveyard, with a horrified, "*Gud!* You are enough to frighten us, mistress. You look like a drowned woman. How could you do such a thing!" (280). He takes her home, where the loyal Signa gives the mistress a footbath—particularly appropriate, in view of what Ivar has recently told her about feet—and puts her to bed. More important, Ivar's rescue sets up the three great puzzles of the novel's conclusion: Alexandra's waking vision of a male figure in a white cloak whose shoulders "seemed as strong as the foundations of the world" (283); her visit to Frank Shabata, imprisoned for murdering his wife, Marie, and Alexandra's brother Emil, which concludes with her declaring her intention to get him pardoned for his crimes; and the revelation, in the novel's closing paragraphs, that she and Carl Linstrum plan to marry. Each of these odd moves is in keeping with Ivar's and the community's preoccupation with maintaining bodily and social order: Alexandra's vision is triggered by her longing to be freed from the weight and demands of "her own body" (282); the killings of Emil and Marie seem just, or at least explicable, punishment for their violations of the institution of marriage; she and Carl are "safe" to marry because they are "friends" and therefore won't "suffer like—those young ones" (308) from the disasters wrought by excessive desires.

In a discussion aimed at situating Cather's second novel in dialogue with the turn-of-the-century's medicalization of sex, C. Susan Wiesenthal has contended that Cather responds "in a creative and challenging way to dominant contemporary theories of sexuality, quietly establishing in *O Pioneers!*, her own alternate paradigms of human sexuality" (56). She sees Alexandra as the locus of this subversion, claiming that Cather endows her heroine with "a healthy, hermaphroditic nature" that "works to break down the contemporary myth of the diseased and degenerative woman of 'intermediate sex' " (52–3) and noting that heterosexuality is frequently associated in the novel with images of decay, sickness, and pain. I would argue that Cather's engagement with the sexologists and racial suicidists is challenging but also deeply conflicted, as I hope this discussion of "queer," "Crazy" Ivar (who is left out of Wiesenthal's account) has demonstrated.

Beyond Ivar, *O Pioneers!* is obsessed with bodies and the ways in which they matter, the ways in which they signify desire, disorder, power, pain, deviance, horror, glory, and nation. We glean from these images both the "corporeal utopianism" Michael Moon has described as the heart of Walt Whitman's challenge to the nineteenth century's demonization of nonprocreative sexualities ("Disseminating Whitman" 253)[7] as well as a pronounced corporeal dystopianism—a tendency toward erotophobia, homophobia, and general ambivalence toward the condition of embodiment. These competing impulses push and pull at one another, making the "vast checker-board" (75) of the settled prairie a space of greater instability and tension than is usually recognized, particularly with the recent emphasis on Alexandra as a heroine who succeeds through "yielding" rather than through struggling (*EV* 434). The land itself, as readers of *O Pioneers!* have often noted,[8] is imaged in contradictory bodily terms, initially through Carl's young eyes, as an Amazonian "stern frozen" country that is enigmatic and withholding, wanting "to be let alone, to preserve its own fierce strength, its peculiar, savage kind of beauty, its uninterrupted mournfulness" (15), and ultimately through the narrator's eyes, as a happily yielding American Girl whose "open face" is "frank and joyous and young" (76). Such a stark contrast may accurately reflect the transformation the landscape undergoes in the blank space between part 1 ("The Wild Land") and part 2 ("Neighboring Fields") of the novel, but it also underscores several problems in the oft conjoined strategies of reading the world as if it were a body and reading the body as if it were a world. It suggests, for example, the subjective and often duplicitous character of the gaze as well as the shifting nature of "bodies" and the unreliability of the evidence they present. It also exposes the overdetermined nature of the relationship between physical spaces and human beings, particularly as it is figured in the American expressive traditions that came down to Cather from Whitman.[9]

For the most part, though, the narrator ignores such complications and blithely operates, as an observer of human beings, with a faith in bodily types derived from the positivism of the nineteenth century and the nativism of the twentieth, relying quietly but systematically on physical appearance as a means of judging and classifying individuals.[10] *O Pioneers!* may be steeped in classical myth and in allusions to British and American Romanticisms[11], but the text abounds in bodily diversity and documents the conditions and characters of each type as carefully as Frank Norris's *McTeague*, which Cather praised in an 1899 review as "realism of the most uncompromising kind," noting approvingly that "his characters are personalities of flesh before they are anything else, types before they are individuals" (*WP* 2:746–8).

Governed by the twin principles of realism and organic form, Cather's prairie resembles the dioramas mounted by taxidermist Carl Akeley in the American Museum of Natural History's African Hall. As Donna Haraway has said of Akeley's scrupulously detailed and lifelike efforts to create a "peephole into the jungle" (quoted in "Teddy Bear Patriarchy" 242), Cather's immigrants and pioneers seem at times to be specimens selected on the basis of their typicality and placed into habitat groups to tell a true story of "natural history."[12] In creating her own "peephole into the [prairie]," Cather includes in her gallery of physical types: *abject* bodies (Ivar trampling in filth, Alexandra drenched in the rain); *idealized* bodies (Alexandra, as Carl recalls her carrying her milk pails, "coming with her free step, her upright head and calm shoulders . . . as if she had walked straight out of the morning itself" [126], or the athletic Emil, mowing with a scythe, "a splendid figure of a boy, tall and straight as a young pine tree, with a handsome head, and stormy gray eyes, deeply set under a serious brow" [77]—who, it should be noted, is judged by the girls at university dances to have "something queer about him" because of his air of intensity and preoccupation [180]); *monumental* bodies (the so-called yellow man of Alexandra's early morning fantasies, who is "much larger and stronger and swifter" than any man she knew [206] and who reappears in the previously noted vision with an arm "dark and gleaming, like bronze," which Alexandra recognizes as "the arm of the mightiest of all lovers" [283]); *criminal* bodies (in prison, Frank's "shaved head, showing the conformation of his skull, gave him a criminal look which he had not had during the trial" [293]); *ethnic* bodies (Alexandra recalls that as a child, Marie's "dark red cheeks" made her look like "some queer foreign kind of a doll" [192]); *weak* bodies (Carl is "slight and narrow-chested" [9], a bodily trait that links him to Paul and accurately predicts the frustrations he will encounter in the masculine roles of pioneer and suitor when he faces opposition from the land and from Alexandra's brothers, respectively).

The most elaborate of the bodily moments in O *Pioneers!* is, however, the tableau of the *dead* bodies of Emil and Marie, which Ivar comes upon in the orchard just as the sun is rising. Here, Cather's semiotics of the body and her somatizations of story converge in an extended description that is at once highly aestheticized and brutally scientific:

> The story of what had happened was written plainly on the orchard grass, and on the white mulberries that had fallen in the night and were covered with dark stain. For Emil the chapter had been short. He was shot in the heart, and had rolled over on his back and died. His face was turned up to the sky and his brows were drawn in a frown, as if he had realized that something had befallen him. But for Marie Shabata it had not been so easy. One ball had torn through her right lung, another had shattered the carotid artery. She must have started up and gone toward the hedge, leaving a trail of blood. There she had fallen and bled. From that spot there was another trail, heavier than the first, where she must have dragged herself back to Emil's body. Once there, she seemed not to have struggled any more. She had lifted her head to her lover's breast, taken his hand in both her own, and bled quietly to death. She was lying on her right side in an easy and nat-ural position, her cheek on Emil's shoulder. On her face there was a look of ineffable content. Her lips were parted a little; her eyes were lightly closed, as if in a day-dream or a light slumber. After she lay down there, she seemed not to have moved an eyelash. The hand she held was covered with dark stains, where she had kissed it.   (268–9)

Aggressively installed in narrative and spectacle, the bodies of the dead lovers are queered by their to-be-looked-at-ness and by the play of dif-ferences registered in the tableau. Whether or not the adulterous hetero-sexual couple occupies a " 'homosexual' position" in Cather's ambivalent rendering of the heterosexual plot,[13] the lovers' corpses are made to appear self-textualizing, naturalizing the relationship between death and representation so that dying and storytelling seem to be not merely related but in fact identical activities: "The story of what had happened was written plainly on the orchard grass."

Though Frank Shabata with his "murderous 405 Winchester" (261) is the author of the crime, Marie is figured as chief author of the story written on the grass, despite the presence of her collaborator in adultery and in dying, Emil. The arrangement of the scene, then, denaturalizes the relationship between death and representation by exposing the gender asymmetries of a cultural system that constructs the feminine body as "the superlative site of alterity" and uses representations of the dead feminine body to "repress and articulate its unconscious knowledge of death which it fails to foreclose even as it cannot express it directly" (Bronfen xi). The details of the scene foreground these asymmetries, as the dead man's body is markedly reticent while the dead woman's body is rendered in a state of hyper-expressivity: Emil's "chapter" is "short," while Marie's is long and excruciatingly detailed. He is identified by first name only, which makes him seem both innocent and less Swedish (and therefore, perhaps, more "American"), while "Marie Shabata" identifies her as married and "ethnic." He is shot once, in the heart, and seems to die without bleeding, while Marie bleeds profusely from one ball that had "torn through her right lung" and another that had "shattered the carotid artery." His neatly wounded "heart" is the romantic heart of a stormy-eyed "boy" (as Alexandra and Frank both call Emil after his death [305, 293]) who would run off to Mexico in order to escape erotic temptation, but there is little romance in Marie's shattered body parts or in the narrator's anatomical precision—"right lung," "carotid artery." With his face turned up toward the sky, Emil presents "the romantic image of the beautiful corpse," while Marie, despite her "look of ineffable content," suggests "the realistic image of the ugly corpse" (Bronfen 164). Only in the woman's case does the narrator follow the track of the bullets beneath the skin, opening the body up for inspection and performing a kind of autopsy to prove, contra Poe, that the death of a beautiful woman is anything but "poetical," though the pastoral elements of the scene—the orchard setting, Marie's eyes "lightly closed, as if in a day-dream or a light slumber" (as if Sleeping Beauty and Prince Charming have nodded off in mid-fairy tale)—call attention to its artfulness. Prolix and prosaic, Marie's body—feminine, leaky, grotesquely mobile in dragging itself back and forth across the orchard—writes its story not in Cixousian "white ink" but in the "dark stains" of its own blood. In death, her mouth is open—her lips "parted a little"—but instead of words it, too, issues blood, marking Emil's body (in, literally, kisses of death) as well as the ground. In death, the beautiful, vivacious woman is finally still and silent, delivered simultaneously to art, to science, and to a process of bodily decomposition that her bleeding "quietly to death" both initiates and presages. The story begun in blood will end, as Emma Bovary's ends,[14] in the still darker stains of putrefaction.

O Pioneers! is transfixed by the spectacle of the bodies in the orchard, offering three views of the scene in addition to the narrator's extended description of it—Frank Shabata's flight from the tableau he created in a moment of drunken rage when "his blood was quicker than his brain" and he shot blindly at "the two dark figures under the tree" (263); Ivar's horror in the moment of his discovery when he falls "upon his knees as if his legs had been mowed from under him" and groans "Merciful God!" (270); Alexandra's "awe" when she reaches and immediately reads the bodies: "There was something about those two lying in the grass, something in the way Marie had settled her cheek on Emil's shoulder that told her everything" (285). But the "something" that clarifies "everything" is quickly banished, for the lovers' bodies are disentangled and buried in the Norwegian and the Catholic graveyards[15] and order is systematically restored. Interestingly, that restoration is signaled in Alexandra feeling herself "immune from evil tidings" (299) after she has visited Frank in prison. Like all "immune" systems, particularly as they were constructed in turn-of-the-century biomedical discourses, Alexandra's is bolstered by expulsion of elements perceived to be alien and threatening to it,[16] a move that is crucial to reestablishing (reconsolidating, reharmonizing) Alexandra's sense of individuality ("Oh," Signa laments, before Ivar goes to rescue their mistress in the graveyard, "I wish she would be more like herself!" [277]) and to restoring the vision of nation signified by the "gleaming white body" (206) of the farmer heroine.

In this regard, it is worth noting again that both Emil and Marie are called "queer" in the course of the novel—he because he frightens the girls who watch him "wonderingly" and assiduously at dances, she because Alexandra judges her face to look "foreign." As individuals, their "queerness" designates (perceived) sexual ambiguity in Emil's case ("Are you stuck up, Emil," asks his friend Amédée at one point, "or is anything the matter with you? I never did know a boy twenty-two years old before that didn't have no girl. You wanna be a priest, maybe?" [160–1]) and ethnic otherness in Marie's. Together, the deviance that requires their expulsion from the prairie arises not only out of their transgressions against marriage but also their violations of a code that defines safe sex as intercourse with one's own (ethnic) kind. That Alexandra subscribes to and actively enforces this code is made clear in her comments on the all-Swedish wedding of Signa and the grumpy Nelse. After the wedding celebration, as the couple sets off with each leading one of the milk cows Alexandra had given them as a present, she declares, "Those two will get on. . . . They are not going to take any chances. They will feel safer with those cows in their own stable." When Marie complains about the match, saying she would have preferred Signa to marry a more congenial Bohemian boy who had shown an interest in her the previous winter, Alexandra remarks, "I suppose she was too much afraid of Nelse to marry anyone else. Now that I think of it, most of my girls have married men they were afraid of. I believe there is a good deal of the cow in most Swedish girls. You high-strung Bohemians can't understand us. We're a terribly practical people, and I guess we think a cross man makes a good manager" (228–9).

Swedish "cow"-girls and Bohemian dolls, cross men as good "managers"—Alexandra's smug pronouncements are contravened by the particularities of her own case (e.g., her plans to marry a kind, narrow-chested man who is not a manager at all but a passive partner in a mining venture in the Klondike) and by the text's blurring of precisely the boundaries and categories Alexandra seeks to maintain (e.g., the Swedish Emil and the Bohemian Frank physically resemble one another: both are tall and fair, with good teeth and blond hair [77, 143], and Emil crosses and subverts ethnic lines both in his affinity for the French immigrants and in the exotic Mexican costume he wears to the church supper where he and Marie first kiss). In the end, though, the narrative scale of *O Pioneers!* is tilted in Alexandra's favor, as she clearly stands at the pinnacle of the novel's bodily and ideological hierarchy—healthy, wealthy, and "immune" from further attack by "queers" in her family or community. The narrative finally cannot escape the logic of the systems of representation (semiotic and political) that its proliferating figures of the body have served to interrogate, and so we are left with the "gleaming white body" of the un-queer entrepreneur who recognizes that a "good manager" is necessary to the successful operation of any business. Far from showing Cather's rejection of putatively "masculine" values and cultural activities, Alexandra's triumph is the apotheosis of Progressive Era values of systemization and efficiency in matters of business and discipline in matters of the body, values that converge in her remark to Carl that "I think, myself, it is more pleasant to do business with people who are clean and healthy-looking" (132).

Alexandra's bolstered immunity and her commitments to health and hygiene make possible a movement into transcendence that clarifies the body politics of *O Pioneers!* and situates them within U.S. social and literary history. From this standpoint the mysticism evinced in Alexandra's concluding paeans to the abiding nature of the land and the temporality of human claims upon it are a massive yet predictable denial of her life's work, which has at every point involved expanding her holdings in land, using the law to protect her claims to them, and seeking ways to maximize their profitability. "Suppose I do will my land to [my brother's children]," she says to Carl, "what difference will that make? . . . How many of the names on the county clerk's plat will be there in fifty years? I might as well try to will the sunset over there to my brother's children. We come and go, but the land is always here. And the people who love it and understand it are the people who own it—for a little while" (307–8). Only those who are secure in their titles can assert that titles don't matter, but Alexandra's question, "What *difference* will that make?," registers a desire to make invisible (or at least irrelevant) the economic system and the regulatory practices that have mediated her relationship to the land and to erase the struggles over "difference" that have marked "her" prairie as a site of U.S. history.

The narrator's final words similarly conspire in the effort to take Alexandra out of history and install her in myth in the apostrophe to the "Fortunate country, that is one day to receive hearts like Alexandra's into its bosom, to give them out again in the yellow wheat, in the rustling corn, in the shining eyes of youth!" (309). Both Alexandra and the narrator seek to turn her real possessions into imaginary ones, claiming for her the pure, unassailable title of "love" and "understand[ing]" instead of (but actually in addition to) the shifting, contestable titles worked out in the marketplace and in courts of law, where, as Priscilla Wald and others have shown, natural rights arguments about property and ownership have been pivotal to the processes through which the United States constitutes subjects and citizens.[17] The gesture aims to secure for Alexandra the transcendent, disembodied subjectivity of liberal individualism by echoing Emerson's claim that the poet would be "true landlord! sea-lord! air-lord!"—a claim previously echoed by the mentor and precursor to whom *O Pioneers!* is dedicated, Sarah Orne Jewett. In her excursion narrative "An October Ride," Jewett declares, "Each of us has truly a kingdom in thought, and a certain spiritual possession. . . . I have trees and fields and woods and seas and houses, I own a great deal of the world to think and plan and dream about. The picture belongs most to the man who loves it best and sees entirely its meaning" (*Country By-Ways* 97–8) Jewett's formulation makes a "man" out of the imaginary possessor, while Cather figures Alexandra as a "land-[lady]!" whose literal and symbolic ownership of the prairie is beyond dispute, even as she agrees with Carl that she "belong[s] to the land" (307). Alexandra is an author as well as an owner, having usurped the role played by Marie in the orchard and revised the tale written in the blood of the dying woman into "the old story" written "with the best we have" (307). The queers are gone (unless, like Ivar, they have made themselves useful as zealous servants of an anti-queer order), and Alexandra extolls the virtues of a timeless "land" whose nationhood she erases and—capably, dazzlingly—signifies.

Tonic Queers, Diva Citizens

My goal thus far has been to read *O Pioneers!*—so genial and familiar a text—in an antimystical, antiessentialist way that disrupts the coziness of Cather's second "first" novel by attending to the anxieties that underlie her portrait of a powerful, autonomous woman. Viewed through the lens of gender alone, Alexandra may indeed seem worth celebrating, supplying as she does a salubrious alternative to the Isabel Archers, Edna Pontelliers, and Lily Barts who live and die or resign themselves to death-in-life in American fiction with such grim regularity. Alexandra's triumphant personhood is considerably more vexing, however, when viewed along the axes of ethnicity and sexuality as an allegory of nation-building predicated on the repudiation or containment of the "queer" and emblematized in skin so smooth and white it is said to possess "the freshness of the snow itself" (88). Such disruptions are necessary in order to demonstrate Cather's entanglement in her own historical moment and to suggest the limitations of feminist critical models that, because of their particular investments in identity, insist upon drawing clear and stable boundaries between "male" and "female" and read female characters as if they were real women. Alexandra interests me not because she is an exceptional girl whose developmental plot concludes satisfactorily but because she is a semiotic field where important cultural work occurs. Having generated a model for reading—queering, as it were—Cather's early fiction, we may proceed to place *O Pioneers!* in dialogue with what comes before and after it. This survey will be guided by several questions: Who occupies the space of the queer in these texts, and how do they fare? How do queer and un-queer bodies signify, both in themselves and in relation to one another? Does the queer ever stand in the fiction, as it does, for example, in Cather's letters to Louise Pound, as a mark of aesthetic value or of privileged marginality? What vision of nation is ratified or repressed in images of the queer and the un-queer? How does Cather's interrogation of genre inform her representations of queerness? How do the texts negotiate the tangled issues of ownership, citizenship, authorship, and authority? Do they ever revel in a defiant anti-assimilationism, or do they valorize, as my reading of *O Pioneers!* suggests, an anxious determination to control or expel the "queer" from a "prairie" that serves as a synecdoche of the nation?

As in *O Pioneers!*, "queer" often functions throughout Cather's early fiction as the name of a bodily difference that is perceived as socially unassimilable, whether that difference is a matter of sex or gender "troubles," racial or ethnic otherness, or nonnormate physical appearance or ability—or, as is frequently the case, some combination of these factors. "Queer" is generally a judgment rendered in a context of terror and threat, making the term's invocation, as Judith Butler describes it, a "linguistic practice whose purpose has been the shaming of the subject it names or, rather, the producing of a subject *through* that shaming interpellation" (*Bodies* 226).[18] Thus, Jim Burden remarks of Ántonia's brother Marek, when he and his grandmother go to visit the Shimerdas during the Bohemian family's first difficult winter on the prairie, that he "slid cautiously toward us and began to exhibit his webbed fingers. I knew he wanted to make his queer noises for me—to bark like a dog or whinny like a horse—but he did not dare in the presence of his elders. Marek was always trying to be agreeable, poor fellow, as if he had it on his mind that he must make up for his deficiencies" (*MÁ* 62). The implication, of course, is that, try as he may, "poor" Marek cannot be "agreeable," because the differences he feels compelled to "exhibit" and to voice as "queer noises" are too great.

Similarly, when Ernest Havel, the Bohemian friend of Claude Wheeler in *One of Ours*, is informed that Claude has been injured in a bizarre plowing accident, he thinks to himself, "It's queer about that boy, . . . He's big and strong, and he's got an education and all that fine land, but he don't seem to fit in right" (120). Though able-bodied, Claude's wounded and infected face makes him "unclean and abject" in his own eyes (123) and provokes his best friend and comrade in homosociality to articulate his suspicions of an inchoate but disturbing difference that he calls "queer" and that some readers have called "homosexuality."[19] Finally, in *The Song of the Lark*, Thea Kronborg's Aunt Tillie is described as "a queer, addle-pated thing, at thirty-five as flighty as a girl, and overweeningly fond of gay clothes" (24). Tillie is called "queer" due to the unconventional nature of her gender performance—because she dresses "gay" and acts like a "girl" long after her body shows her to be a mature "woman"—but in this case "queerness" proves also to be an asset, a mark of nonconformism and superior insight. Tillie is right, for example, in her "intuitions" about her niece's talent and her "brilliant future" (83). The novel's epilogue even returns to Thea's hometown and her chattering "queer old aunt" (578), lapsing into a congenial second-person address to assure the reader that "If you chanced to be passing down that Moonstone street" and saw Tillie out on her front porch "you might feel sorry for her, and how mistaken you would be! [for] Tillie lives in a world full of secret satisfactions" (577–8).

Marek's queerness earns Jim Burden's pity and disgust, because he reads it as rooted in pathologies of the body that are not amenable to change, have no obvious social value, and likely signal a weakness in the Shimerda family constitution (a weakness subsequently confirmed in the father's suicide and Ántonia's sexual fall). With Tillie, however—and a few other figures, including Claude Wheeler, as we shall see—Cather opens up a different set of queer possibilities, redeploying the mark of shame and using it as the staging ground for a critique of the homophobic categories of the sexologists and, though in a more limited and ambivalent way, the virulent xenophobia of the racial suicidists. The narrator of *The Song of the Lark* literally smiles on Tillie, insisting that the "wildest conceits" of this queer "romancer" (580), far from threatening the prairie, are essential to its imaginative and economic life, as her stories of Thea's success—celebrated as an example of "Moonstone enterprise" (580)—give her provincial neighbors "something to talk about and to conjecture about, cut off as they are from the restless currents of the world" (581). Rather than being the source of contagion, as it was in *O Pioneers!*, here the queer is a tonic presence, for Tillie's stories make Moonstone "habitable and wholesome" by "bring[ing] refreshment" to the community, just as nightly tides bring "fresh brine" into "the seemingly stagnant water of the lagoons" surrounding Venice (581). As with so many of the spinster-story-tellers of Jewett's fiction, Tillie's eccentricity is not coded as pathology, and the instability she brings to her community is viewed as productive rather than destructive. Unlike Ivar, who battles to subject himself to an anti-queer order, Tillie is proud and unregenerate in her queerness and saves Moonstone from the narrowness and rigidity—i.e., the stagnation— of an excess of order.

Tillie's prophylactic power suggests a good deal more than that Cather had learned to follow Jewett's lead in crafting an affable narrator with a soft spot for eccentric elderly women, though it does show that. The agent and not just the object of a "queering" on the prairie, Tillie as storyteller and "romancer" also throws into relief a vital pattern that shapes Cather's first decade as a novelist. That pattern, which has not been sufficiently explored, may be stated in the form of a proposition: *The further Cather moves away from realism as the structuring principle of her narratives, the more likely it is that white heteronormativity will be challenged by a "queerness" marked not as individual pathology but as forceful oppositionality.*[20] Cather never comes close to abandoning narrative altogether, as some of her modernist contemporaries did, but she does challenge many of the governing assumptions of realism as well as what Judith Roof has described as the "heteroideology of narrative," which articulates the reciprocal relation between narrative and sexuality that tends to produce "stories where homosexualities can only occupy certain positions or play certain roles metonymically linked to negative values within a reproductive aegis" (xxvii). Nor does she seriously attempt to " 'lesbianize' language," as de Lauretis has suggested Monique Wittig does in her assaults on personal pronouns ("Sexual Indifference" 149). Nonetheless, Cather's steady movement away from realist technologies of representation—e.g., detached and impersonal narration, the striving for verisimilitude and the illusion of unmediated transcriptions of a world, plots driven by conflicts and the rhythms of heterosexual desire—is a movement toward the generic instability and the profound subversiveness of her ambitious narrative experiments of the 1920s, *The Professor's House* (1925) and *Death Comes for the Archbishop* (1927).[21]

Examined under the logic of this pattern, *Alexander's Bridge* and *O Pioneers!*, which Cather and generations of readers have labored to distinguish from one another, are more alike than different, each similarly invested in realist logics and tactics. They share, for example, a predilection for reading the body through limited taxonomies and an ambivalent fascination with the chaotic force of illicit sexuality, a fascination that ultimately leads to the elimination of threat and the restoration of a conservative sexual order. Cather's doomed engineer, Bartley Alexander, is by no means "queer," though his old friend and teacher, Lucius Wilson, finds his former pupil an enigma, admitting there is something about him that "simply wouldn't square" (12). Like the narrator of *O Pioneers!*, however, the narrator of *Alexander's Bridge* has an eye for bodies that exemplify a type, which Bartley emphatically does:

> There were other bridge-builders in the world, certainly, but it was always Alexander's picture the Sunday Supplement men wanted, because he looked as a tamer of rivers ought to look. Under his tumbled sandy hair his head seemed as hard and powerful as a catapult, and his shoulders looked strong enough in themselves to support a span of any one of his ten great bridges that cut the air above as many rivers.   (8)

Like the "gleaming white" skin of Alexandra, Alexander's "hard and powerful" body both captivates and signifies. With his "rugged blond good looks" (8), Bartley presents the manly white body of American civilization, the turn-of-the-century body that is part organism and part machine, the modern nervous body that is never truly at rest and never fully at ease.[22] If Alexandra is a rural, female, and generally stable version of this busy body, Bartley is an urban (though by birth Western), male, and highly unstable version of it. But where Alexandra disciplines her body through hard work and the cold baths she "prosecute[s] . . . with vigor" (206) as the penalty for sleeping late and indulging in erotic fantasies, Bartley's instability leads to bodily vulnerability and a fatal indulgence in his passion for the actress Hilda Burgoyne. (Bartley's infidelity is "fatal" in that his affair with Hilda prevents him from receiving a telegram informing him of problems on his Moorlock Bridge. Had he received it, he would have halted work and not been on the bridge, along with a crew of workers, when it collapsed [see 81].) The logic and the deep structure of both stories are the same: the disciplined body is the basis of a narrative and social order that the realistic novel, exemplified for Cather in the works of James and Wharton, seeks to maintain, however critically or reluctantly; the undisciplined body must be brought into order, as happens with Alexandra and Ivar, or destroyed, as happens with Emil, Marie, and Bartley.

When *Alexander's Bridge* was first published in the February, March, and April 1912 issues of *McClure's* (with the title *Alexander's Masquerade*), its first two installments ran concurrently with the last two installments of a five-part series on prostitution by Hull House founder, Jane Addams. F. Graham Cootes's illustrations for the novel depict Bartley as a burly man whose body visually dominates every picture and whose face bears a distinct resemblance to the young Teddy Roosevelt (who, elsewhere in the pages of *McClure's*, was being encouraged to enter the presidential race of 1912).[23] Given Cather's long association with *McClure's*, even though she was on leave from her position as managing editor when the novel ran, she likely had some say in how it was presented in the magazine, so it is unlikely that these intertextualities are entirely coincidental. Coincidental or not, however, they suggest how fully—even literally—enmeshed her story of the adulterous bridge-builder is in Progressive discourses of sexual and racial hygiene. By 1912 Roosevelt—as Rough Rider, president, and big game hunter—had been promoting "the strenuous life" and all it implied—"manly virtue, masculine violence, and white American racial supremacy"—as the "antithesis of overcivilized decadence" (Bederman 192–3) for nearly fifteen years. Meanwhile, Addams and other crusaders against "the social evil," whose exposés of how conditions for immigrant working-class women in the cities fueled the traffic in "white slavery" were featured regularly in the pages of *McClure's*,[24] had succeeded in gaining passage of the Mann Act in 1910, which "forbade the transportation of women across state lines for 'immoral' purposes" (D'Emilio and Freedman 202). Still, the battle for sexual/social purity raged, and Addams, in the installment of her series that ran the month before Cather's novel began, called for a program of moral education and "sex hygiene" in order to protect society from "the havoc wrought by the sexual instinct when uncontrolled." "Unrestrained stimulation" of the sex instinct may make a young man's imagination so "perverted" and "evil" that it may "swamp his faculties" and inhibit his power for "normal living." Addams invokes the specter of "race deterioration" as the greatest threat posed by illicit sexuality and offers this bit of advice to her readers: "The wise men in every age have known that only the power of the spirit can overcome the lusts of the flesh" ("Lack of Moral Education" 339–40).

Bartley's lust of the flesh leads not to prostitution but to marital infidelity, and male infidelity was lower on the scale of sexual sins than female infidelity (Haller and Haller 237–8), which may be why he suffers less in death than does Marie Shabata. His loyal and deceived wife, Winifred, washes his body "clean of every mark of disaster," and the narrator reports that "For Alexander death was an easy creditor" (87–8). Nevertheless, in the throes of his obsession for the Irish actress and in his obvious sexual incompatibility with his "very proud, and just a little hard" Boston wife (47), Bartley seems a middle-aged version of Addams's erotically overstimulated schoolboy, his death by drowning neatly literalizing the "swamp[ing]" of his faculties by a sex instinct run amuck. Bartley experiences the rekindling of his desires for Hilda, whom he had loved as a youth (and student) in Paris and whom he encounters years later in London, as a corruption of his whole being, comparing himself to horses crazed by loco and to the beseiged Dr. Jekyll, telling Hilda in a frantic and manipulative letter:

> I feel as if a second man had been grafted into me. At first he seemed only a pleasure-loving simpleton, of whose company I was rather ashamed, and whom I used to hide under my coat. . . . But now he is strong and sullen, and he is fighting for his life at the cost of mine. That is his one activity: to grow strong. No creature ever wanted so much to live. Eventually, I suppose, he will absorb me altogether. (69)

Exiled though he may feel from all the civilized spaces of his former life—garden, home, study, "all these quiet streets where my friends live" (68)—Bartley is clearly thrilled by the "unnatural excitement" and the "enervating reveries" that "torture" and "batter" him (47) throughout his duplicity. For Bartley the affair is a prolonged masturbatory fantasy, a reunion with the Rooseveltian "boy he had been in the rough days of the old West" and a relief from the feeling that he was "being buried alive" in the "dead calm of middle life" (27–8) by his public and professional responsibilities. Crossing the Atlantic to see Hilda, he is "continually hammering away at himself" in an effort to resolve to end the relationship, but his "hammering" gives way to "a sudden painful delight at being near another shore" (53).

Elizabeth Ammons reads Bartley's personal collapse and his professional failure—both so spectacularly evident, at least to readers, who know about his betrayal of his marriage, in the collapse of his great cantilever bridge—as proof that the novel aims to "demythologize the myth" of the American engineer and the values of "conquest and rugged masculinity embedded in" that heroic image. Cather's depiction of Bartley as a "flesh-and-blood dynamo, a well-equipped muscular mechanism" stands as a "negative judgment of Progressive Era America and of the social construction of masculinity in the United States at the time" ("The Engineer as Cultural Hero" 754–6). Despite Bartley's obvious chafing against social constraints and the dehumanizing effects of having turned his own "internal heat" into "functions of a mechanism useful to society, things that could be bought in the market" (28), the narrator's judgment seems to weigh more heavily against Bartley than it does against the society that produced him and whose values Ammons sees him as signifying. The narrator's epitaph on Bartley frames his death as a matter of mental deficiency, suggesting that he is the cause and not the effect of another type of "social evil":

> When a great man dies in his prime there is no surgeon who can say whether he did well; whether or not the future was his, as it seemed to be. The mind that society had come to regard as a powerful and reliable machine, dedicated to its service, may for a long time have been *sick within itself and bent upon its own destruction.* (88, emphasis added)

Society may be partly to blame for having regarded Bartley's mind merely as "a powerful and useful machine," but the language of a mind made "sick" and "bent" by desire—which implies that Bartley is perhaps a bit "queer" after all—localizes pathology and indicates that Cather's novel is a cautionary psychosexual tale surprisingly similar to Addams's cautionary stories of schoolboys and immigrant girls. Sexual activity other than what is "essential to the continuance of the race," as Addams puts it (339), is an activity likely to lead to the deterioration of the race. Bartley, whose marriage produces no children and whose affair brings only "ugliness . . . into the world" (79), perfectly exemplifies the turn-of-the-century's pathologization of nonprocreative sexualities. His indulgences are shameful and self-destructive, and the world quietly reconstitutes its old boundaries once he is gone out of it: his widow maintains her "beautiful and dignified sorrow" (91) in Boston; his mistress, as hostess, excels at "making people comfortable" (89) in London; and his old friend Lucius Wilson shuffles back and forth between the two women, sipping tea and being careful not to know too much about what had gone on between Bartley and Hilda. Jane Addams couldn't have scripted a more complete restoration of a safe sexual order.

Bartley Alexander's transformation from exemplary citizen to masturbating boy and unmarked corpse represents his betrayal of the Progressive mania for building and efficiency rather than Cather's clear rejection of those values. Though harshly judged and severely punished for his sexual misconduct, Bartley's involvement in the project of designing and building the American future elicits from other characters and the narrative itself a mixture of awe and anxiety, admiration and fear. His death leaves an ordered but seemingly empty world, as though the loss of his tremendous energies had turned the novel into a blank text. The novel ends in the blankness of silence, as Wilson and Hilda fall quiet while discussing his recent visit with Bartley's widow:

> "...We shouldn't wonder too much at Mrs. Alexander. She must feel how useless it would be to stir about, that she may as well sit still; that nothing can happen to her after Bartley."

> "Yes," said Hilda softly, "nothing can happen to one after Bartley."

> They both sat looking into the fire. (93)

That reiterated "nothing" and the pervasive immobility of this conclusion underscore again the structural similarity of Cather's two "first" novels: shaped by realism's will to mastery of the body and the visible world, *Alexander's Bridge* ends in death and *O Pioneers!* ends in the promise of marriage. Vice is punished, and virtue rewarded—as the conventions of the bourgeois novel have demanded since the genre's inception in the eighteenth century. The neatness of these finishes would prove, however, to be the exception rather than the rule in Cather's career as a novelist. In the other three novels produced between 1912 and 1922, *The Song of the Lark* (1915), *My Ántonia* (1918), and *One of Ours* (1922), Cather would continue to bring the body into story and probe the range of its significations, but as she deploys technologies of representation that gesture toward realism only to subvert and problematize them, her bodies are less likely to be pinned down into the immobilities of death or excessive order.

In *The Song of the Lark*, for example, Tillie's prophylactic queerness is only one aspect of the text's radical circumventions of order. Thea Kronborg's story is above all else, I would argue, a tale of glorious embodiment, and her collosal, expressive form has made her something of a cult figure in lesbian literary and cultural criticism.[25] Thea's body can properly be called "queer" because it is marked from the beginning as different, though in this case difference is positively valued as the aura of a special destiny, the allure of the celebrity she will become, and, most importantly, as the grounds for reimagining the relations between politics and the body in the U.S. From the first and without singing a note, Thea embodies what Lauren Berlant has wittily termed "Diva Citizenship," "an unrealized form of political activity" whose subversive possibilities are glimpsed in figures who expose the contradictions between America's "universalizing logic of disembodiment" and its social practices of domination over the minoritized bodies of those persons deemed "illegitimate, far beyond the horizon of proper citizenship."

The Diva Citizen aims "to create national publics trained to think, and thus to think differently, about the corporeal conditions of citizenship." She "mobilizes her contradictions to unsettle the representational and political machinery of a dominant culture that desires her" but does not recognize her (564–6). She does what is, within the logic of that machinery, unthinkable: she uses voice and body to address the nation and change the conditions of nationality. All of this Thea does, with gusto. When she first appears in the novel, Thea is eleven years old and has pneumonia. A strangely predatory Dr. Archie unveils her sick body and thinks to himself "what a beautiful thing a little girl's body was—like a flower," while the narrator explains that Archie's childless marriage "was a very unhappy one." In this moment of undressing and redressing (as the doctor "sew[s] her up" in a flaxseed jacket [11]), Thea's otherness is emphatically and multiply marked: she is foreign (a "little Swede, through and through," though she was born in Colorado of American-born parents), female, young, ill, "different" ("he believed that there was something very different about her"), and erotically stimulating (12). However, Thea's "milky white" skin (12) marks her as the assimilable ethnic, for it signals, as does Alexandra's, both a strong physical "constitution" (13) and the political "constitution" of that nation made out of immigrants, the United States. Thea is thus a good candidate for American Girl and Diva Citizen because she images both the national fantasy of "becoming American" as well as the refusal, the critique of that ideal. Though racially assimilable and legally "beyond the horizon of proper citizenship" only because as a woman she lacks the right to vote, Thea has no interest in becoming "the same." Instead, she moves constantly between categories, exposing their contingency and reveling in their contradictions. Initially, Thea is "very sensitive about being thought a foreigner" (19), but she eventually sees a benefit in claiming an ethnic identity, explaining to Archie later that "Swedes are kind of common, but I think it's better to be something" (105). To be "American" is by implication to be "nothing" or, worse perhaps, to be Anna, the sanctimonious older sister whose mind has "really shocking habits of classification" and whose "conventional" face has not "the Scandinavian mould of countenance." " 'Anna, she's American,' Mrs. Kronborg used to say" (166–7).

Thea is native-born but not "American," and though she and her mother suggest that being Swedish is an identity—a "something"—fixed in the body or the genes, Thea's mobility and her powerful subjectivity enact an assault on the "habits of classification" that underlie such claims. What I am calling Thea's mobility is also, importantly, an attribute of her body, which "had the elasticity that comes of being highly charged with the desire to live" (282). That elasticity is crucial to Thea's success as a singer, since her discovery of her vocal power hinges upon the recognition that voice is "vitality[,] a lightness in the body," and that she could only sing "when her body bounded like a rubber ball away from its hardness" (381). It is also crucial to *The Song of the Lark*'s fierce and exuberant reclaiming of the body as a site of power, pleasure, and utopian possibility, for the text stands not simply as a resistance to coercive heteronormativity but as a positive alternative to it. Cather's soprano may be drained and disciplined by the rigors of "operatic routine" (544), but Thea's hard work and her strong, cherished, elastic body represent a caring for and cultivating of self that is radically at odds with the punitive notions of self-discipline that characterize Alexandra Bergson and Bartley Alexander (as well as most of the other characters in Cather's early fiction).

The singer's discipline is more like the "ascesis" or practice of self that Foucault describes in *The Use of Pleasure* as "those intentional and voluntary actions by which men not only set themselves rules of conduct, but also seek to transform themselves, to change themselves in their singular being, and to make their life into an *oeuvre* that carries certain aesthetic values and meets certain stylistic criteria" (10–11). In contrast to Alexandra's cold baths and Bartley's guilty "hammering away" at himself, Thea's relationship to her body is not a matter of shame but of reverence and profound pleasure, not a matter of avoiding the forbidden but of discovering and honoring the sacred. In Panther Canyon her baths come to have "a ceremonial gravity" (378), as she luxuriates in the warmth and the solemn history of the place. Conducting her own summer course in women's studies, Thea comes through the rituals of bathing and arduous climbing on the water-trail to have "intuitions" about the Anasazi women who had been custodians of the "precious water" in the canyon and made "graceful jars" not simply to hold the water but to express their desires for beauty (377–9). In her apartment in New York her bathroom is "a refuge," where she does "Swedish exercises," "fairly play[s] in the water" with her brushes and sponges, and admires the "cheering sight" of her own body in the mirror (515), even on the morning after a particularly grueling performance as Elsa in *Lohengrin*.

These are the moments, I have to confess, when I find myself astonished and delighted by Thea Kronborg, no matter how skeptical I am about the identificatory fantasies that shape such readerly responsiveness. Still, Thea gets me every time: a woman who works on her body, plays with her body, finds satisfaction instead of torment in looking at her body, actively wishes to nourish and have more body rather than trying to starve herself to death in an effort to have less. To get a sense of how remarkable Thea is in this regard, try comparing her to other fictional women before the mirror. See, for example, Wharton's pathetic Charity Royall, the young heroine of *Summer* who, though obviously pretty, "look[s] critically at her reflection, [and] wishe[s] for the thousandth time that she had blue eyes like Annabel Balch" (8), or Lily Bart who, after a night of losing money at the bridge table, sits before the mirror and notices that her twenty-nine year old face looks "hollow and pale." Schooled by her mother to believe that trading on her beautiful face was the only way to avoid the fate of "dinginess," Lily is "frightened by two little lines near her mouth, faint flaws in the smooth curve of her neck" (25). In contrast to their shrinking and self-loathing, Thea as a young woman tells Dr. Archie she hopes she'll keep growing because she "particularly" wants to be tall (105). As a diva at the height of her success, she has an enormous postperformance appetite, which Fred Ottenburg, to his credit, both accommodates and admires. "Aren't you hungry, though!" he gasps, as she devours a plate of grilled chops and kidneys after her thrilling debut as Sieglinde. "It's beautiful to see you eat." "Glad you like it," she replies. "Of course I'm hungry" (535). For the satisfaction of this moment alone, I have always thought Cather was wrong to regret having let *The Song of the Lark* go on for so long, following Thea beyond her period of apprenticeship and on into "the full tide of achievement," as she put it in her 1932 preface to the novel. "Success is never so interesting as struggle," she claimed. Perhaps, but the latter parts of Thea's story—those luscious details on the care and feeding of the diva, on the powerful body knowledge that drives her performances and holds audiences in thrall, and on her shrewd determination to "hold out for a big contract" with the Met because she knows "the next five or six years are going to be [her] best" (555)—show the novel's full-throated, if you will, commitment to exploring a woman who is the subject of her own desires and the extraordinary possibilities unleashed in the artful channeling and cultivation of excess.

Opera and romance, which figure prominently in *The Song of the Lark*, are both discourses of excess that serve to liberate Cather's third novel from the confines of literary realism, making possible the text's corporeal utopianism and its wide-ranging critique of white heteronormativity. "The savage blonde" (224) is the ideal vehicle for such a critique, in part because Thea's "Sapphonic" voice, as Elizabeth Wood describes it, is a "border-crossing," "transvestic enigma, belonging to neither male nor female as constructed—a synthesis, not a split." Challenging the polarities of gender and sexuality, "the Sapphonic voice is a destabilizing agent of fantasy and desire," which, in its "capacity to embody and traverse a range of sonic possibilities and overflow sonic boundaries, may vocalize inadmissible sexualities and a thrilling readiness to go beyond so-called natural limits, an erotics of risk and defiance, a desire for desire itself" (32–3). Where *Alexander's Bridge* and *O Pioneers!* were, as we have seen, preoccupied with defining limits and policing borders, *The Song of the Lark* is concerned with "go[ing] beyond" limits not by transcending them but by constantly pushing up against them, sneaking around them, shaking them up from within. "You'll always drive ahead," Fred tells Thea in a moment of angry insight. "You will always break through into the realities" (444). Driven and forceful, Thea is also a pragmatist—she has a way of finding and profiting from what she needs. She parlays the $600 Ray Kennedy leaves her and the money Dr. Archie loans her into a career that earns her "a thousand dollars a night," as Tillie is fond of reminding her neighbors in Moonstone (576). She is as skilled an entrepreneur as Alexandra, but she is also a defiant queer: larger than life, disruptive of familial and social order, fabulously accessorized. (On the night she is summoned to fill in for a soprano stricken with fainting fits mid-performance, Thea orders Dr. Archie into her trunk-room and points him toward a white trunk " 'full of wigs, in boxes. Look until you find one marked "Ring 2." Bring it quick!' While she directed him, she threw open a square trunk and began tossing out shoes of every shape and colour" [527].)

"Romance" serves in *The Song of the Lark* as a measure of the emotional and imaginative investments other characters have in Thea Kronborg and of the narrative's investment in blurring the lines between generic categories, a blurring that will come increasingly to characterize Cather's relationship to genre. Aunt Tillie's status as a "romancer" has already been noted. Her "wildest conceits" about her niece are confirmed by the reports she reads in the New York papers (580). Dr. Archie, too, belatedly acknowledges to Thea the extent to which he has lived off and through her, noting that life "would have been a pretty bleak stretch" had she not been part of it. "I guess I'm a romantic old fellow, underneath," he explains. "And you've always been my romance" (549). Fred's prediction that Thea "will always break through into the realities" ascribes to her powers of hubris and revelation often associated with romance and romancers in American fiction and critical discourse. Indeed, his language uncannily echoes Ahab's claim that "All visible objects . . . are but as pasteboard masks" concealing reason and reality, as well as the captain's maniacal determination that "If man will strike, strike through the mask!"

In the end Thea does "break through" to the "truthfulness" and the "passion" that is "every artist's secret," according to Harsanyi, the piano teacher credited with discovering Thea's voice (570–1). The terms of that breakthrough connect the romance of *The Song of the Lark* to Hawthorne, Whitman, and Frank Norris as well as Melville, for Hawthorne and Norris had both defined buried truths and truthfulness as the province of romance, while Whitman's influence is apparent in a description that articulates Thea's triumph as a movement into open space: "this afternoon the closed roads opened, the gates dropped" (571).[26] The romance of *The Song of the Lark* is Whitmanesque in broad terms as well as in specific details—in the capaciousness of the narrative and its genial embrace of contradiction, in its celebration of the body in action and in the world. The diva whose body is "absolutely the instrument of her idea" (571) puts the lie to the ideal of disembodied subjectivity and proves that corporeality can and must be the grounds for a "dynastic, dignified, and pleasuring" notion of citizenship (Berlant 565). Even Thea's mother participates in the romances spun out of her daughter's impressive physicality, taking pleasure in Thea's "good looks" and recalling that "as a baby, Thea had been the 'best-formed' of any of her children." She even conducts her own hands-on examination of Thea's developing body when she is home for a summer visit, "feeling about" on her chest and declaring, "You're filling out nice" (282–3). Such maternal interest and approval elicit from Thea the recognition that "There was no sham about her mother," which is the basis of an affection that endures long after Thea has left home for good, having recognized that she is not a part of her family, that her siblings in particular, instead of being *"of her kind,"* were in fact "among the people whom she had always recognized as her natural enemies" (301, emphasis in original).

Thea's amplitude, her "filling out," is "nice," but it is also complex, predicated as it is to some degree on her "filling [up]" on the labor and cultures of other people. In some ways Thea signifies a vision of nation that is not "queer" at all but is in fact perfectly "normal," unproblematically "American": in a consumer culture, she triumphs by recognizing that "anything good is—expensive" and managing her career accordingly (557); in an imperialist culture, she identifies happily with Ray Kennedy's "feeling of empire," seeing as "the real element of companionship" between herself and the dreamy railroad man his feeling that "all the Southwest really belonged to him because he had knocked about over it so much, and knew it, as he said, 'like the blisters on his own hands' " (277); in a racist culture, she assumes that lost laundry has been stolen by some "nigger" (563), and the narrator casually describes "Spanish Johnny" as "a grey-haired little Mexican, withered and bright as a string of peppers beside an adobe door" (572). Such moments suggest that the subversive, celebratory mood of *The Song of the Lark* is at times undercut by signs of dis-ease and anxiety about the security of white racial power and civilization. The text manifests some superficial awareness of these anxieties when, for instance, Mrs. Kronborg admonishes her children not to spoil their Sunday dinner "with race prejudices" (298) after they attack Thea for singing at a party in Mexican Town or when the narrator explains Johnny's refusal to respond to an insult by one of Thea's brothers: "A Mexican learns to dive below insults or soar above them, after he crosses the border" (61).

In *The Song of the Lark* the crossing of borders is fraught with risk, though it does not result in death, as it does in *Alexander's Bridge* and *O Pioneers!*. When Johnny comes north, he encounters racial hostility. When Thea ventures south on her trip to Mexico with Fred Ottenburg, she faces the sexual and social vulnerability of being an unmarried woman traveling with a man who, unbeknownst to her, is married to someone else at the time. Still, the crossing of borders and the blurring of boundaries is necessary to the "queering" of "America" that *The Song of the Lark* finally if at times ambivalently enacts. That "queering" is rooted in Thea's denial of her family, for in rejecting a blood-based system of kinship— which she does in marking her siblings as "natural enemies" who are not "*of her kind*"—she attacks as factitious the racial and sexual logic of a representational system that constructs her own ultrawhite body as clean and Johnny's nonwhite body as "dirty," the epithet her brother Gunner hurls at Johnny. The narrative may cryptically deliver Thea to heterologic in slipping in an allusion to her marriage to Fred in the epilogue, but it never delivers her to reproduction,[27] and the narrative proper ends in homologic, in the queer space of the opera, where Thea performs for "her kind," claiming kinship not with her family—none of whom is present at this performance, though Spanish Johnny is—but with an audience whose response is "almost savage in its fierceness" (569). Interestingly, the only moment of the opera, Wagner's *Die Walkure*, that is fully detailed in the diegesis of the novel is the duet in the first act in which Sieglinde and Siegmund, who are sister and brother, recognize their passion for and relationship to one another. The duet ends with the incestuous couple racing off together into a beautiful spring night. Thea and the audience thus join ecstatically in celebrating the Volsung pair's violation of the taboo that defines and sustains the patriarchal family, a taboo rooted in the impossible desire to stabilize the boundary between the natural and the unnatural, between endogamy and exogamy. The "savage blonde"—as Diva Citizen, Viking soprano, Cliff-Dweller, American Girl, and anti-American Queer—unsettles those boundaries and with a "flaming cry" (568) invites us to revel in the wrecked machinery of the sex-race-gender system. With "savage . . . fierceness," we comply.

Bohemian Girls, Soldier Boys

For Cather, the body that signifies the nation is a queer body indeed— never fully the property of the "person" who inhabits it, never fully in control of the symbolic resonances arising from it, never stable in its relationship to official and unofficial notions of citizenship or to medical notions of the normal and the abnormal. This examination of her first three novels has established the poles that define Cather's vexed engagement with processes of national self-imaging that judged and marked every body. *Alexander's Bridge* and *O Pioneers!* point, on the one hand, to a dystopic fear of the queer (understood as a range of deviations from white heteronormativity) that images difference as a form of contagion requiring strict mechanisms of bodily and social control. Bartley Alexander's death and Alexandra Bergson's passionless efficiency attest to the smooth operation of these mechanisms. *The Song of the Lark* gestures, on the other hand, toward the utopic possibilities of queerness as a positive counterdiscipline motivated not by terror but by reverence and a sense of play. On stage or in her bathtub, Thea Kronborg is a celebration of power and plenitude—of a corporeal "filling out" that is "nice" because excess is the art and soul of the diva. Having staked out these parameters, I will conclude this chapter by looking at *My Ántonia* and *One of Ours*, texts whose divergent critical histories (the one novel so beloved, the other so marginalized) have obscured their important connections to one another and their place within the literary and cultural project I have been describing.

My Ántonia represents a significant tactical shift and a movement away from the optimism of *The Song of the Lark*, as Cather abandons realism in favor of the fully subjective mode of first-person narration, deploying a middle-aged Jim Burden as the main teller of a story that is chiefly about himself, though his title calls attention to a woman with whom he grew up on the Nebraska prairie. In the uncertain balance between the teller and the tale, Cather grapples—in a novel written in the midst of World War I and revised for a second edition in the midst of the xenophobic 1920s—with how a southern European immigrant woman figures into the contest to signify "America." Ántonia's remoteness and her lack of access to the possibilities of Diva Citizenship are foregrounded by the novel's imbricated narrative structure, doubly layered in that an introduction appended to Jim's narrative shows an unnamed speaker who clearly or subtly calls Jim's point of view into question, depending on which edition of the novel—1918 or 1926—one accepts as authoritative.[28] Judith Butler has argued that such layering and repetition—particularly the convergence between Jim's title for his manuscript and Cather's title for the novel—results in a false transfer of narrative authority, so that the text that "Cather" appears to give away in letting Jim tell the story actually stays in her control. The "false transfer" is important as "a figure for the crossing of identification which both enables and conceals the workings of desire" (*Bodies* 148–9). For my purposes, however, the transfer from "Cather" to Jim, true or false, is crucial to the text's interrogation of the sociopolitical technologies of vision and visibility, the conditions that determine access to cultural power and narrative authority. Transfixed by and yet never able to re-present directly "a Bohemian girl . . . [who] seemed to mean to us the country, the conditions, the whole adventure of our childhood" (5), *My Ántonia* is profoundly pessimistic about the possibility of altering what de Lauretis calls "the standard of vision, . . . of *what can be seen*" ("Sexual Indifference" 152).

Jim is the arbiter of "what can be seen" in his narrative. "Cather" lets us know that he doesn't see clearly or neutrally, being endowed with a "romantic disposition," a disposition that, in the 1918 version of the introduction, is written on a body that seems unmarked by time yet is carefully particularized in terms of gender, race, region, and nation: "[Jim Burden] never seems to me to grow older," "Cather" remarks. "His fresh color and sandy hair and quick-changing blue eyes are those of a young man, and his sympathetic, solicitous interest in women is as youthful as it is Western and American" (5). However, these details, which show the situatedness of Jim's point of view, are excised from the 1926 version of the introduction, as are comments from "Cather" that place his view of Ántonia in relation to her own: "He had had opportunities that I, as a little girl who watched her come and go, had not" (6). The excision of such details, as well as the occlusion of "Cather's" status as a writer and her active role in shaping Jim's manuscript, destabilizes the text by making uncertain the connection between the introduction and Jim's narrative and by making the few editorial marks upon his narrative—such as the footnote on the pronunciation of Ántonia's name and the insertion of the illustrations by W. T. Benda—seem in a sense to have come from nowhere. That destabilization reveals the novel's uneasy preoccupation with the gendering of the power struggle at the heart of language as an ideological system. "Cather" is the only woman in the book who speaks in her own voice rather than through Jim's, but her speaking, confined to the supplementary textual space of the introduction, underscores rather than overcomes the muted state of women's voices that characterizes *My Ántonia* and contrasts so dramatically with the "flaming cry" of Thea Kronborg's powerful soprano. Elusive and self-effacing, "Cather" is barely a presence in her own brief narrative, receding away from the reader as she swerves continually toward Jim, her conversation with him, and their shared experience of growing up "in a little prairie town,"

> buried in wheat and corn, under stimulating extremes of climate: burning summers when the world lies green and billowy beneath a brilliant sky, when one is fairly stifled in vegetation, in the colour and smell of strong weeds and heavy harvests; blustery winters with little snow, when the whole country is stripped bare and grey as sheet iron. (3)

"Buried," "stifled," and "stripped bare" aptly describes the condition of women's voices in *My Ántonia*, and Cather's revisions to the introduction indicate more clearly that "Cather" suffers as fully from this condition as the women whose voices are selectively recalled, transcribed, and contextualized by Jim Burden. Jim may not be fully credible and his perceptions may on a few occasions be challenged by critical female voices that erupt out of his narrative, but he is still creator and sovereign of the world he calls into being from the opening "I first heard of Ántonia on what seemed to me an interminable journey across the great midland plain of North America" (9). By 1926, "Cather" had been "stripped bare" of the power or authority necessary to challenge the larger claim Jim makes to Ántonia. Unwilling or unable to offer a glimpse of "her" Ántonia, "Cather" stands as a sign of Cather's deep skepticism about women's ability to compete in the contest to figure themselves in a culturally powerful way.

Jim is the policeman on the prairie, seeking to impose order on a space that is initially so undifferentiated that to him, "There seemed to be nothing to see" (12). As part of bringing the prairie from "outside" to inside "man's jurisdiction" (12), in his narrative Jim functions as a sexual-linguistic gatekeeper, translator, and monitor of female and immigrant language and behavior. Ántonia is on more than one occasion criticized for using language deemed inappropriate to her gender, as Jim notes disapprovingly that "she could talk of nothing but the prices of things, or how much she could lift and endure" (100). He also chastises her for "jabber[ing] Bohunk" (41) when the two confront a rattlesnake in prairie-dog town. Jim's harsh judgments of Ántonia in these situations contrast with the respect he accords the native-born Frances Harling for her linguistic dexterity—i.e., her ability to talk with her father "like two men" on business matters and to understand the country grandmothers "who spoke no English" (119–20)—indicating that for the immigrant woman language is a field mined with much greater risks. Ethnic difference compounds and complicates the difficulties created by gender difference, making Ántonia doubly vulnerable and doubly burdened. Just as he polices her appearance for signs of masculinization in her youth and diminishment in middle age, Jim polices Ántonia's speech for evidence of gender or ethnic transgression, both of which, in his judgment, she commits: she talks (and works) "like mans" (97) and "jabber[s] Bohunk."

Uncertain as *My Ántonia* is about the prospect of altering the conditions of vision or of mounting an effective counterstory to Jim's narrative of white male subjectivity, the "queering" of Jim's prairie is an irreversible process of social and cultural change that exceeds his policing powers and his control of authoritative discourse. "Queer" and "Bohemian" generally function as synonyms in *My Ántonia*, but each term retains a sexual as well as an ethnic resonance and each marks the failure of Jim's imaginative and ideological project. In addition to the "queer noises" issuing from the extraordinary and Bohemian body of Ántonia's brother Marek, the crossing and the mingling of the two terms throughout the text signal anxiety about proliferations of difference. Such proliferations had, by the time of *My Ántonia*'s republication, been attributed by nativists such as Lothrop Stoddard to "the rising tide of color" in the U.S. population, but they were also visible in the emergence of lesbian and homosexual communities and subcultures—in places such as Harlem and Cather's own Greenwich Village—in the 1910s and 1920s.[29]

Thus, fears of the Bohemian—included among the "hordes of swarming, prolific aliens" whom Stoddard warned were "crowd[ing] out" the Nordic (i.e., northern European) groups that had originally settled the country (165)—and fears of the queer were pervasive in the culture surrounding *My Ántonia*. Within the novel the mushrooms gathered "in some deep Bohemian forest" and offered to Jim's grandmother as a gift are fearfully tossed into the stove, their recipient suspecting "they might be dried meat from some queer beast" (64–5), and Mr. Shimerda's gun is "a queer piece from the old country," which Jim is relieved to be offered only as a promised rather than an actual gift (37–8). The suicide of the homesick Bohemian is judged by Jake Marpole to have "something mighty queer about it," while Otto Fuchs insists that Mr. Shimerda "done everything natural" (78–9). The opposition of the "queer" and the "natural" is telling, for it recalls the tension in Cather's letters of the 1890s between fears of looking and feeling queer and her protests against the supposed unnaturalness of female same-sex love.

Significantly, one of the few instances in *My Ántonia* in which "queerness" is imputed to a person or object that is not ethnically Bohemian occurs when Jim reports that he has been the subject of rumor and suspicion because of his fondness for "the hired girls": "People said there must be something queer about a boy who showed no interest in girls of his own age, but who could be lively enough when he was with Tony and Lena or the three Marys" (166). In this case "queerness" presses in the direction of the other type of "Bohemianism"—i.e., the contempt for conventional morality, art, and sexuality that Cather had privately renounced and publicly attacked in 1896.[30] Jim, too, will renounce "Bohemianism," giving up his Saturday nights of dancing with the immigrant girls when his grandmother weeps her disapproval and eventually leaving the prairie and settling into a socially advantageous if disappointing marriage to a woman "of like nationality" (154), which, as in *O Pioneers!*, is one of the primary norms constituting the regime of heterosexuality.[31] The persistence of his attraction to Ántonia suggests, however, that the renunciation is incomplete and that he remains drawn to some forms of "Bohemianism." Indeed, though Cather dismissed the figurative "Bohemia"—which defies accepted standards of art and which, as "the last inevitable step," defies nature—as "the kingdom of failure" in her 1896 review (*WP* I: 295–6), she would have Jim travel to the other "Bohemia" and send Ántonia photographs of "her native village" (245). Later, visiting Ántonia for the first time in many years, he momentarily plays at being "Bohemian," imagining himself one of "Cuzak's Boys" as he walks between two of her "straight, well-made" older sons (256).

The mobility of the terms "queer" and "Bohemian" is a function of their substitutability in relation to one another and their movement, jointly and independently, along the axes of gender, sexuality, and ethnicity. Such mobility, which Jim finds both attractive and unnerving, makes impossible the movement into sameness that fueled what Cather herself described in 1924 as the "passion for Americanizing everything and everybody" (Bohlke 71–2).[32] Cather rails that this passion is "a deadly disease among us," and its spread certainly contributed to the postwar movement to institutionalize anti-immigrant feeling in the U.S., leading, for example, to passage of legislation in her home state prohibiting the teaching of foreign languages in 1919 (Reynolds 80) and to passage of the Johnson Act in 1924, which ended unrestricted European immigration to the United States. Despite Cather's professions of support for a multicultural, multilingual prairie/nation (Bohlke 94), *My Ántonia* wavers uneasily between the poles of an impossible but coercive assimilationism and a perhaps inevitable yet uncontrollable pluralism. Jim flirts in his youth with Bohemian girls and in middle age with the fantasy of being a Bohemian boy, but in the end he is a childless man made dizzy by the "explosion of life" (252) he perceives in seeing Ántonia's children burst together out of the darkness of the fruit cave and into the sunlight, a sign that Jim harbors some of Stoddard's ambivalence about "swarming, prolific aliens." His whole narrative, which he refers to in both versions of the introduction as merely "the thing about Ántonia" (6, 280), is an effort to stop proliferation and mobility by turning her into a static symbol—but even as a symbol she moves and multiplies. As an emblem of "immemorial human attitudes" (261) and "the incommunicable past" (273), Ántonia seems safe, "universal" (261), and within Jim's control. However, the fecundity that compels him to describe her as "a rich mine of life, like the founders of early races" (261) is for Jim and *My Ántonia* the source of profound racial and sexual anxiety because she's the agent as well as the emblem of the queering of the nation. Unlike the other "queer" agents of difference, disorder, and anti-assimilationism who crop up elsewhere in the early fiction—Paul (and perhaps Bartley), who dies; Ivar, who serves; Thea, who performs—Ántonia reproduces, with gusto, raising a large brood of "strong" children who speak Bohemian—or "jabber Bohunk," as Jim had earlier described it—at home and don't learn English until they get to school. Her family thus marks the point where, as Walter Benn Michaels suggests, nativists such as Stoddard and cultural pluralists such as Horace Kallen meet: Stoddard attacks the "shibboleth of the 'melting-pot' " on the grounds that "each race-type . . . is a stubbornly persistent entity" (165), while Kallen speaks of "dissimilation"—the opposite of assimilation—as a repudiation of Americanization aimed at preserving "culturally autonomous" and "ancestrally determined" ethnic groups (quoted in *Our America* 11, 64). Settled into marriage with a man "of like nationality"— who is so "like" Ántonia that his name, Anton, is a masculine version of hers—and recovered from the sex/race crime of producing a child out of wedlock with a man (Larry Donovan) of unlike nationality, Ántonia has "forgot my English" (250) and created a self-sustaining Bohemian enclave that welcomes visitors but is largely impervious to outside influences. "It was a Bohunk crowd, for sure," reports her husband upon returning home from a street fair (264). Linguistically, socially, culturally, and economically, as Katrina Irving points out, Ántonia has rejected Americanization, though her "enclave of 'European-ness' . . . is still set amid, and serves, the economic and cultural imperatives of the American culture" (101).

In canonizing Cather as a "nativist modernist," Michaels ignores Cather's first five novels and implies that all resistance to assimilation is racially motivated (a move that flattens out and decontextualizes John Higham's nuanced definition of nativism in his still authoritative *Strangers in the Land: Patterns of American Nativism, 1860–1925*)[33]. If, however, we view sex and gender as interwoven with race but never simply the tools for advancing an exclusively racial agenda, it is possible to see another form of resistance, another type of anti-assimilationism. Cather's early fiction does indeed show the persistence through time of racial characteristics, and it sometimes hierarchizes those characteristics in ways that suggest some races are superior to and some more threatening than others. It also demonstrates, however, that normativity is dangerous and destructive, differences can be salubrious, and transgressions can produce beneficial change, possibilities that are obscured in Michaels's hypostatization of Godfrey St. Peter's ambivalence toward his Jewish son-in-law in *The Professor's House* (as well, I think, as in Michaels's assumption that

St. Peter's point of view is the text's or Cather's point of view). In *My Ántonia* miscegenation, far from being criminal, produces the mulatto pianist Blind d'Arnault and Ántonia's cherished daughter Martha,[34] moves that unsettle the stability of racial taxonomies and offset the apparentethnic purity and isolation of the Bohemian family at the end of the novel. Moreover, Jim's residual "Bohemianism" and his desire to make himself part of that family suggest that he is, like Thea Kronborg in her critique of the biological family, an agent of the "queering" of "America," for through him and Ántonia "Bohemianism" emerges as a technology for the creation of racial and sexual ambiguity—i.e., for the making of women who work "like mans" and of men who study Virgil together and then abandon the prairie for Harvard, for the destabilization of a bland Americanism, a cruel nativism, and a facile, messy pluralism.

In *My Ántonia* the challenge to assimilationism is staged through sex and gender as well as race, and the result is a brilliant uncertainty. The seductive, violet-eyed Lena Lingard earns her living as a dressmaker, catering to the tendency in consumer culture to view women's bodies as objects of display and exchange. She is imaged in Jim's narrative as just such a figure, a figure of alluring and threatening feminine excess—"a comely woman, a trifle too plump, in a hat a trifle too large" (259)—but Lena is clearly detached from the spectacle he and other men make of her body and deftly resistant to sex and gender normativity. Explaining to Jim that marriage turns men "into cranky old fathers" and that family life is "all being under somebody's thumb" (217–18), Lena stays outside institutionalized heterosexuality, opting instead for work and companionship with Tiny Soderball in San Francisco. Jim's childless marriage probably does signal the nativist fear of declining birth rates in the American-born population, but it also suggests that Jim belatedly discovers the wisdom of Lena's critique of family and resists becoming a "cranky old father" himself. After all, Jim reports in his narrative that he discussed with Ántonia "the difference" Gaston Cleric's death had made in his life (239–40), but he never specifies for the reader what that "difference" is, though it seems to explain his decision to go to New York to study law.

In calling attention to this unnamed "difference" and Jim's unfinished mourning for his lost male companion, I do not wish to claim that he is a homosexual who stumbles in his grief into the mistake of marriage. My point, rather, is to emphasize that Jim is, like the other figures examined throughout this discussion, a semiotic field where competing cultural possibilities are interrogated and put into play. By claiming, even without naming, the difference within himself, Jim acknowledges his failures as a policeman, his reluctance to subject himself to a law of sameness—except for the queer sameness of his devotion to Gaston Cleric. Jim's and the text's resistance to assimilation is the mark not only of the nativist aversion to racial intermixture, which, when the parent stocks are too "diverse," according to Stoddard, results in "a mongrel—a walking chaos" (166); it is also the sign of an inextinguishable longing for difference— from the norm of heterosexuality and from the increasingly vituperative and contested discourse of Americanism.[35] "You really are a part of me," Jim remarks to Ántonia near the end of the conversation in which they discuss Cleric's death and then separate for twenty years (240). This gesture of incorporation, which in some ways seems odd,[36] makes sense in light of the multiple meanings of "queerness" and "Bohemianism" that are in play in the novel. Having lost the object of his (same-sex) "Bohemian" desires, Jim declares the (ethnic) "Bohemian" woman a "part" of himself and beats a hasty retreat from the prairie—space of the difference he craves and fears. His incorporation of difference and his departure from the prairie stand in marked contrast to Alexandra Bergson's denial of difference—"What *difference* will that make?" she muses to Carl on the subject of wills and titles—and her quiet determination to stay on the prairie and make it a space of sameness. The contrast succinctly conveys the contradictory signifiying functions of the prairie and the crucial role it plays throughout Cather's early novels.

One of Ours is in many respects a transitional text, and so it is appropriate to conclude this survey of Cather's early fiction with a glance in its direction. Published in 1922, it marks the end of the decade that began with *Alexander's Bridge*, a decade of steady productivity, rising confidence, and growing critical stature. (H. L. Mencken had praised *My Ántonia* as "not only the best [novel] done by Miss Cather herself, but also one of the best that any American has ever done."[37]) *One of Ours* is the first of Cather's novels published in the 1920s, a watershed period in both her career and in America's career as an international cultural power. It is also the first of her novels to be published with Alfred Knopf, the shrewd young New York publisher who wooed Cather away from the staid Boston house of Houghton Mifflin by promising to market her books more aggressively. Finally, it is the last of her books to engage so fully with the prairie as cultural and discursive space. Her next novel, *A Lost Lady* (1923), is set in the town of Sweet Water, which is said to be in "one of the prairie States" (3), but the story of Marian and Daniel Forrester assiduously avoids telling the tale of his role in subjugating the prairie as a contractor for the Burlington railroad. The story is remote from its setting, despite Niel Herbert's belated attempts to connect the two in reading the Captain's invalidism and his wife's infidelity as an allegory of "the very end of the road-making West" (144). Cather would return to the prairie in one later novel, *Lucy Gayheart* (1935), which harkens back to *The Song of the Lark* and *One of Ours* in its preoccupation with the figure of an artistic or sensitive individual struggling to escape the provincialism and the painful intimacy of small towns where "loves and hates beat about, their wings almost touching" (167), but Haverford and its stark surroundings serve chiefly as the cold, static backdrop to the story of Lucy's disappointment and death. *Lucy Gayheart* is by no means a "prairie novel" or, as Cather called it, a "novel of the soil," in the way that the books from this earlier period are.

Until it is clothed in the uniform of the U.S. Army, Claude Wheeler's body seems to signify the dystopic fear of the queer evident in earlier characters such as Paul and Crazy Ivar. His first action in the narrative of *One of Ours* is to "douse his face and head in cold water, and . . . to plaster down his wet hair" (3), gestures that signal his preoccupation with and discomfort in embodiment. Even as a child Claude is marked by a "physical restlessness" and a habit of imposing "physical tests and penances upon himself" (26–7). At nineteen his self-consciousness and self-loathing are so acute that he regards himself in the mirror while shaving and thinks that the pale color of his eyebrows and lashes gives "a look of shyness and weakness to the upper part of his face. He was exactly the sort of looking boy he didn't want to be" (17). He particularly hates his large head and is even humiliated by his name. Claude experiences himself as different and difference as deviance: "Claude knew, and everybody else knew, seemingly, that there was something wrong with him." His whole family speculates about Claude's reticence and discontent and the neighbors "laughed at him," while he is aware that "his energy, instead of accomplishing something, was spent in resisting unalterable conditions, and in unavailing efforts to subdue his own nature" (90). The battle against his "nature" is part of what motivates Claude's disastrous decision to marry the erotophobic Enid Royce: "His marriage would be the first *natural*, dutiful, expected thing he had ever done" (127, emphasis added), but during the wedding "Claude was so pale that he looked *unnatural*,— nobody had ever seen him like that before" (165, emphasis added).

Again, such compelling evidence of bodily dis-ease and the character's awareness of deviance make it tempting to examine Claude's story as a case study in "the homosexual temperament" (Cramer). Given, too, the psychological realism of the first three books of *One of Ours*—the attention paid to Claude's attachment to his mother and his aversion to his father's "rugged masculinity" (25) and to his sense of being stymied, trapped, and defeated by an unbearably alien environment—such an approach may be justified. Beyond telling the story of Claude's suffering as an individual, however, *One of Ours* brings to a spectacular conclusion Cather's decade-long interrogation of the relationship between queer bodies and national bodies in the contest to authorize "America." Out of uniform, as I have already noted, Claude is called queer even by his friend Ernest and laughed at by neighbors. In uniform, he compels admiration, as "the townspeople" come down to the train station expressly to see him arrive in his "close-fitting khaki" (208) when he comes home on a leave from training camp. His difference is now the mark of superiority and the impetus for his extraordinary transformation in the eyes of the community. His own father-in-law wonders if Claude hasn't grown taller, yet avers that "He always was a manly looking boy" (214). One need not diagnose Claude as homosexual (though such clinical language would be appropriate given the novel's social context) in order to appreciate the way his queer body intervenes in American discourses of sexuality and citizenship, for the doughboy is finally most like the diva Thea Kronborg in unsettling and reimagining the meanings of the body politic. In the very moment that efforts to exclude homosexuals from military service in World War I (largely through the Navy's investigation of allegations of homosexuality and "immoral conditions" at the Newport Naval Training Station[38]) made the homosexual, as Jared Gardner puts it, "the paradigm for *decitizenship*" in the United States (33), Cather turns the queer Claude into a soldier hero and an exemplary American.

To claim Claude as "one of ours," then, is not merely, as hostile readers of the novel have suggested, to indulge in warmongering, an unreflective patriotism, or the nativist zeal for distinguishing "us" from "them."[39] It is also to demand that the queer not be excluded from the terms and conditions of citizenship, to insist, indeed, that the queer be understood to articulate and exemplify precisely those terms and conditions. "You'd last about ten minutes in the American army," Claude says to a group of boys who are taunting an elderly German woman who runs a restaurant on the prairie. "You're not our kind" (212). Claude's uniform

invests his words with national authority, but he brings to the prairie a
queer (in the sense of being broadly anti-assimilationist) rhetoric of
national identity that will allow an old woman to speak of her homesick-
ness for the country he will soon go off to fight. Rather than a stable,
homogeneous entity rooted in a biological conception of race, "our kind"
is a dynamic and always incomplete category, a coalition mobilized to
achieve a particular goal. Seen in this light, Claude's idealism about
the war, which has had readers cringing for more than seventy years,
elucidates his similarity to Thea Kronborg. Each is the vehicle for a
utopian challenge to American fears of the queer.

War, I would suggest, functions in *One of Ours* much as opera functions
in *The Song of the Lark*, as a counterdiscourse of excess that affords the
queer a broader field for action or performance and opens up a narrative
alternative to the grim realism of the prairie sections of the novel. I
concur with critics who argue that Claude's romantic views of the war are
substantially undercut by the narrator,[40] particularly as the novel returns,
after Claude's death, to his mother, who recognizes that her son had
"hoped and believed too much" and likely could not have stood the disil-
lusionment of the postwar period. Still, the mother's elegy is not unlike
Nick Carraway's elegy for Jay Gatsby in celebrating even as it questions an
idealism rooted in naiveté. Claude was among "the ones who had hoped
extravagantly," and though his hopes are, like Gatsby's capacity for wonder,
wasted on a futile cause, fixed on an inadequate object, they enable him to
act heroically and then to die with his "beautiful beliefs" intact (390).
Feminist critics are right to focus on the ending's attention to the female
survivors of the war—not only Claude's mother, but the servant Mahailey
who "speak[s] for" Claude and seems also to have replaced Mrs. Wheeler's
husband as companion and helpmate. The women's devotion to Claude's
memory and to one another and their ability to endure disappointment
stand as an implied critique of a masculinity that seems to require the violence of war in order to realize itself.[41] The novel's critique of the gendering of men cannot, however, be disarticulated from its exploration of the
boundaries between homosociality and homosexuality, boundaries whose
uncertainties were thrown into relief by the Newport investigations and by
the broader social upheavals of the World War I era. If Claude's blindness
to Enid's true desires and motives is a measure of a "fatal idealization of
women" that Cather is determined to expose (Ryan 70), it is also proof of
his desperate determination to "subdue his own nature." As marriage
proves to be a bitter disappointment, Claude is relieved that Enid decides

to go to China to care for her missionary sister who has fallen ill, though he had previously admonished her to give up the idea of traveling there because "wandering off alone like that ... makes people queer" (109). Once she is gone, Claude feels himself condemned to a life of "actions without meaning" and wonders, "What was it—what *was* the matter with him? Why, at least, could he not stop feeling things, and hoping? What was there to hope for now?" (193).

War is the answer to all of Claude's questions, in part because it gives him manly, meaningful work to do and in part because it gives him love, companionship, and a new relation to his body: "Claude loved the men he trained with,—wouldn't choose to live in any better company" (193). For Claude, the discipline of soldiering is, like Thea's operatic routine, a positive and liberating alternative to the terroristic sex and gender regime enforced on the prairie by such disparate figures as his hypermasculine father and his puritanical brother, Bayliss. Claude, "born with a love of order" (30) yet appalled by his father's petty tyrannies, delights in being part of the uniform, homological world of the army, in riding on trains crowded with "passengers all of the same sex, almost all of the same age, all dressed and hatted alike" and with strikingly similar physical features such as "clipped heads and tanned faces" (229). On board ship, during the crossing to France, Claude ministers to men suffering from seasickness and influenza and cultivates friendships with exceptional men such as Albert Usher and Victor Morse. As men die all around him, Claude is giddy with a sense of freedom and purpose, of something "elastic" (the same quality Thea's active, loved body has) in him that bounds up and says, "I am all here. I've left everything behind me. I am going over" (265). For Claude, the war in France is a spectacle of love, death, and male bonding, as he finally finds in the soldier/violinist David Gerhardt "some one whom he could admire without reservations; some one he could envy, emulate, wish to be" (350). All of the romantic, emotional intensity of their relationship is gathered in the single sentence that initiates the brief, idyllic interlude the two men enjoy with the Joubert family: "Claude and Gerhardt were going off on their leave together" (342). In contrast to the abstemiousness and reticence of the prairie—where his brother worries about his mother having a second cup of coffee because "it's a stimulant" (79)—during the "perfect bliss" (343) of his leave with David, Claude enjoys twelve-egg omelettes washed down with pots of coffee and brandy and is able to get David to tell the story of his past. They tramp through the woods together, and Claude dreams of staying in France "for the rest of his life," having realized "There was no chance for the kind of life he wanted at home" (345). Even his body changes during this period of "hazy enchantment" (349). The enervated farm boy whose face looked shy and weak stretches out in the forest for a nap and has "the relaxed, deep-breathing body of the American soldier" (349).

In *One of Ours* war makes the queer a hero and gives him a space for love, allowing him to reconstitute a family, enter history, state his faith in his "wonderful men" (385), and die for a glorious cause, but all of this exaltation is predicated upon the twin violences of war and misogyny, implying that men who love men do so because they feed on death and the hatred of women.[42] During the crossing Claude comes to feel that "years of his life" are "blotted out" in the fog of the open sea, and he notices that "Enid's pale, deceptive face" (259) seldom rises up in his consciousness, a process of erasure that links him to the psychiatric patient in the hospital who has "forgotten almost everything about his life before he came to France. The queer thing is, it's his recollection of women that is most affected. He can remember his father, but not his mother; doesn't know if he has sisters or not" (287). Such a construction of homosociality is undeniably homophobic, though it is hard (and per-haps unnecessary) to say whether the source of the homophobia is Cather or the discursive field she is interrogating. Nevertheless, the nar-rative's latent homophobia becomes manifest in such crucial scenes as the one in which three male couples—David and Claude, Sergeant Hicks "and his chum Dell Able," and the two second lieutenants Bruger and Hammond—bathe in and relax around a shellhole, "all more or less naked" and "examining various portions of their body with interest" because they hadn't had their clothes off for some time. When Claude comes to take his bath, he steps on something sharp, dives down into the water, and pulls up a German helmet, in the process "open[ing] up a graveyard" of bodies that begin emitting noxious bubbles (311–12). Male intimacy is intoxicating when Claude and David are alone and fully clothed, but six naked men fascinated by their bodies are literally toxic, stirring up the deadly possibility that American "chums" are too close for comfort to hidden, unsuspected horrors. Those horrors break through to the surface, as it were, in a later scene in which Claude and his men encounter a German sniper whose killing of Dell Able so enrages Sergeant Hicks—"my buddy—He's worse than dead!" (367)—that he delivers a gratuitous shot through the temples of the dying enemy, whom Claude has already bayoneted in the back.

Many readers have noted the sniper's strangely effeminate appearance—his carefully manicured nails, "gorgeous silk dressing gown," and the locket he wears around his neck, which has inside it a painting of "a young man, pale as snow, with blurred forget-me-not eyes" (367)—and Claude and David's contrasting readings of the locket.[43] Claude "studie[s]" the object and "wonder[s]," supposing the young man who "looks like a poet, or something" was "a kid brother, killed at the beginning of the war." David merely "glance[s]" at the locket with "a disdainful expression" and instructs the men who are rifling the sniper's pockets to let the dead man keep it. He then "touche[s] Claude on the shoulder to call his attention to the inlay work on the handle of the officer's revolver" (367). Julie Abraham is correct to read this strange scene as a mutually fatal encounter (because the sniper kills Dell and Dell's comrades kill the sniper) between innocent American homosociality and German homosexuality[44] that demonstrates "the violent stricture of the system of permission and suppression" (46) that undergirds Cather's story of unarticulated same-sex love. As she points out, however, David's reaction in the scene suggests not innocence but understanding and complicity. He touches Claude and looks at him "as if he were very pleased with him,—looked, indeed, as if something pleasant had happened in this room" (367). Instead of touching the body of the dead German homosexual, as the other men do, David touches the living body of his American pal and finds pleasure in the aftermath of death.

The mixture of horror and pleasure, killing and touching, the *blue* eyes of Willy Katz, the Austrian boy from Omaha whom the sniper shoots as he and Claude enter the room, and the *blurred* eyes of the young man pictured in the locket marks the scene as a site of boundary crisis and disavowal. Jonathan Ned Katz has traced the origins of the phrase "homosexual panic" to the work of Dr. Edward J. Kempf, a psychiatrist at a U.S. government mental hospital in Washington, D.C., who relied heavily on case histories of World War I soldiers and sailors to document the type of anxiety attack that occurs "due to the pressure of uncontrollable perverse sexual cravings" arising "wherever men or women must be grouped alone for prolonged periods" (quoted in *Almanac* 391–2).[45] Claude is "unnerved" in the scene because the German sniper speaks English "with no foreign accent" and shouts at his killers, "You swine, go back to Chicago!" (366–7). His panic is engendered by intimate proximity with an enemy who is less "foreign" than Claude might have wished, an enemy who speaks his language and who, like him, wears a wristwatch, an accessory he had "despised as effeminate" until he discovered its usefulness during the war (254). In this confrontation of intimate and similar enemies, *One of Ours* stumbles into the panic of its own No Man's Land, that "dead, nerveless" space where "life was a secret" (309) and the lines between queer and un-queer, enemy and ally, pervert and chum, foreign and native collapse as two massive armies struggle to control and fortify them.

One of Ours overcomes its panic not by resolving its boundary crisis but by aggressively acknowledging it in two key moments involving Claude and the parapet, the wall built up in front of the trench to protect soldiers from nearby enemies. On his first morning at the front Claude studies the enemy lines by cautiously "peep[ing] over the parapet between the sandbags" (309). On the last morning of his life he springs up onto the parapet to encourage his men and direct their fire, making himself the perfect target for the advancing "Hun line," which, in Claude's judgment, had been "behaving queerly." In that moment of grandiose self-display and self-destruction, the young man who hated the sight of his own face in the mirror is both maximally powerful and maximally vulnerable. Campy in its excess and its theatricality—both in Claude's performance and Cather's narration of it—the soldier's death dance releases his long pent-up desire to be conspicuous,[46] his hunger to be looked at, his long-ing to "behav[e] queerly," one might say. The uptight kid from Nebraska proves to be an in-your-face drama queen who revels in the visceral reac-tions and the adoring looks he gets from half of his audience—his men "become like rock" and "their eyes never left him" (385)—and seems oblivious to the bullets rained down upon him by the other half of his audience. Claude's death is a diva moment of erotic and ideological mastery: "With these men he could do anything" (385). The queer body is no longer stigmatized (though it seems a bit stigmatic, as the blood from Claude's wounds drips down his coat) but monumental in its signifying force. If the prairie functions, in the last of Cather's major prairie novels, as a space of shame, the parapet represents a coming out and into power, as the metaphors of vision and visibility woven throughout the scene suggest, though the "anything" Claude might do with the hard bodies of his "wonderful men" is pointedly unspecified. Small wonder, however, that Lieutenant Wheeler dies in their arms—unaware that David has already been "blown to pieces" (386)—with a smile on his face.

In these pages I have resisted the temptation to read *One of Ours*—or any of Cather's early novels—as lesbian love stories under cover or in drag. I am reluctant even to embrace the more nuanced Sedgwickian refraction model because it is still more or less invested in tracking the movement from lesbian writer to male characters whom the critic calls "gay" (*Tendencies* xiii). The recognition that Willa Cather was a lesbian is important in puzzling out her relationship to a signifying practice that I have termed "queering 'America' " (and that David Van Leer has called "the queening of America"[47]), but my emphasis on bodies as tropes has been aimed precisely at *not* turning characters into authorial surrogates, at *not* turning critical inquiry into a detective's search for the lesbian in the text. I began this discussion with an analysis of the twists and turns the word "queer" takes in documents from a pivotal moment in Cather's life—the 1890s—partly to establish its salience in her experience of "unnatural" love and her long-running performance as "William Cather," but my primary goal was to contribute to the historiography of the "queer" by demonstrating that it was a name for sexual deviance— and specifically for female sexual deviance—well before World War I and in a region far removed from the Eastern, urban enclaves of long-haired men and short-haired women analyzed by Chauncey and others. Years later, as a resident of Greenwich Village if not quite as a citizen of Bohemia, Cather would produce a series of novels in which the "queer" would serve as a fulcrum for getting at the incoherences of sex and gender, the instabilities of race and ethnicity, the incomparable and anxiety-inducing diversity of a nation falling in love with the sound of the word "America."

In the first novels, *Alexander's Bridge* and *O Pioneers!*, "America" is seldom invoked and merely designates a vague set of attributes or a body of laws. The insipid Englishman Maurice Mainhall likes Bartley Alexander, for example, because he is an engineer and Mainhall's "idea about Americans was that they should be engineers or mechanics. He hated them when they presumed to be anything else" (*AB* 17). Nevertheless, one sees in these texts the gathering force of the term "America" and the role that the queer and the un-queer play in the contest to authorize it. Alexandra Bergson is a Swedish immigrant who resists assimilation in the cultural sense, retaining ties of language and custom to the country of her birth, but she succeeds economically because of her shrewd understanding of American laws of property and the mechanisms of agricultural commerce. She is also a tireless crusader for bodily and social order, embracing the queer when—as with Ivar—it is held in check by guilt and proves to be both useful and entertaining, rejecting it when—as with

Emil and Marie—it leads to illicit sex across ethnic boundaries. By *The Song of the Lark*, "American" is a term of derision, naming a distinctly negative set of traits—e.g., provincialism, intolerance, fear of the imagination—that are positively offset by the queerness of figures such as Tillie and Thea Kronborg. The diva's unambiguous triumph marks *The Song of the Lark* as Cather's most sustained contribution to a discourse of corporeal utopianism that is radically anti-assimilationist and queer-affirming, committed to a notion of citizenship rooted in the body rather than in flight from it.

With World War I, "America" was irredeemably queered by its new resonance within the context of an unprecedented geopolitical conflict into which the nation was reluctantly and belatedly drawn. Cather's fiction from this period, *My Ántonia* and *One of Ours*, wrestles with the crisis of visibility engendered for a range of ethnic and sex/gender queers within a representational system in which the meaning of "America" came to be increasingly calcified and narrow. The story of the southern European immigrant woman, who can and cannot signify "America," must be told indirectly, through the voice of a man marked as "youthful," "Western," and "American" (*MÁ* 5) who is ambivalently drawn toward a "Bohemianism" that is partly ethnic and partly sexual. With *One of Ours*, Cather ends her first decade as a novelist with a text that is doubly fractured, first by its fears of and affection for a queer boy who must leave the prairie in order to find and then gloriously to lose his life, and second by its grave doubts about "America"'s role in world affairs and in the domestic politics of Prohibition and anti-immigrationism that took hold during the postwar period. With Claude, *One of Ours* moves through corporeal dystopianism to a fragile utopianism that perishes because it must, as his own mother puts it, be "safe, safe" from disillusion (*OO* 390). The queer body may be a figure and an agent of resistance, but after Claude's fortunate death the grounds of resistance would shift decisively for Willa Cather. That new terrain and the new terms for negotiating it are the subject of part 2 of *Queering "America."*

Cather as "William Cather, Jr."

Louise Pound and Willa Cather as undergraduates at the University of Nebraska, proving, perhaps, the validity of Theresa de Lauretis's claim that "it takes two women, not one, to make a lesbian."

Willa Cather in Wyoming, 1905—"Hang on, Toto—I have a feeling we're not in [Nebraska] anymore."

Annie Pavelka (seated, right) and her large family inspired Cather's sometimes anxious study of "Bohemianism" as a technology for the creation of racial and sexual ambiguity in My Ántonia.

Cather's cousin, G. P. Cather, who was killed in action in World War I and served as the model for Claude Wheeler in One of Ours. *Cather uses the doughboy as an exemplary figure of queer citizenship.*

Part II

Queering the "Classics"
Willa Cather and the Literary History of the United States

Willa Cather's place in "gay and lesbian literary history" is at this point prominent and secure. She has a story in Lillian Faderman's *Chloe Plus Olivia: An Anthology of Lesbian Literature from the Seventeenth Century to the Present*, although Montaigne, Henry Fielding, and Freud are also represented there. She has an entry, which I wrote, in Claude J. Summers's compendious *The Gay and Lesbian Literary Heritage* and a volume, which Sharon O'Brien wrote, in the Chelsea House series *Lives of Notable Gay Men and Lesbians*. Even popular culture offers evidence of Cather's power as a signifier of lesbianism and literariness. In the spring of 1997 the episodes that focused on the coming out of TV's *Ellen* contained a cryptic but important Cather allusion that had particular resonance in my household, perhaps the only household in the country containing one Dickinson scholar and one Cather scholar who are both lesbians and fans of prime-time sitcoms, though we generally pass ourselves off as cultural studies specialists. Ellen's homophobic boss, a literate yet bigoted bookstore owner, didn't want Ellen babysitting for his two young daughters when he found out she was gay. His daughters, whom he acknowledged adored Ellen, were named, not Gertrude and Alice (too obvious) nor Ruth and Naomi (too likely to offend), but Emily and Willa. The Belle of Amherst and the Tomboy of the Prairie sneak into the family of the man who loves literature but hates lesbianism as if to say, "You can't have one without the other." Sisterhood, it seems, is still powerful. My partner and I replayed the joke several times and nearly fell off the couch laughing every time we heard it. I can't imagine how it was received in other living rooms.

What, however, is—or would be—a "queer" literary history? Is it the same thing as the "gay and lesbian" literary history of which Cather is already a part, or does the anti-identitarian stance of much queer work disallow the making of history in the name of a stable and coherent group of individuals defined by something as quaintly modernist and humanist as their genders and sexualities? Does the phrase "queer literary history" refer only to queer people (whoever they might be, however we might decide to name that willfully unnameable group) as producers of literature, or might it refer more broadly to "queerness" as a fact of or force in literary history itself? If that is the case, what, then, is an "un-queer" literary history? In the U.S., where the notion of a national literature took hold during the same period in which "queer" came to signify sexual deviance, is there any such thing? Indeed, aren't all literary histories in some sense "unnatural formations," as Michael Moon suggests in a recent issue of *American Literature* devoted to examining "the inseparability of questions of 'unnatural' sexualities from histories of American literature and culture" (3)? All writers, not just gay and lesbian ones, dream of installing themselves in something called "literary history," and they often do so through metaphors of family and biology that play upon the blurriness of the line between the "natural" and the "unnatural" in the wholly artificial world of the literary. Thus, the un-queer Hawthorne, in the prefaces to his tales, articulates his anxieties about literary productivity and reputation in terms of potency and paternity, secrecy and publicity—terms that could be said to have a queer inflection.

"Queer literary history," if it does not merely document the achievements of "queer" writers, must, at a minimum, account for such inflections, for the bodily terms through which many writers negotiate questions of literary power, authority, marginality, and history. In part 1 of this study, I focused on tracking the "queer" as a deviant, disruptive figure in Cather's early fiction. Moving forward in her career, I will in part 2 shift the ground of the inquiry, to consider her interventions into the postwar debates concerning the "Americanness" of American literature. Here, the "queer" is less a figure in the text than a strategy in the argument, a way of calling into question the terms of the debate and the canons those terms were in the process of establishing. At times in this analysis, gender will move into the foreground while sexuality might seem to slip into the background, but that is because Cather's participation in the culture wars is marked particularly by concern about the masculinization of American literary history. By 1931 Cather would even acknowledge that it was a distinct disadvantage to be a woman writer, noting, in an obvious reference to *A Room of One's Own* (1929), that Virginia Woolf had made a pretty fair statement of the disadvantages.[1] Chapter 3 will focus on letters, literary criticism, and Cather's major editorial project of the 1920s—her preparation of *The Best Stories of Sarah Orne Jewett* for Houghton Mifflin—as well as *The Professor's House*, to situate her squarely within these debates and show how grim she could be about their likely outcome; chapter 4 shows her back in the mode of *The Song of the Lark*, presenting in *Death Comes for the Archbishop* the queering of America as a kind of dreamwork, a love story, a utopian fantasy of sexual/literary history.

3

"In a Prohibition Country"

The Culture Wars of the 1920s

> The most sensuous of writers, Willa Cather, builds her imagined world as
> solidly as our five senses build the universe around us. . . . Miss Cather has
> within herself a sensitivity that constantly presents her with a body of mate-
> rial which would overwhelm most of us, so that we would give up all idea
> of transmitting it and would sink into a state of passivity; and *she has also a*
> *quality of mountain pony sturdiness that makes her push on unfatigued under her*
> *load and give an accurate account of every part of it.*
> —Rebecca West (emphasis added)

First, though, another tracking: the queer appears in a critical
text of the early 1920s, Cather's loving essay in memory of
Annie Adams Fields, which was originally published as "The House on
Charles Street" in Henry Seidel Canby's *The Literary Review* of the *New
York Evening Post* in November 1922 (and subsequently revised and
published as "148 Charles Street" in *Not Under Forty* in 1936). Cather had
gotten to know Fields, widow of publisher James Fields and companion
to Sarah Orne Jewett, when she was in Boston on assignment for
McClure's in 1908. Her essay pays tribute to the preeminent New England
hostess and posits a genteel vision of literary history as a series of comings
and goings by "the aristocracy of letters and art" presided over by Fields's
talent for maintaining "an atmosphere in which one seemed absolutely
safe from everything ugly" (56, 58).[1] The piece is mostly backward-looking, as Cather seems awestruck and reverential in her verbal tour of a
house in which "the past lay in wait for one in all the corners" (61), but
at one crucial point she acknowledges Fields's "genius of survival," a
genius that kept her open to the present and applied to both her personal
and her cultural lives. Cather notes that Fields, who died in 1915, survived

her husband by thirty-four years and the much younger Jewett by six, but she also survived—and even embraced, according to Cather's account—a number of significant transitions in the world of art:

> She was not, as she once laughingly told me, "to escape anything, not even free verse or the Cubists!" She was not in the least dashed by either. Oh, no, she said, the Cubists weren't any queerer than Manet and the Impressionists were when they first came to Boston, and people used to run in for tea and ask her whether she had ever heard of such a thing as "blue snow," or a man's black hat being purple in the sun!   (67)

The Annie Fields of Cather's essay is thus no Miss Havisham, sealed up in her house with the decaying remnants of an ever more remote past, though the revised version tends somewhat in that direction, with its concluding vision of Annie dying "with her world . . . unchallenged," "in that house of memories, with the material keepsakes of the past about her" (75). Even within the context of the generally sardonic mood of *Not Under Forty*—which is aggressively backward-looking, as Cather's explanation of her title indicates ("It means that the book will have little interest for people under forty years of age," she grouses in her preface [v])—Fields laughingly greets the "queer" as a signifier of aesthetic originality, a boldness and newness that are clearly welcome at her tea table. Though Cather herself was neither a proponent nor an exponent of the kind of modernist experimentation associated with free verse or Cubism, her attributing to Fields such receptiveness and the shrewd recognition that what is "queer" today may be aristocratic tomorrow underscores both her hunger for the older woman's approval and the struggle for cultural authority that is apparent in all of Cather's work in the 1920s. During this middle decade of her career as a novelist—the decade in which she reached the pinnacle of her popular and critical success—that struggle reached crisis proportions, fueling some of her greatest fictions and marking them with fissures and tensions that are absent from or less apparent in most of the earlier novels. The imbricated narrative structure of *My Ántonia* hints at the turn she would make away from depictions of powerful, memorable heroines and toward a more troubled analysis of what was being made visible and invisible in the nation's rush to formulate an "official" culture and history. In the 1920s Cather lived and wrote, like her out-of-sorts professor, Godfrey St. Peter, "in a Prohibition country" (*PH* 257), and she did so with keen sensitivity and responsiveness to the forces that were shaping the nascent American canon and the increasingly professionalized field of American literary study.[2] Her essay on Annie Fields is but one of many examples of her efforts to propound a model of literary history that might accommodate the gentility of nineteenth-century Boston and "the tumult" of twentieth-century New York,[3] the traditional and the "queer," the male-authored and the female-authored. She was by no means alone in dissenting from the narrow, masculinist view that would come to dominate American notions of the literary, so in the pages that follow I will put her in dialogue with allies as well as opponents in the project of "queering the 'classics.' "

To say that Cather "queers the 'classics' " is to say first that she brought the acute sense of difference she had always felt as a writer and as a lesbian into the whole discussion of the literary and the national that permeates the periodicals, anthologies, and criticism of the 1920s. Second, it is to say that she responded directly and resistantly to the all-male pantheon of duplicitous swashbucklers erected by her acquaintance D. H. Lawrence in his controversial *Studies in Classic American Literature* (1923), a book that crystalized the stakes in the culture wars and exerted a lasting influence on the discipline. Lastly, it is to say that, even acknowledging the aristocratic pretensions of Cather's fondness for the "kingdom of art," her ideas and those of friends and allies such as Mary Austin and Louise Pound would have constituted a radically different field of study had they succeeded in defining "American literature." As Americanists in the postmodern, postcolonial environment of the contemporary academy scramble to reconstitute or deconstitute the discipline—to figure out, as Peter Carafiol puts it, "what to do after American literature"[4]—we might find it useful to attend to the period of dissensus and contestation that came "before" "American literature" and see what might be gained by going back, as it were, to the future of the discipline.

An Ounce of Enthusiasm: Marketing "Difference," Making History

Like the queerness imaged in the novels we have already examined, the sense of "difference" that punctuates Cather's efforts throughout the 1920s to position herself in the literary marketplace and in literary history is multivalent, seeming at times to be a source of pride and power—an aspect of what Rebecca West describes as her "mountain pony sturdiness"—and at others to be a source of significant anxiety. As a young woman, Cather's fundamentally heroic and voluntarist notion of the self is apparent in the confidence of her pronouncements (on a breathtaking range of subjects) and in her persistent attempts to minimize or deny in particular the differences made by gender. Writing under the pseudonym "Helen Delay" in 1897, for example, Cather admonished readers of the Pittsburgh *Home Monthly* to avoid making the "hateful distinction" between "boys' books" and "girls' books" for as long as possible, saying she preferred the books that are for both (*WP* 1:337). Several months later, writing again as "Helen Delay," she boasted that as a child, acting out the plot of Eugène Sue's *The Wandering Jew*, "the fact that I was a girl never damaged my ambitions to be a pope or an emperor" (*WP* 1:368). Years later, as a mature woman managing a literary career, Cather's ambitions are still clearly intact, but they also seem tempered by the concern that differences of region and class as well as of gender might be greater impediments to success than the girl who had played at being a pope had perhaps imagined.

This volatile admixture of ambition and doubt fuels two pivotal moves Cather made in the 1920s that would have significant short-term and long-term consequences vis-à-vis her career and her role as an agent of literary history. The first was her decision, finally reached in January 1921, to leave her publisher Houghton Mifflin—the distinguished Boston house, descended from the firm of Ticknor and [James T.] Fields, which had published all of her novels from *Alexander's Bridge* through *My Ántonia* and which had also published all the major works of her friend and mentor Jewett—for the younger, more adventurous publisher from New York, Alfred A. Knopf. The second was her decision to return to her literary mother's (publishing) house, briefly, in 1924 to edit for Houghton a posthumous collection of Jewett's stories. (Jewett had died in 1909, just a year after she and Cather met, but their brief friendship was, as biographers have noted, the catalyst behind the younger writer's decision to leave journalism and devote herself fulltime to the writing of fiction, as she took to heart Jewett's advice, offered in a letter from 148 Charles Street, to "find your own quiet centre of life and write from that" in order to "keep and guard and mature your force, and above all, have time and quiet to perfect your work" [Fields 248–9].) Both of these moves are documented in rich detail in Cather's correspondence with Ferris Greenslet, her legendary editor at Houghton Mifflin, and the details are worth examining, because, beyond their importance as biographical documents, Cather's letters to Greenslet elucidate the tensions involved in the changing dynamics in author-publisher relationships in the U.S. as corporate mergers and the rise of professional literary agents transformed the institutions of book publishing in the early decades of the twentieth century.[5]

Cather's departure from Houghton Mifflin was a major loss for the firm, and in the annals of the company it is still recalled as a singular instance of a greed and ambition associated, somewhat cryptically, with both gender and sexuality. In a 1983 address to the Newcomen Society, Houghton Mifflin chief executive officer Harold T. Miller spoke proudly of the tradition of loyalty Houghton has enjoyed from its authors, noting that "Most of [them] have stayed with us throughout their careers, but occasionally a few have become disgruntled and transferred to another house where they hoped that the grass, or perhaps the money, would be greener." From the 150-year history of the firm, Miller cites but two examples of authors who left the house, and one of those ultimately came back: "Cigar-smoking Amy Lowell was one author who left and then returned a number of years later, but Willa Cather, insulted because her editor addressed her by her first name in a letter, took her books to a young man named Alfred Knopf who would treat her more respectfully" (12). The butch Lowell proves loyal in the long run, but the femme—at least as Miller constructs her—Cather, a stickler for gender propriety, takes off with a clever young man who would always call her "Miss Cather." He would also, by the way, help her to achieve the financial security that had eluded her throughout her association with Houghton Mifflin and carefully manage her career and reputation in an association that would last until her death (LL 316–17).

Not surprisingly, Cather's take on her decision to leave Houghton Mifflin differs significantly from Miller's anecdote of the prickly lesbian in search of respect, though her language in the letters to Greenslet similarly mixes sexual and familial vocabularies of loyalty to the house along with a modern vocabulary of economic self-interest and the commodification of the book and the author. Such a mixture suggests how conflicted she was about making a move that was clearly shrewd and necessary, for Cather, who needed to earn a living and whose years with *McClure's* had given her a healthy respect for the value of publicity, had long been dissatisfied with what she described to Greenslet as the cautious spirit in which the firm handled her work.[6] As early as 1915 she took an active interest in how her books were marketed and promoted, arguing that *The Song of the Lark* ought to be pushed a good deal harder than *O Pioneers!* had been because she believed it had more momentum in it and ought to go farther—and because she wanted to sell a good many copies. Already, though, Cather seems quietly concerned that Greenslet or Houghton might not fully appreciate the book, commenting that unless one had lived all over the West, she didn't think one could possibly know how much of the West this story has in it.[7] Within months concern had turned to anger and frustration, and Cather's focus shifts from regional communication problems to Houghton's failure to promote her growing critical stature aggressively enough. So disappointed was Cather in advertisements for *The Song of the Lark* that she actually remade an ad Houghton's publicity department sent her, using quotations from reviews that she felt had some pull and enthusiasm in them instead of the wooden remarks that had been used in the original. In advertising, she icily remarked, it seems to me that an ounce of enthusiasm is worth a pound of approbation, arguing that a reviewer's excitement would make one want to read a book, while mere commendation is worth nothing.[8] By 1919, when Knopf was wooing her with a long-range strategy aimed at building and marketing her reputation while Houghton was billing her—she thought excessively—for proof corrections on *My Ántonia*, Cather complained bitterly to Greenslet about the firm's timidity in promoting her and its failure to recognize the unique publicity needs of work like hers. Such phrases—books like mine, work like mine—crop up repeatedly in her analyses of Houghton's shortcomings, but Cather never clearly defines the difference she felt the publicity department overlooked. She is emphatic, however, on the firm's refusal to capitalize on positive reviews, pointing out that one advertisement that quoted from a number of notices edited out the strongest sentences of praise and such expressions as "a new and great writer." Now I don't want Houghton Mifflin to pronounce me a great writer, she tells Greenslet, but why are they so shy about quoting anything of that sort when other people say it?[9]

Region is the most explicitly articulated difference in Cather's announcement to Greenslet, in a letter from January, 1921, of her decision to let Knopf publish *One of Ours*. Despite her successful shift away from "Eastern" literary models and materials after *Alexander's Bridge*, Cather continued to fear that the "Western" qualities of her work eluded or annoyed even such sympathetic readers as Greenslet. You've always groaned a great deal about the West, she reminds him, and this novel is so wholly West that maybe you will feel a little relief at not having to be responsible for it.[10] Finally, though, sex and gender find their way into Cather's struggle to choose between Houghton and Knopf, as she seems to have worried that the obvious ambitiousness of the move would be perceived—as, indeed, Houghton's CEO would still describe it more than sixty years later—as an act of betrayal fraught with sexual overtones. Despite her effort to define the choice as a business decision based entirely on the conviction that Knopf's publicity work on *Youth and the Bright Medusa*, the volume of short stories he had persuaded her to let him bring out in 1920, had been much more spirited and effective than Houghton Mifflin's had ever been, she cannot bring herself to say that the break is final, and, more important, she lapses into a vocabulary of marriage and family in order to defend her decision and soften the blow to Greenslet. Assuring her editor that she has not forgotten his early encouragement and the fact that he published her first novel, Cather insists that she is only going away from Houghton temporarily and for Claude's health, because she feels strongly that he needs a certain kind of publicity work. But, she continues, unless you see it otherwise, I shall refuse to say that I have "left" you. I would like to say that indeed I have not left you, though it is true that Knopf is going to publish this next book.[11]

Cather's concern for the "health" of her protagonist Claude Wheeler elaborates on a metaphor drawn in an earlier letter to Greenslet when, in reporting on the progress of *One of Ours*, she told him that Claude is getting big enough to look after himself. Still, she concludes somewhat ominously, I won't hand him over to anybody who won't do a good deal for him.[12] As a mother acting in the best interests of her "child," Cather, even as she exits her own "mother's" (publishing) house, appropriates the trope Jewett had used in defending one of her favorite stories, "A White Heron," after its rejection by the *Atlantic Monthly*: "I love her, and I mean to keep her" (Fields 60), wrote Jewett of her plan to save the story for the beginning of her next collection. That Cather's "child" is a strapping soldier boy and not a delicate "her" is a sign of the gulf in history and sensibility that stood between her and the women of Jewett's generation, but that she deploys the same maternal metaphor to justify what was clearly a wise business decision is a sign of a similar need to find a culturally acceptable way for a woman to stake an author's proprietary claim to her text.

Even at that, Cather's refusal to say that she is "leaving" Greenslet suggests a profound and unresolved ambivalence: her language personalizes the issue she has sought to describe in the impersonal terms of publicity and advertising and traps her in a web of metaphors she probably wanted to avoid. If she is Jewett's "daughter," Claude's "mother," and Greenslet's "wife," then Alfred Knopf is her illicit "lover," and her departure from the house of Houghton is an act of betrayal and abandonment that neither her concerns for her child's health nor her refusal to call the separation permanent can entirely justify. Cather's compulsion to draw this choice as an erotic triangle indicates that the most significant professional decision she ever made was undertaken with considerable guilt and anxiety, as the image of fiction-making as an enterprise that is both textually and sexually generative suggests that the writer in some sense condemned herself of both baby-selling and prostitution.[13] For Cather, New Woman and lesbian, the metaphorical links between literary and biological (pro)creativity prove to be both enabling and troubling, an anxious mark of the changing meanings of female authorship within the larger context of the transition from a familial, nineteenth- to a corporate, twentieth-century model of publishing.[14]

Unlike Thea Kronborg, who left home with an emphatic vow to stay away "forever!," Cather left the house of Houghton Mifflin with a wishy-washy refusal to say she was leaving, even ending her letter to Greenslet with a plea that he not reject the next novel she sends him. Three years later, however, in replying to Greenslet's invitation to come back to the house for a visit—i.e., to take on the *Jewett* project—her tone and stance are markedly different, understandably so, since she had in the intervening period won a Pulitzer Prize and earned both critical and popular acclaim for *A Lost Lady*. By the terms of her own metaphors of textual and sexual generativity, Greenslet's proposal offered Cather a rare and peculiar opportunity to be temporarily reunited with her ex-husband and to preside over the rebirth of her own literary mother. Cather seems to have jumped at the chance, teasing Greenslet that she would much rather tackle this project than make her fortune at the various lucrative commissions that are constantly pressed upon her. Jewett was in need of a rebirth, Cather implies, because her local librarian has reported to her that the young intellectuals of Greenwich Village sometimes ask vaguely for some of Jewett's books, but when she produces volumes such as *A White Heron* they finger them, say they look like children's books, and leave them on the desk. The librarian thinks their physical appearance is much against them with this generation.[15] Despite her zeal for the endeavor, the concatenation of psychological and historical issues involved in her making of *The Best Stories of Sarah Orne Jewett* leads to a fascinating series of switches and mix-ups, as Cather wrestles to do many things simultaneously: to present a warm tribute to her friend and precursor, to depict and lay claim to an enabling model of female creativity, and to establish a context, a precedent, a history, and a favorable climate of reception for the nondramatic—and in many ways "queer"—narratives she was working on at the time, *The Professor's House* and *Death Comes for the Archbishop*.[16]

Both a material and a critical recreation, Cather's editing of Jewett is an act of daughterly revisionism and of canon-formation that demonstrates how fully she was engaged with, in, and against the American literary history that was being invented all around her at this crucial moment in her career. Aside from her obvious professional interest in the formation of that history, Cather had personal connections to several of its important makers, including Carl Van Doren, one of the four editors of the *Cambridge History of American Literature* (1917–21), whose chapters on American fiction helped to establish the distinction between "novel" and "romance" that has driven so much subsequent criticism and contributed to the marginalization of women writers, as shown in Nina Baym's still useful analysis of the masculinist assumptions underlying theories of American fiction (70–5);[17] Louise Pound, her former college crush, by then a prominent folklorist at the University of Nebraska, whose chapter on oral literature in the fourth volume of the *Cambridge History*, is an eloquent plea for the value of "the great body of this floating literature . . . of old ballads and songs, nursery jingles, game songs, and popular satires and sentimentalities" (502) to the cultural history of the United States; Mary Austin, a friend in New York as well as New Mexico, whose discussion of aboriginal literature in the fourth volume of the *Cambridge History* was but a small piece of her tireless work throughout the period to expand the historical timeframe and un-do some of the racial biases already being built into still inchoate definitions of "American literature," as she exhorted scholars and critics to embrace the complex task "of competently knowing not one vast, pale figure of America, but several Americas, in many subtle and significant characterizations";[18] and D. H. Lawrence, the novelist whom Cather had excoriated in "The Novel Démeublé" as a writer of prose "crowded with physical sensations" that reduced his characters to "mere animal pulp" (*NUF* 50–1), whose *Studies in Classic American Literature* was greeted by reviewers with a mixture of shock, scorn, envy, and the begrudging recognition that "Classic American literature is a new phrase to most of us" and that Lawrence's take on the subject is, though eccentric and unscholarly, exciting.[19] Cather and Lawrence met in New York in the spring of 1924 when she was at work on the Jewett volume—according to her compan-

ion Edith Lewis's account in *Willa Cather Living,* Lawrence amused his
hostesses by imitating the sounds of leopards, which he had heard on a
recent trip to Ceylon (139).[20] Given, too, the wide and intense critical
response to his *Studies* in the Eastern literary press, Cather would doubtless have been familiar with its essential arguments and may well have
used the preface to *Jewett,* in part at least, as a way of responding to and
counteracting them.

That Lawrence was on Cather's mind as she worked on the volume is
evident first in her concern that contemporary readers might reject Jewett
as a writer of children's books—a concern raised in the first sentence
of the *Studies* regarding his selection of texts: "We like to think of the
old-fashioned American classics as children's books. Just childishness, on
our part" (*SCAL* 7). Lawrence looms even larger, however, in a dispute
Cather had with Greenslet over whether the volume should be intro-
duced by a sonnet (written by neither her nor Jewett) she described as distinctly third-rate. Explaining to Greenslet that she had hoped this would
be an edition of Miss Jewett for writers, she imagines with horror
Lawrence or Middleton Murray picking up these volumes and running
them over, and the first thing their eyes would light upon would be a tire-
some piece of "old-lady-poetry." Why, she forcefully concludes, put a
piece of feeble, foolish verse into a volume whose avowed excuse for
being is its literary excellence? Cather was so appalled by this vision of
writers reading her *Jewett* that she threatened to pull her preface from the
collection if the offensive sonnet were included. Not surprisingly, it was
withdrawn, as was the story, "Decoration Day," which Jewett's sister Mary
had hoped to include but that Cather dismissed as scarcely belonging in
the second grade of her work, much less the first.[21]

As her stubbornness on the point of the sonnet suggests, Cather had a
great deal at stake in the Jewett project, something even more serious than
the possibility that Jewett's talent or her own critical acumen might be
called into question by a piece of "old-lady-poetry." Her desire to defend
Jewett, as she tells Greenslet, alongside any really first-rate writer of any
country stems in part from the satisfaction of returning to the house of
Houghton and promoting Jewett as aggressively and enthusiastically as she
believed she had once deserved to be promoted, but it stems, too, from an
even deeper need to counter Lawrence's all-male canon and his image of
female creativity in America, which emerges so vividly in his reading of
Hester Prynne as a "destructive malevolence which eat[s] out the inner life
of a man, like a cancer" (*SCAL* 99).[22] Cather's Jewett, with her "gift of

sympathy" and her head "full of dear old houses and dear old women" (*SOJ* xii, xvi), is an exemplary figure of female creativity as constructive, a domestic artist whose sketches were designed on principles markedly similar to those Cather had recently enunciated in "The Novel Démeublé" (1922) and whose rhetorics of kinship and neighborliness consistently resulted in the kinds of blendings and boundary-crossings Cather aimed at in *The Song of the Lark*. Jewett's ability to "understand by intuition the deeper meaning of all she saw" (*SOJ* xvi) suggests that the American fondness for symbolism and ambiguity did not have to signal, as Lawrence insisted, subterfuge and self-division, turning the romance, which he, like Carl Van Doren, saw as the preeminent mode of American fiction, into a duplicitous "earthly story with a hellish meaning" (*SCAL* 89).

The Jewettian model of artistic power as loving or at least benign is one that both attracted and perplexed Cather. Indeed, much as she wanted to refute Lawrence and pay tribute to her predecessor, her effort to do so in the preface to the Jewett volume is marked by signs of gender trouble, as her use of the third-person generic pronoun makes a linguistic "man" out of Jewett:

> If [the artist] achieves anything noble, anything enduring, it must be by giving himself absolutely to his material. And this gift of sympathy is his great gift; is the fine thing in him that alone can make his work fine. He fades away into the land and people of his heart, he dies of love only to be born again. The artist spends a life-time in loving the things that haunt him, in having his mind "teased" by them, in trying to get these conceptions down on paper exactly as they are to him and not in conventional poses supposed to reveal their character; trying this method and that, as a painter tries different lightings and different attitudes with his subject to catch the one that presents it more suggestively than any other.   (*SOJ* xii)

At the beginning of her preface, Cather acknowledges that the notion of art as an effort to give shape to impressions that have "teased" the artist for a long time came to her directly and in a very personal fashion from Jewett herself: "In reading over a package of letters from Sarah Orne Jewett, I find this observation: '*The thing that teases the mind over and over for years, and at last gets itself put down rightly on paper—whether little or great, it belongs to literature*'" (*SOJ* ix). In choosing to emphasize the artist rather than the "thing" that teases the artist's mind, however, Cather's development of Jewett's observation cross-dresses her "mother" and cloaks her art of sympathy and suggestion in terms that define it as a masculine achievement. Cather's Jewett, though radically different from Lawrence's Hawthorne, is thus a manly mother or a womanly father, nurturing and loving, and yet the source of an inheritance that the daughter seems compelled to mix up and obscure. As she "fades away" into he, Cather succeeds not in queering or problematizing the Lawrentian notion of the classic but in queering the figure of the woman author so that s/he can be assimilated into an all-male tradition.

Another mix-up in Cather's *Jewett* stems from her desire not only to turn her mother into a father but to turn her in other respects into herself as well. That desire includes and goes beyond her promotion of Jewett as a first-rate writer. It extends even to Cather's concern that the physical appearance of Jewett's books is a liability in the contemporary marketplace. Telling Greenslet that she rather loves those dumpy little [4 1/2" X 6"] books herself, she recommends nevertheless that they be reissued in standard-size volumes with good clear type—and she suggests that a type like that used in *My Ántonia* would be appropriate.[23] Because readers do judge books by their covers, better that the late-Victorian Jewett should be repackaged as a New Woman of the twentieth century, and so Cather asks that the mother/father be made over in the image of the daughter. Cather remained a fierce critic of materialism within fiction—praising *The Country of the Pointed Firs* in her preface for being "so little encumbered with heavy materialism that deteriorates and grows old-fashioned" (*SOJ* xix)—but her preoccupation with typography, jacket design, and the size of the volumes indicates a pragmatic awareness that the materiality of texts is a significant factor in shaping their reception, even among the writers and Greenwich Village intellectuals to whom she hoped to appeal.

As editor, however, Cather's makeover of Jewett is a refurbishing that involves the substance as well as the appearance of her predecessor's oeuvre. In selecting stories to be included in the volume, Cather's eye was squarely on literary history, but a certain self-interest is also apparent in the editor's justification of her choices. "I have tried," she writes in her preface, "to gather into these two volumes the very best of Miss Jewett's beautiful work; the stories which, read by an eager student fifty years from now, will give him the characteristic flavor, the spirit, the cadence, of an American writer of the first order—and of a New England which will by then be a thing of the past" (*SOJ* xii–xiii). Equal parts "New England" and "America," a regionalist and a "writer of the first order," a recorder of the past destined to appeal to "eager" readers of the future, Cather's Jewett embodies and reconciles the tensions that emerged in her own struggles with the publicity department at Houghton. She is an idealized projection of the younger writer's ambitions and insecurities, and her "best stories" certify Cather's claims to greatness in ways that even a Pulitzer Prize could not. Devoid of "Othellos and Iagos and Don Juans," Jewett's stories about "the people who grew out of the soil and the life of the country near her heart, [and] not about exceptional individuals at war with their environment" (*SOJ* xv-xvi) are both "beautiful" and different in the strong, positive sense, and her antiheroic, "tightly yet so lightly built" (*SOJ* xix) narratives established a context for the novel Cather was then at work on and the one she had already begun to plan. Her argument that *The Country of the Pointed Firs* should be designated, along with *Huckleberry Finn* and *The Scarlet Letter*, as one of "three American books which have the possibility of a long, long life" because "no others . . . confront time and change so serenely" (*SOJ* xviii) might just as easily be offered in favor of *The Professor's House* or *Death Comes for the Archbishop*, which is perhaps the subconscious aim of Cather's mingling of promotion and self-promotion in the preface to *Jewett*. In selling Jewett, she sells herself. In assuring a bright future for *Pointed Firs*, she assures a continued demand for books cut from the same cloth—thus achieving what Knopf viewed (according to Cather) as the aim of advertising: to give an author a certain standing that would insure his future and interest in his future books.[24]

Like her decision to leave Houghton, Cather's remaking of Jewett shows signs of strain and ambivalence. In this instance the difficulty seems to arise out of the daughter's fear that she has used the precursor/mother selfishly or unfairly—a fear Adrienne Rich confronts and tries to alleviate in her "third and last address" to Emily Dickinson through a solemn promise: "with the hands of a daughter I would cover you/from all intrusion even my own/saying rest to your ghost."[25] Cather seems to have worried that her encounter with Jewett was also something of an intrusion, and that possibility made her uneasy. In April 1924 she sent Greenslet a draft of her preface and asked for his opinion. She tells him that, though her heart and mind had been full of ideas on the subject for years, when she sat down at the desk, it was not an easy piece of work to do. The tone, she explains, is the difficult thing; I have tried for a tone which would not have displeased Miss Jewett herself, but in these things one never knows.[26] Her desire to please Jewett and her uncertainty about whether or not she had succeeded indicates that the "ghost" of this precursor had hardly been laid to "rest."[27] The tone that so concerned Cather is occasionally and slightly condescending, as she refers once to "the *almost* flawless examples of literary art that make up these two volumes" (*SOJ* x, emphasis added) and points out that the writing in "William's Wedding," which was unfinished when Jewett died, "is in places a little vague, lacks the last coordinating touch of the writer's hand" (*SOJ* xiv–xv).

More than her tone, however, or the high claim she was making for Jewett and for herself in the preface, what perhaps haunted the editor was her decision to place that unfinished story and two other Dunnet Landing stories into the main body of *The Country of the Pointed Firs*. Cather had told Greenslet in the beginning that the safest way to prepare the new *Jewett* was for him to send her a complete set of the original editions and she would cut them up herself and bind them into volumes in the sequence that seemed best.[28] That Cather defines her editorial power in physical terms—and as the possibly violent actions of cutting and binding—suggests that this literary daughter, despite the affectionate bonds that connected her to Jewett, fought hard and for many years to establish a sense of autonomy and separateness,[29] and her efforts to do so included violating the integrity of the maternal text she was promoting as a masterpiece of style and structure. Though history seems to have vindicated most of Cather's choices regarding the "best stories" of Jewett,[30] she has been roundly criticized for the cut-and-paste job that for years served as the standard edition of *The Country of the Pointed Firs*.[31] Her insertion of the additional Dunnet Landing stories—two of which ("The Queen's Twin" and "A Dunnet Shepherdess") Jewett had already published separate from *Pointed Firs* in *The Queen's Twin and Other Stories* (1899)—mars Jewett's carefully patterned narrative significantly because the three stories are longer than most of the other sketches and are broken down into brief, numbered "chapters." The unfinished "William's Wedding" also confuses the chronology established in the 1896 edition because the narrator is describing an event that occurred on a return visit to Dunnet Landing—before the scene of farewell and departure that concludes the original. Moreover, the story awkwardly installs *The Country of the Pointed Firs* into precisely the narrative logic of the heterosexual love plot that Jewett's text had assiduously avoided. Cather's editing is to some degree, then, a "de-queering" of a story whose primary narrative interest had been in the world of love, particularly between women, outside of marriage. If Cather's visit to Jewett's "country" may be compared to Thea Kronborg's exploration of the cliff-dwellings in Panther Canyon, she seems to have overlooked her heroine's remonstrances to herself that "she was a guest in these houses, and she ought to behave as such" (*SL* 379).

Cather is a guest who feels entitled to remodel the house while the landlady is, as it were, indisposed.

Whether Cather's takeover of Jewett's "country" is hostile, friendly, or, as I have tried to suggest, some potent mixture of both, the move serves simultaneously to strengthen the mother figure by positioning her alongside Twain and Hawthorne and to weaken her by suggesting that even her masterpiece would benefit from the helping hand of the daughter/editor. Cather's engagement with the literary past is thus creative as well as destructive, since her remaking of her predecessor did reintroduce Jewett's work to contemporary readers, though with flaws resulting from the editor's zeal for cutting and binding. Most likely, however, Cather found the preface to *Jewett* a difficult piece of work to do for reasons that go beyond her personal relationship with its subject or the uncertainty she might have felt regarding the license she had taken editorially. The greater difficulties arise from the complex of issues that had "teased" her mind for years and would emerge as central preoccupations of both *The Professor's House* and *Death Comes for the Archbishop*: the relationship of "boys' books" to "girls' books," the relationship of "regionalism" to "nationalism" (or whether, indeed, a meaningful distinction could be made between the two), the power of the "masterpiece" and the terms that define it to shape American cultural history and critical debate.

In yoking together *Pointed Firs*, *Huckleberry Finn*, and *The Scarlet Letter*, Cather constructs, albeit in miniature, a canon of American fiction that appears to be gender-blind as well as familial, as she casually connects male- and female-authored texts by two New Englanders and a well-traveled Missourian, eliding the significant differences between and among them with the vague assertion that each of them "confront[s] time and change so serenely" (*SOJ* xviii). In two simple sentences, she buries the anxieties that had plagued her in her relationship with Houghton and begins to build a model of American literary history as a sexually egalitarian and happy family. The somber Hawthorne, long ago credited with "showing Miss Jewett how to write,"[32] seems a father to her and her romances of "every-day life" (Fields 59) as *The Scarlet Letter* is reclaimed from the Lawrentian canon and transformed from "an earthly story with a hellish meaning" (*SCAL* 89) into one defined instead by its serenity. Chronologically, of course, Hawthorne could be "father" to Twain as well as Jewett, and that odd (and metaphorically incestuous) couple—the satirist and the comedian, the southern steamboat pilot and the old-guard New Englander, the teller of tall tales and boy's adventure stories and the sketcher of the daily, extraordinary lives of women—could easily have produced Willa Cather. The conclusion of her preface to *Jewett* and much of the fiction published after it suggest that she believed that is precisely what happened.[33] Like many families, however, Cather's often proved difficult to keep together—as she had already learned in her decision to "leave" Houghton for the sake of Claude's "health."

Cather's fictions of the family, as we saw in part 1, often emphasize its social and ideological functions—i.e., its role in policing the queer or in reproducing sameness—and celebrate those powerful individuals such as Thea Kronborg who manage to escape its tyranny. An essay from the 1920s suggests that Cather continued to view the family as coercive. Writing on Katherine Mansfield for *The Borzoi 1925*, Cather observes, "in most families, the mere struggle to have anything of one's own, to be one's self at all, creates an element of strain that keeps everybody almost at the breaking point" (*NUF* 136). In the preface to *Jewett,* though, her implied familialization of literary history serves, much as more explicit metaphors had served in her negotiations with Houghton, to mask a risky and deeply radical act as a conservative or apolitical one. She disguises her resistance to Lawrence's masculinization of the American classics as a non-ideological "family" matter in order to avoid defining it as a "feminist" issue, but by "serenely" slipping Jewett into a canon of fiction that also included Twain and Hawthorne she deconstructs the major critical and philosophical premise of the *Studies*—i.e., men write, women seduce—and offers in reply an alternative, more inclusive vision of literary history.

In this regard, her preface to *Jewett,* resembles the contributions by Louise Pound and Mary Austin to the *Cambridge History of American Literature*, as her effort to revitalize Jewett's reputation is comparable to the efforts of her two friends and contemporaries to bring the ballads and folksongs of the lower classes and the poetry and literature of the continent's indigenous peoples into the canons of American literature. Cather was more invested in the notion of the "masterpiece" than was Pound, who argued in an essay of 1918 that "literature is not really the matter of a few outstanding names but of the whole activity" and sought to examine the relationship between masterpieces and the background that helps to define them.[34] She was less interested than Austin in immersing herself in and promoting the arts and cultures of the Southwestern tribes. Nonetheless, all three sought to forestall the processes of racial, sexual, and class exclusionism that were already evident in the compendious *Cambridge History* and that Lawrence's *Studies* legitimized by so narrowing the range of "classic" "American" "literature." For Cather, the stakes in this debate could hardly have been higher, and the fantasy of integration underlying her family portrait of Hawthorne, Twain, and Jewett(/Cather) is one she fought to maintain not only in her view of American literary and cultural history but in the structure of her fiction as well. She recognized that if her own increasingly nondramatic narratives were to stand a chance of enjoying "a long, long life," Lawrence's dark yet powerful psychocultural analysis would have to be effectively countered and a more favorable climate of reception and interpretation established. Her preface to *Jewett* is her effort to establish such a climate, which perhaps explains why she found it a more difficult piece of work than she had anticipated. One can also imagine why in writing it she was haunted by the reported scorn of the Greenwich Village intellectuals for Jewett's books and the potential scorn of writerly readers such as Lawrence, but Cather's fantasy that "girls' books" could attain the same cultural power as "boys' books" is a stubborn one, and she builds a compelling case for Jewett's status and ends her preface with a loving and optimistic prolepsis of literary history—a prolepsis that would shortly echo off the walls of *The Professor's House*. Further down in the paragraph that connects *Pointed Firs* with *The Scarlet Letter* and *Huckleberry Finn*, Cather contemplates the "long, joyous future" of Jewett's text:

> I like to think with what pleasure, with what a sense of rich discovery, the young student of American literature in far distant years to come will take up this book and say, "A masterpiece!" as proudly as if he himself had made it. It will be a message to the future, a message in a universal language. (*SOJ* xix)[35]

The closing image of Jewett's text—a text that is also Cather's, since she "made" the "this book" to which she refers—as a time capsule destined to be discovered by some "young student of American literature" is a complex one, and the "message" it offers reverberates forward and backward in Cather's career as well as outward to other significant cultural and textual "discoveries." The mingling of "pleasure" with "a sense of rich discovery" recalls both Thea Kronborg's ecstatic "discovery" of Dvorak's *New World* symphony and Wunsch's claim that "desire" motivated Columbus's "discovery" of the land mass Europeans would call the New World, and it transforms the student's reading of Jewett into an engagement with history comparable to Thea's, Columbus's, and Cather's in her problematic re-presentation of her predecessor's "masterpiece"—"as if

[she] [her]self had made it," indeed. History is recreation and interpretation, and sometimes it is also inevitably exploitation. Cather's conclusion thus recapitulates her own encounter with Jewett's text, while her application of the literary and cultural honorifics "masterpiece" and "discovery" to *Pointed Firs* confers upon Jewett's "little" "sketches" a degree of power that might have surprised their relatively unambitious author. Further, the preface gestures again in the direction of *The Scarlet Letter* in the notion of reading as an act of discovery that is also a remaking. Here, Cather's "student" is allied with "Hawthorne" in the Custom-House, where he happens upon the scarlet letter and Mr. Surveyor Pue's narrative of the life of Hester Prynne in a pile of "heaped-up rubbish"—an encounter described as "a *discovery* of some little interest" approached with "the sense that a treasure would here be brought to light." Like Jewett's text, the discovered narrative contains "a message to the future," an open invitation from the author of the prior text to recreate the past and "bring his mouldy and moth-eaten lucubrations before the public" (26, emphasis added). "Hawthorne's" fiction of *The Scarlet Letter* being "authorized and authenticated by the document of Mr. Surveyor Pue" (28–9), coupled with his sly assertion that, "in dressing up the tale," he has allowed himself "nearly or altogether as much license as if the facts have been entirely of my own invention," defines the literary artist's relationship to history as one of affiliation and exploitation—a precedent that clearly underlies Cather's fiction of the "student" reading *Jewett*.

Silent Screams: Gender, Reading, History, and *The Professor's House*

In reading and writing, Cather's figure of the student suggests, one is always inscribing oneself within the history of reading and writing, rewriting prior texts whose "messages" the future is always already waiting to decipher and rewrite yet again. Having positioned herself in the preface to *Jewett* within an American "family" drama that we might, following Jane Tompkins, call "Masterpiece Theater,"[36] Cather had set the stage for the interrogations of history that would occupy her major works of the mid-1920s, *The Professor's House* and *Death Comes for the Archbishop*. The contrasts between these two texts—the one so divided and despairing, the other as cool and quiet as a deserted cathedral—suggest that Cather remained haunted by the act of canon-formation she had so "serenely" undertaken in her preface, and that her place in the "family" of Hawthorne, Jewett, and Twain was a source of both power and uncertainty. With these two texts, we will conclude the main body of our examination of Cather's entanglement in the cultural politics of postwar "America," not because it ended for her in 1927 but because the dialogue enacted between her *Professor* and her *Archbishop* displays effectively and elegantly what that entanglement signified to her. Finally, too, though, any such conclusion is the more or less arbitrary construct of the interpreter, who, like some overly exuberant "young student," seems to discern some shape in a literary career and eagerly embraces it—"as proudly as if [she] [her]self had made it." It would be wiser, perhaps, to keep in mind Dickinson's advice to philosophers and scholars: "This World is not Conclusion."

The Professor's House is the novel that was in process when Cather was at work on the edition of Jewett, and evidence indicates she used it as a testing ground for the integrative vision of literary history she had articulated in her preface as well as for the self-consciously anti-Lawrentian version of the masterpiece she was struggling to define and promote. Significantly, the student who occupies such an important space in her preface is refigured in the novel as Tom Outland, the brilliant young engineer who for a few years enlivens Professor Godfrey St. Peter's middle life before being killed in the war. Like the student of American literature, Tom, an orphan who grew up in New Mexico, is credited with making a "rich discovery"—of the ruins of an ancient pueblo village on Blue Mesa. Cather's interpolation of the discovery of Mesa Verde by cowboy Richard Wetherill in 1888 opens with Tom's initial finding of Anasazi artifacts in the irrigation trenches across the river from the mesa. Stumbling upon "some pieces of pottery, all of it broken, and arrowheads, and a very neat, well-finished stone pick-ax," Tom realizes that the household he and his pal Roddy Blake had established in their cabin by the river was not the first in that neighborhood, and the language of his realization echoes in key respects Cather's image of the student "discovering" Jewett's "masterpiece":

> To people off alone, as we were, there is something stirring about finding evidences of human labour and care in the soil of an empty country. It comes to you as a sort of message, makes you feel differently about the ground you walk over every day. (173)

Like the prefacer's "message to the future," the young man's "message" from the past is a sign of Cather's involvement in the postwar effort to prove that, from a cultural standpoint, America was not "an empty country"—an effort that again allies her with Mary Austin who, in the *Cambridge History*, insists that the history of the "national literature" of "America" must begin with "aboriginal literature," because it offers "a study of what the land [the American] loves and lives in may do to the literature by which the American spirit is expressed" (*CHAL* 4:610). Like Austin and like Thea in Panther Canyon, Tom recognizes the nonemptiness of the land's indigenous cultures, as the artifacts complete the transformation of the mesa from "a blue, featureless lump" (170) to a "message"-laden landscape, a rich record of "human labour and care," the history of a "colony" of "fixed residents" (173). Cather's personal response to Mesa Verde was strikingly similar to Tom's. After her visit there in 1915, she wrote:

> Dr. Johnson declared that man is an historical animal. Certainly it is the human record, however slight, that stirs us most deeply, and a country without such a record is dumb, no matter how beautiful. The Mesa Verde is not, as many people think, an inconveniently situated museum. It is the story of an early race, of the social and religious life of a people indigenous to that soil and to its rocky splendors. It is the human expression of that land of sharp contours, brutal contrasts, glorious color and blinding light.[37]

As a representative "historical animal," Tom Outland proves to be a highly responsive reader of the "story" told by the ruins of the Cliff City, being so "stirred" by the evidence of this "powerful tribe" (181) that he claims them as ancestors and protests to Blake when the relics are sold that they are "the pots and pans that belonged to my poor grandmothers a thousand years ago" (219). However, as a figure in Cather's effort to demonstrate allegorically that the forms and history of American literature could be made to integrate and accommodate the narrative differences and cultural extremes represented by *The Scarlet Letter*, *Huckleberry Finn*, and *The Country of the Pointed Firs*, Tom is a sign of difficulty. Despite his rather bizarre claim of kinship with the cliff dwellers, his fetishization of the artifacts and his desire to preserve the mesa as an example of "pure" culture (and as an object of study—Tom goes to Washington in the hope of bringing back scholars "who would understand [the mesa], who would appreciate it and dig out all its secrets" [202]) run counter to Cather's desire for cultural dynamism and blending—and they contradict as well her claim that the Mesa Verde was not merely "an inconveniently situated museum." (Tom, with his meticulous numbering of "each specimen" and his daily "account" of their finds, seems determined to make his mesa precisely that.)

"Tom Outland's Story," a first-person narrative dropped into the middle of the third-person story of the professor, is Cather's queering— in the sense of critique and revision—of the American classic as the tale of a free boy's adventures. Tom's Blue Mesa is "a world above the world" (217), and it is, like Huck Finn's Mississippi River, a place where strays and castaways (Tom, Roddy, and their housekeeper Henry Atkins) can make of themselves "a happy family" (176), devising their own patterns of living, working, and caring for one another without interference from the other world below.[38] Tom's resemblance to Huck goes beyond the fact that he, too, is an orphan endowed with ingenuity and imagination. In the freshness and directness of his voice—what St. Peter calls the "austerity" of Tom's style in the diary he had kept of their work and life on the mesa (238)—Tom's narrative has the same lyric simplicity of Huck's at its descriptive finest. Returning to the mesa for his showdown with Roddy over the sale of the artifacts, for example, Tom's voice seems literally to soar:

> When I pulled out on top of the mesa, the rays of sunlight fell slant-ingly through the little twisted pinyons,—the light was all in between them, as red as a daylight fire, they fairly swam in it. Once again I had that glorious feeling that I've never had anywhere else, the feeling of being *on the mesa*, in a world above the world. And the air, my God, what air!—Soft, tingling, gold, hot with an edge of chill on it, full of the smell of pinyons—it was like breathing the sun, breathing the colour of the sky.   (217)

Despite such similarities, however, and Cather's obvious desire to affili-ate her tale with Twain's by way of Tom, his name links him not to the "innocent" narrator of *Huckleberry Finn* but to Tom Sawyer, whose slavish obedience to literary "authorities" fills him with the desire to rob, torture, and kill—much, one might suppose, as Tom Outland's reading of "filial piety in the Latin poets" (227) might have contributed to his self-destruc-tive desire to participate in the war. Tom's narrative is a destabilizing force in *The Professor's House* because Cather's use of the boy's story turns into a critique of the genre by exposing Tom's pitiable naiveté as a reader. He brings *Robinson Crusoe* with him to the mesa and then proceeds, in his relentless attack on Roddy for selling off their "inheritance," to treat him as a sort of Friday in spurs. "I see now," Roddy says sardonically when Tom's attack begins to sink in, "I was working for you like a hired man, and while you were away I sold your property" (222). When Roddy leaves, Tom finds a new text and a new meaning for his experience, as he immerses himself in the Latin poets and claims that he no longer regards the mesa as an adventure but with a "religious emotion." His feelings had "formerly been mixed up with other emotions," which he does not specify, "but now that they were gone, I had my happiness unalloyed" (227). Neither Tom's happiness nor his purity are "unalloyed," however, because he lacks the ironic self-awareness that makes Huck's "innocence" so much more convincing. Tom is trapped by the plots he reads and lapses carelessly into borrowed rhetorics without realizing their implications or that they "alloy" and mediate his experiences in significant ways. When Tom insists that the artifacts "belonged to this country, to the State, and to all the people" and compares Roddy's sale of them to Dreyfus's alleged sale of secrets to the Germans, Roddy rightly dismisses the harangue as "Fourth of July talk" (221), a hypocritical patriotism that masks the fact that, with or without the cash nexus, Tom views the artifacts as his "property." Indeed, Tom's description of his first night alone on the mesa proves the accuracy of Roddy's assessment, as he stakes his solitary claim to the Cliff City:

> This was the first time I ever saw it as a whole. It all came together in my understanding, as a series of *experiments* do when you begin to see where they are leading. Something had happened in me that made it possible for me to co-ordinate and simplify, and that process, going on in my mind, brought with it great happiness. It was *possession*. The excitement of my first *discovery* was a very pale feeling compared to this one.   (226, emphasis added)

Discovery, experimentation, possession: Tom's "religious emotion" is "alloyed" by the vocabularies of science and imperialism that creep unwittingly into his description, undermining the "free" boy's story by investing it with the same "secret [though in this case unconscious] Kind of Pleasure" Robinson Crusoe takes in realizing that the island "was all my own, that I was King and Lord of all this Country indefeasibly and had a Right of Possession."[39] Tom's lack of awareness about his use of language makes his will to possess the mesa far more problematic than the "feeling of empire" shared by Ray Kennedy and Thea Kronborg, because it leads not to the relatively serene blending of rhetorics and crossing of boundaries that occur in *The Song of the Lark* but to a more anarchic sort of textual "pollution," as one story or rhetoric spills over into another, tainting it and making "distinctions" not merely "hateful" but impossible to draw and destabilizing utterly any notion of textual authority. Roddy again calls attention to the problems created by such "pollution" when, as he prepares to make an angry and risky nighttime departure from the mesa, Tom warns him that "the river's high. It's dangerous crossing." "I'm surprised at you, using such common expressions!" Roddy replies. "*Dangerous crossing*; it's painted on signboards all over the world!" (247). Linguistically, Tom is a "dangerous crossing" of literary languages from Virgil to Defoe to Twain along with the low cultural discourses of "signboards" and "Fourth of July talk." Such bristling tensions suggest that Cather was at this point overwhelmed in her attempt to reconcile the competing claims of the three exemplary texts she had named in her preface to *Jewett* and that the effort to do so marks her *House*, like another famous domicile in American fiction, with a fissure at its center—out of which bursts the jarring yet beautiful "Tom Outland's Story."

If Tom Outland is Cather's "free" boy whose freedom proves both false and "dangerous," Godfrey St. Peter, hovering broodingly, fastidiously, and in some ways obliviously over his household in his attic study, is a more ominous refiguring of "Hawthorne" in the Custom-House (as well as a number of other male characters from his tales and romances)—and, by implication, of Cather in Jewett's *Country*. A chair in European history at a university on the shores of Lake Michigan and author of the eight-volume *Spanish Adventurers in North America*, St. Peter is a scholar whose "habit of living with ideas" causes him gradually to come to view the desk in his study as "a shelter one could hide behind, . . . a hole one could creep into" (141). In the years following Outland's death, St. Peter increasingly seeks that shelter, withdrawing so completely from marriage, family, and "the engaging drama of domestic life" that his wife accuses him of becoming "lonely and inhuman" (16, 141). St. Peter, however, defines his existential crisis in more specific and revealing terms:

> He had had two romances: one of the heart, which had filled his life
> for many years, and a second of the mind—of the imagination. Just
> when the morning brightness of the world was wearing off for him,
> along came Outland and brought him a kind of second youth. (234)

When both of his "romances" are brought to an end—the one by death, the other by a crushing yet simple sense of exhaustion—St. Peter comes to believe that "the saddest thing in the world is falling out of love," but for him that process involves much more than the loss of his early passion for his wife: "Falling out, for him, seemed to mean falling out of all domestic and social relations, out of his place in the human family, indeed" (250). Through St. Peter, Cather explores the emotional and aesthetic possibilities of the "romance" as an antisocial discourse of destruction, a renunciation of relationship, a "falling out" or into something that closely resembled a Lawrentian "earthly story with a hellish meaning." Even St. Peter's physical appearance suggests this association, since, with his "silky, very black hair," his "tawny skin," "hawk nose," "hawk-like eyes," and "wicked-looking eyebrows [that] made his students call him Mephistopheles" (5), Cather's "God-free" professor recalls an even more diabolical scholar who had also sacrificed his "best years to feed the hungry dream of knowledge," Hawthorne's Roger Chillingworth (*SL* 57).

As a character in his own "two romances," St. Peter is both selfish and self-divided, but his flaws seem hardly to merit the comparison with the cruelties of Chillingworth, much less the evil doings of the devil himself. He is guilty, as Jean Schwind has pointed out, of despising the female world that occupies the space below the masculine, intellectual space of his study and of ignoring his dependence on women's labor and money when he attacks the acquisitiveness of his daughter Rosamond and her husband, Louie Marsellus ("This Is a Frame-Up" 78–80). St. Peter's wife, Lillian, had "inherited a small income from her father—only about sixteen hundred a year," but, St. Peter admits, "it had made all the difference in the world"—because he believes that if his wife had had to "pinch and be shabby and do housework," she would have become "another person, and a bitter one" (233). Engaged to Outland at the time of his death, Rosamond inherited all the profits from an engine he invented that was "revolutionizing aviation," according to her husband, who ultimately capitalized on Tom's invention (30). Still, on the surface at least, St. Peter seems no more despicable than anyone who has an office at home and worries that in "that perilous journey down through the human house he might lose his mood, his enthusiasm, even his temper" (18). At the university he has fought the good fight, resisting "the new commercialism, the aim to 'show results' that was undermining and vulgarizing education," defending "purely cultural studies," and battling in his own department against such "lax methods" as allowing students to "charge up the time spent in perusing *The Scarlet Letter* to Colonial history, and *Tom Sawyer* to the Missouri Compromise" (43). One must wonder why such laxity did not include using *The Country of the Pointed Firs* to teach the decline of the

New England fishing industry, but one must also consider why Cather's two-time romancer has eyebrows that endow his story with a hellish meaning that seems so at odds with the mere perils of middle life and academe from which he seems to suffer.

St. Peter's devilishness arises primarily out of his status as historian in a text that is so preoccupied with the makings and meanings of history. Events such as the rediscovery of Mesa Verde proved to Cather that the cultural soil of her country was neither "dumb" nor "empty," that it contained, on the contrary, a "record" and a "story." As St. Peter's attacks on using literature to teach history suggest, however, she delighted in exploring and exploiting the boundaries and the relationship between the historical "record" and historically inflected "stories" such as *The Professor's House*. In interpolating Richard Wetherill's narrative (related to her by one of his surviving brothers during her 1915 visit) of entering the mesa in search of lost cattle and seeing "through a veil of lightly falling snow . . . a little city of stone, asleep" (179), Cather does not bother to draw the reader's attention to the similarities between her Blue Mesa and history's Mesa Verde.[40] She thus foregoes the opportunity to muse, à la Hawthorne in his preface to *The Blithedale Romance*, on how the romancer may "make free" with a "romantic episode of his own life" because it offers "an available foothold between fiction and reality." Nevertheless, in crediting Tom Outland with a major archaeological discovery as well as an invention that was "revolutionizing aviation," Cather "make[s] free" with history in flagrant fashion in order to make her young hero's story, as St. Peter calls it, "fantastic" (233). For Cather, two generations after Hawthorne's send-up of the socialist experiment at Brook Farm, history is devilishly slippery, a condition that makes possible the phantasms and "Faery Land" Hawthorne had argued were necessary for the American romancer; for St. Peter, whose *Spanish Adventurers* eschews "all the foolish conventions about that kind of writing," making history is merely "fun" (23).

Hawthorne may have taught Cather that the romancer could have "fun" manipulating the "facts" of history, but such Mephistophelean "fun" had its "hellish" side as well. In *The Professor's House* St. Peter's "falling . . . out of his place in the human family" is a sign that the "serenity" of the literary-historical project undertaken in the preface to *Jewett* was in fact severely strained. Moreso even than Tom's "dangerous crossing" of conflicting rhetorics, the professor's "falling out" and the hollow resignation with which he finally resolves to "face with fortitude the *Berengaria* and the future" (258) reflect Cather's lingering doubts about the viability of the metaphorical family the preface had constructed, her place within it, and her actions as editor and promoter of Jewett. The link between St. Peter's desire, in his "hour of desperation," to "avoid meeting his own family" (250) and Cather's struggle to create a place for the woman writer in American literary history is, perhaps not so strangely, Tom Outland's diary.

Like the "young student" with Jewett's "masterpiece" and "Hawthorne" with the narrative of Mr. Surveyor Pue, Tom's diary is to St. Peter a found manuscript in need of remaking. Technically speaking, St. Peter cannot be credited with discovering this manuscript, but his relationship to it replicates in other respects those of the "student" and "Hawthorne" to the texts they encounter on their own. Tom had taken St. Peter to his diary when they visited the Blue Mesa during a summer of traveling the Southwest together two years after Tom's graduation. They retrieve it from the "Eagle's Nest," a remote group of cliff houses where Tom had sealed up the diary in a "stone cupboard" (235)—and where he and Roddy had discovered the female mummy Henry named "Mother Eve" (192). Since the men remove the mummy and put her in a more accessible chamber in the Cliff City, Tom's diary literally occupies the space of the dead mother, whose well-preserved body is a brutally graphic text of suffering:

> We thought she had been murdered; there was a great wound in her side, the ribs stuck out through the dried flesh. Her mouth was open as if she were screaming, and her face, through all those years, had kept a look of terrible agony. Part of the nose was gone, but she had plenty of teeth, not one missing, and a great deal of coarse black hair. Her teeth were even and white, and so little worn that we thought she must have been a young woman. (192)

The mother's text—the text of the mummy/mommy—is also unfinished, since the fast-acting "water-drinking air" of her death chamber makes her "screaming" and her "terrible agony" seem like ongoing events, sounds that have echoed down "through all those years," as though her "great wound" were still fresh, still causing pain to a body still capable of feeling it. Tom's text replaces the dead mother, who is later "murdered" a second time when, as she is being moved out of the Cliff City with the other sold relics, the box she is in falls to the bottom of Black Canyon (221). Killed again in commodification, Eve is an appropriate "mother" to a "son" who will die in war—and be "resurrected" in an act of textual commodification that strongly resembles *The Best Stories of Sarah Orne Jewett.*

Through most of the novel, St. Peter seems to resist fiercely and judge harshly efforts to trade and profit upon the memory of Tom Outland. When Rosamond and Louie announce that the Norwegian manor house they are building on the shores of Lake Michigan will be named "Outland," in honor of the man whose foresight in securing a patent for his invention and leaving a will had made its construction possible, St. Peter protests to his wife that the Marselluses should "be quiet" about their good fortune and "not convert [Tom's] very bones into a personal asset" (36). Then, when Rosamond lets her father know that she and Louie would like to "settle an income on you, so that you could give up your university work and devote all your time to writing and research" because it's "what Tom would have wanted," St. Peter immediately and indignantly refuses on the grounds that "my friendship with Outland is the one thing I will not have translated into the vulgar tongue" (48, 50). He concurs with the assessment of his younger daughter Kathleen, who bemoans the fact that Tom has turned out nothing but "chemicals and dollars and cents" for everyone but her and St. Peter. But, she adds, "Our Tom is much nicer than theirs" (112–13). Ultimately, though, St. Peter becomes a direct participant in the commodification of Outland, as he devotes part of the summer of his discontent—once his wife and the Marselluses have sailed for France on the *Berengaria*—to preparing Tom's diary for publication. Left alone, St. Peter abandons the new house the prize money for his *Spanish Adventurers* had just built and returns to the old house with his beloved attic study. Curiously, however, he finds himself avoiding the study and sitting all day in his garden instead, because "the task that awaited him up there was difficult. It was a little thing, but one of those little things at which the hand becomes self-conscious, feels itself stiff and clumsy" (150).

"Stiff"-handed and full of dread, St. Peter seems puzzled that such a "little thing" should prove to be so "difficult"—just as Cather had confessed to Greenslet that writing the preface to *Jewett* had not been an easy piece of work to do. For Cather, the tone was the difficult thing. For St. Peter, the "bother" was that he would have to write an introduction, because Tom's diary only covered the six months of his work on the mesa and contained "almost nothing about Tom himself." "To mean anything," St. Peter realizes, "it must be prefaced by a sketch of Outland, and some account of his later life and achievements" (150). To reduce Outland to the fixity and the diminished scale of a mere "sketch"—when, in dreams, the blue-eyed boy was still "com[ing] back again through the garden door" (239)—and to turn Tom's "plain account" (238) into an edited and anno-tated "publication" was, though St. Peter never acknowledges it, to "con-vert his very bones into a[n] . . . asset," to "translate" their friendship "into the vulgar tongue" of commerce. That, of course, was precisely what Cather had done in the making and the marketing of her *Jewett*—and the clearest indication of her ambivalence about that project is that readers of *The Professor's House* never see either the "sketch" St. Peter works at all summer "in a desultory way" or Tom's "almost beautiful" diary (238). What we are offered instead is St. Peter's memory of Tom's telling him his own "story."

Sarah Orne Jewett was a writer of "sketches," and Cather had in effect "sketched" her into literary history in the succinct preface to *Jewett*. But of the three masterpieces placed side by side in her prediction about American books destined to enjoy "a long, long life," *The Country of the Pointed Firs* is the one whose presence in *The Professor's House* is the most elusive. Jewett is arguably "the thing not named" in this troubled narrative, the ineffable something "felt upon the page without being specifically named there" (*NUF* 50), and, indeed, her influence is apparent in, for example, the narrative set-up for the shift into "Tom Outland's Story." The careful situating of Tom and St. Peter in the intimate, sensuous, enclosed atmosphere of "one of those rainy nights, before the fire in the dining-room" (155) recalls the "chilly night of cold northeasterly rain" (*SOJ* 98) when Jewett's speaker lights a fire and passes the narrative off to Mrs. Todd and Mrs. Fosdick for the crucial tale of poor Joanna. The ease of movement in this transfer of narrative power is a sign of Jewett's faith in the functional fluidity of storytelling, and Cather's appropriation of her predecessor's trope for such a movement indicates at least a desire for a similar faith. Too, Tom's initial assessment of the Cliff City—"It all hung together, seemed to have a kind of composition" (179–80)—seems to echo Mrs. Todd's decla-ration, apropos of Captain Littlepage's "great narratives," that, "Some o' them tales hangs together toler'ble well" (*SOJ* 44). But in the crisis of lit-erary author-ity that puts a crack in Cather's *House*, Jewett's romances of "every-day life" are, like Twain's adventure stories and Hawthorne's histor-ical allegories, tested, and the results are similarly ambiguous.

Though cryptically rather than specifically, Jewett is a "thing . . . named" in *The Professor's House*, and her name is Mother Eve. Clearly, Jewett was for Cather an enabling Anasazi, a powerful ancestor whose stories enriched the soil of a never-empty country and provided an alternative to the prevailing cultural model of female creativity as destructive and/or debased. The figure of the twice-murdered mother, however—doomed in the first instance by a jealous husband, according to Father Duchene's theory of "a personal tragedy" (201), and in the second by Tom's displacement of the mother he then fails to defend because he is off in Washington looking for someone to come "dig out [the mesa's] secrets"—suggests that Cather saw this model as hopelessly embattled. Eve's silent, endless "screaming" and her unassuageable, "terrible agony" signal the collapse of maternal author-ity, while St. Peter's offstage "sale" of Tom's diary seems a confession of Cather's complicity in that collapse. In an elaborate series of switches in gender and generation, Cather disperses far and wide the anxieties she experienced as daughter/author/editor and the fears about the cultural power of women's texts she had buried beneath the "serene" surface of her preface to *Jewett*, but the sense of failure and guilt is nonetheless pervasive: in the son's failure to save his mother from sale and murder, the father's failure to save his son from war, the father's reduction of the son's "bones" to a "sketch." Tom's "happy family" on the mesa collapses from Roddy's sale of the artifacts and Tom's betrayal of their friendship, while St. Peter loses his place in the "human family" because finally all he can love is a dead boy. Similarly, the literary "family" of American writers Cather had envisioned feels the immense strain of trying to stay together in one *House*, and, as Mother Eve goes crashing to the bottom of Black Canyon, logic would seem to suggest that the family and the *House* fall to pieces along with her.

Cather's *House* is not quite, however, a House of Usher, and, though extensively damaged, it is saved at the last moment from collapsing utterly by a figure who, like Thea Kronborg's Aunt Tillie, seems on loan from Jewett's "country." Augusta, the St. Peter family's sewing-woman, is a "reliable, methodical spinster" (8) whose dressmaker's forms occupy a corner of the professor's study and whom he acknowledges as "a corrective, a remedial influence" (255). On the stormy night when wind blows out the old gas stove in his study and slams shut the window while he is in a deep sleep, however, Augusta is literally a lifesaver, arriving in the nick of time and dragging the overcome St. Peter out of the noxious room. The spinster/seamstress/nurse, who seems patterned after so many of Jewett's women who are similarly "seasoned and sound and on solid earth" (256), spends the remainder of the night watching over her employer, as she is frequently called upon to do by the families for whom she sews. To

St. Peter, she is "like the taste of bitter herbs," but he finally sees in her solidity and her lack of sentimentality—"She talked about death as she spoke of a hard winter or a rainy March, or any of the sadnesses of nature"—a way to live "without delight[,] . . . without joy, without passionate griefs." Following, he thinks, her example, St. Peter believes that he can live in a world of such tragically diminished expectations, that at last he feels "the ground under his feet" and can "face with fortitude the *Berengaria* and the future" (256–8).

Readers do not see enough of Augusta to be able to judge whether the grim "fortitude" St. Peter derives from watching her watch over him through his "half-closed eyes" is a valid interpretation of her. As a gloss on the "dear old women" (*SOJ* xvi) who were the imaginative core of Jewett's fiction, however, St. Peter's reading of Augusta conflicts dramatically with the warmth and the optimism of Cather's preface, which emphasizes sympathy and humor as well as a quiet acceptance of life's limitations. In appropriating Augusta's "matter-of-factness" to justify the sardonic conclusion that he felt no obligations toward his family and that they would be "too happily preoccupied with their own affairs" to notice his "apathy" (258), St. Peter transforms the romance of "every-day life" into a bleak parable of renunciation that is a remaking of Jewett's text even more radical and problematic than Cather's insertion of the additional Dunnet Landing stories. Despite Augusta's assertion of physical power in saving the professor's life— and he compliments her on her "strong arm" (254)—St. Peter's assertion of interpretive power over the woman's text suggests that the historian's "arm" is ultimately stronger and longer than the seamstress's.

To reduce the Jewettian model of fiction that Augusta seems to represent to a bland tale made joyless and passionless by the absence of "Othellos and Iagos and Don Juans" was to engage in precisely the kind of misreading Cather sought to circumvent in her preface to *Jewett*. That St. Peter's misreading prevails in his final vision of the "future" proves, moreover, that Cather was far from "serene" about the prospect of her "message to the future" holding sway in the cultural contest to define "American literature" and shape its canon. Augusta may barely succeed in keeping the *House* from collapsing, but the seamstress's severely limited "victory" indicates that Cather suspected her effort to a-mend literary history by stitching *The Country of the Pointed Firs* into a small sampler of American masterpieces was for some reason doomed to fail. Early in the narrative, St. Peter expresses a perverse desire to keep Augusta's forms in his old study when she needs to move them to the new house to get on with her work. "You shan't take away my ladies," he protests (12), and, indeed, she does not. The ending of *The Professor's House* enacts the defeat of Cather's proposal that the "forms" of the American classics should be many and various by seeming to acquiesce to the controlling power of devilish readers and misreaders like St. Peter and D. H. Lawrence. St. Peter's misreading of Augusta turns Jewett into a grim realist—"And when you admitted that a thing was real," St. Peter thinks as he contemplates Augusta's new importance to him, "that was enough—now" (257)—whose earthbound stories seem the literary equivalent of Prohibition, that brainchild of the female reformers so vilified by Lawrence in the *Studies*. St. Peter even makes that comparison explicit as he watches Augusta reading her little religious book: "he would have to learn to [live without delight], just as, in a Prohibition country, he supposed he would have to learn to live without sherry" (257). Augusta reads silently. Mother Eve "screams" silently. The dressmaker's headless, voiceless "forms" stay put in St. Peter's study. In a book of failures, defeats, disappointments, and despairs, surely Cather's failure to believe in her own ability to shape the "forms" of American critical discourse must be regarded as one of the most spectacular.

There is, of course, another way to read *The Professor's House*. I always tell my students to read it backward after they have read it forward, by which I mean: read it first, as I have done here, as an allegory of male authority and misogyny in a masculinist culture—i.e., as a feminist critique along the axis of gender—which begins and ends with Godfrey powerfully misreading Augusta; then reread it from St. Peter's concluding ruminations on his alienation from an adult life that had been "shaped by the penalties and responsibilities" incurred by a "secondary social man, the lover" (240). Such a move turns his story into a critique along the axis of sexuality of the regulatory practices that create and sustain the regime of compulsory heterosexuality. By the terms of this critique, St. Peter's search for a way to live "in a Prohibition country" seems poignant rather than sardonic, a measure of his weariness in the face of a profoundly corrosive social machine. His aversion to his own family is an aversion to that machinery, but unlike Thea Kronborg he lacks the tools or the energy for wrecking it and building something else in its place. All he can summon is a hollow "fortitude" for facing a "future" he is powerless to change. Both readings are, it seems to me, in play in the text, each pushing up against and unsettling the other. If I have emphasized one rather than the other in these pages it is because I think the gender critique primarily fuels Cather's forays into the culture wars and gives rise to the pessimism of *The Professor's House*. Regardless of her personal politics and her tendency to depict political workers as zealots and fools,[41] Cather's anxious intervention into the discussion of "classic" "American" "literature" is marked by a suspicion that the radical changes in the meaning of citizenship for women brought about by passage of the Nineteenth Amendment would do little structurally to alter the balance of power between men and women.[42] For Cather, writing "in a Prohibition country" meant writing in a country that was rushing to push women writers to the margins of literary history.

4

Comrades and Countrymen

Queer Love and a Dream of "America"

As I lay with my head in your lap camerado,
The confession I made I resume, what I said to you and the open air I
    resume,
I know I am restless and make others so,
I know my words are weapons full of danger, full of death,
For I confront peace, security, and all the settled laws, to unsettle them,
I am more resolute because all have denied me than I could ever have been
    had all accepted me,
I heed not and have never heeded either experience, cautions, majorities,
    nor ridicule,
And the threat of what is call'd hell is little or nothing to me,
And the lure of what is call'd heaven is little or nothing to me;
Dear camerado! I confess I have urged you onward with me, and still urge
    you, without the least idea of what is our destination,
Or whether we shall be victorious, or utterly quell'd and defeated.
                                                    —Walt Whitman

To many eyes, *Death Comes for the Archbishop* may seem to evade or repress massively the conflicts and anxieties that so bedeviled Cather in *The Professor's House*. One could argue that, in replacing her angst-ridden scholar in the attic with a constitutionally mellow man of the cloth, Cather signals the first phase of a retreat Marxist critics of the 1930s would attack as escapist.[1] Sharon O'Brien has suggested, however, that *Archbishop* is in fact a more diverse and conflict-ridden text than Cather's self-conscious attempt to "do something in the style of legend" (*OW* 9) has led critics to believe, that history and ideology both disturb the serene, even static, surface of the narrative to expose the shifting and contradictory systems of representation hovering just beneath it.[2] O'Brien's point is both useful and refreshing, if only because it disentangles the ideologically monolithic viewpoint of Cather's French priest from the more divided yet in some ways more generous stance evinced in the narrative's easy movement among Catholic, Mexican, Native American, and Anglo-American myths and experiences of the Southwest. Still, if the text does not, either through the consoling evasions of religion or a postcardish sentimentalism, swerve entirely past the violence and instability endemic to what ethnohistorian James Axtell has termed the "contest of cultures" waged in early North America,[3] how does it confront such problems without succumbing to the kinds of tensions that, just two years earlier, had nearly brought down Cather's *House*?

Part of the answer to this question is doubtless that the personal crisis of authority that editing and promoting Jewett seems to have engendered had passed by the time Cather was at work on *Archbishop*, though that crisis is still in evidence in her short, bitter novel of 1926, *My Mortal Enemy*. Cather's portrait of the charismatic Myra Henshawe, who forfeits a substantial inheritance to marry for love and ends up plump, poor, and confined to a wheelchair—"strong and broken, generous and tyrannical, a witty and rather wicked old woman, who hated life for its defeats, and loved it for its absurdities" (65)—is punctuated by such sardonic commentaries on twentieth-century American art and culture as Myra's description of modern poetry as "ugly lines about ugly people and common feelings" (80). She likes Whitman but calls him a "dirty old man" (80) and, under the influence of opiates given to kill the pain of a tumor, she lapses into paranoia and religion and takes to "murmuring to herself long passages from her old poets" (91). Taut and despairing, *My Mortal Enemy* is a nightmarish analysis of the destructive powers of wealth and romance (as erotic illusion) that suggests that Cather's battle to establish her place as American woman writer in the marketplace and in literary history by no means ended with *The Professor's House*. With *Archbishop*, however, it takes a radical and optimistic turn, and her optimism is even in Cather's account of the novel's composition. Of her last and most extensive narrative exploration of the Southwest, Cather remarked that, "Writing this book . . . was like a happy vacation from life, a return to childhood, to early memories" (*OW* 11).

In such a sunny mood, Cather crafted in *Archbishop* an American historical novel that is also—in the smallest and largest senses and to a greater extent than anything else she ever wrote—a love story. It succeeds as such not because she chose to take a "vacation" from the historical and psychological dilemma she created for herself in affiliating her and Jewett's fictions with those of Hawthorne and Twain but because she reapproaches that dilemma determined to prove that love—as discursive practice and force in history—could be as powerful as the despair that had so beautifully fractured her *House*. Her *Archbishop* is a text that engages with the past but does not seem haunted by it. Thus, one sees in its slow-moving vignette structure traces of *The Country of the Pointed Firs*; one hears echoes of a Huck-ish adventure story in the appearance of Kit Carson (who spent his years "from fourteen to twenty picking up a bare living as cook or mule-driver for wagon trains, often in the service of brutal and desperate characters," but nevertheless "had preserved a clean sense of honour and a compassionate heart" [76–7]); one detects the influence of Hawthorne both in the bold strokes of color that mark Cather's desert tableau and in the allegorical portraits of evil priests and troubled women worked into the background of that tableau. Here, though, as in *The Song of the Lark*, the narrative aims at integration rather than disintegration, reconciliation rather than conflict, and author-ity resides not in any particular version of literary or cultural history but in a flexibility that serves ambiguously to tolerate and to contain difference. In *Archbishop* Cather achieves, if only for a moment, the alternative to Lawrentian diabolism that eluded her in *The Professor's House*, and she does so by exploiting the radical cultural and literary potential of love.

That love is central to the ethic and the aesthetic shaping *Archbishop* is made clear in a disagreement the missionary bishop Jean Marie Latour has with his friend and confrere Joseph Vaillant regarding miracles. To Joseph, a miracle is "direct and spectacular, not with Nature, but against it," a sort of spiritual teddy bear that the faithful "can hold in our hands and love" (29, 50). To Latour, however, love is the means to rather than the end of making miracles, as he replies to his impulsive vicar that, "Where there is great love there are always miracles." He continues:

> One might almost say that an apparition is human vision corrected by divine love. I do not see you as you really are, Joseph; I see you through my affection for you. The miracles of the Church seem to me to rest not so much upon faces or voices or healing power coming suddenly near to us from afar off, but upon our perceptions being made finer, so that for a moment our eyes can see and our ears can hear what is there about us always. (50)

Love corrects, transforms, and reveals, turning the homely, bow-legged Father Joseph into something other than one of the ugliest men "the Lord had made" (37) and making it possible to recognize the miraculousness of "what is there about us always." Latour's discourse on love's power to alter and heighten perception suggests that the serenity of *Archbishop* rests in part on a recuperation of Jewettian optimism, as his emphasis on sight and sound echoes a late statement of faith by Cather's predecessor: "I always insist that love isn't blind: it is only love that sees!" (Fields 230). Ironically, in a text in which the Virgin Mary is the most prominent "female" "character," a narrative marked on so many levels by a similar faith signals a restoration of the maternal authority that seemed so endangered in *The Professor's House*.

The subversive, redemptive story of Latour's "great love" for Vaillant ranks as something of a "miracle" in Cather's career, since intimacy in her fiction tends to breed at best alienation and at worst mortal enmity. Here, though, is a homosocial romance more "gorgeous" than "Tom Outland's Story" or Claude Wheeler and David Gerhardt's experience of love (and death) on the battlefield because it is the story of an affection and a partnership played out over a lifetime and often over great distances. Further, the continual shifting of roles and boundaries in the relationship suggests that Latour and Vaillant are complementary companions comparable to the same-sex pairs who turn up so frequently in Jewett's fiction—such as, for instance, the narrator and her landlady/herbalist Mrs. Todd in *The Country of the Pointed Firs* or Abby Martin and Queen Victoria, who never meet but are powerfully linked in "The Queen's Twin"—making *Archbishop* a study in what might be termed "pa(i)rapsychology," an examination of the oscillating nature of identities formed in relationship. In *Archbishop* Cather offers a rare depiction of the couple as a site of nurturance and productive collaboration. At times Latour plays the mother to Vaillant, going to fetch him when he is stricken ill on his missionary journeys, tending happily to him and to the garden at home in Santa Fe while the impatient, childlike Joseph longs for recovery and his next departure (e.g., 118–32, 199–210). Conversely, though, as the more socially and politically adept of the two, Joseph often plays the "wife"—cook, hostess, peacemaker—to Latour's more withdrawn and cerebral "husband." Latour may enjoy a "father's" power to recall his "son" from Tucson when he wants to see him, but of the two he seems to suffer most during their lengthy separations, like a twin or a lover who seems incomplete without his complementary other. Indeed, the two priests ride matching mules, Angelica and Contento (who "are always ridden together and have a great affection for each other" [60]), wear twin cloaks made from cloth they had purchased together in Paris before their first voyage to the New World (212), and share the memories of boys who grew up in the same town, attended the same seminary, and resolved together to leave home and country in order to become missionaries.

Their separations are severe emotional and spiritual trials for Latour, who undergoes his peculiar ordeal at Stone Lips, the cold December night of his soul ("one of those periods of coldness and doubt which . . . had occasionally settled down upon his spirit and made him feel an alien, wherever he was" [210]), and three days of reflective isolation in an "almost perpetual sand-storm" (222) at Eusabio's as a result of his longing or concern for Vaillant. When Vaillant is dispatched to Pike's Peak, a move Latour approves as bishop, he realizes that "as a man, he was a little hurt that his old comrade should leave him without one regret," because he senses this departure is "a final break; that their lives would part here, and that they would never work together again." Latour insists upon the naturalness of their ties to one another—"We are countrymen, and are bound by early memories. And that two friends, having come together, should part and go their separate ways—that is natural, too"—but when Joseph leaves he rides "home to his solitude," acutely aware for a moment of his "personal loneliness" and allowing himself to indulge "in such reflections as any bachelor nearing fifty might have" (249–53).

Comrades, companions, countrymen: the rhetoric and the spirit of Cather's brotherly love story recalls the celebration of manly "adhesiveness" that constitutes the driving force of the "Calamus" poems—by that "dirty old man" admired by Myra Henshawe (and, somewhat reluctantly, by Willa Cather[4])—as well as the legacy of paired figures passed on to her from Jewett. In this instance the prior texts are pre-texts, cover stories that present same-sex love as unthreatening, enabling, and even ennobling. Elsewhere in Cather's fiction, Jewett and Whitman are deployed together, sometimes directly and self-consciously—as in *O Pioneers!*, with its dedication to Jewett and its title's allusion to Whitman—sometimes indirectly and probably unconsciously—as in *The Song of the Lark*, which owes something to Whitman for its corporeal utopianism and something to Jewett for the narrative of an excursion into nature that is pivotal to the development of the woman artist. Here, though, Jewett and Whitman function in a much deeper and more complex way, for the rhetoric of relationship that permeates *Archbishop* and comprises its affective core is a direct inheritance from two American writers who celebrated same-sex love not, as Leslie Fiedler famously claimed, as a flight from adulthood, community, or nation-building, but, indeed, as a primary means of achieving all of those goals.[5]

Death Comes for the Archbishop begins where *Huckleberry Finn* ends, with a movement into the territories—in this case, the recently annexed territory of New Mexico (6)—which is not a "lighting out" but a settling down, a bringing into order, though I will put on hold for the moment the question of whether that order is queer or anti-queer. Both Jewett and Whitman figure prominently into Cather's rendering of Latour and Vaillant as the authors of order and love. Jewett's vision is more local than national, but her mostly female neighborhood—"the country of our friendship," as she once described it (Fields 200)—is presided over by figures such as Almira Todd, "a stern and unbending lawgiver" (*SOJ* 50) who teaches both intimacy and wisdom. For Whitman the "songs" of "the life-long love of comrades" are invested with the power to "make the continent indissoluble" and are offered in service to "Democracy . . . ma femme!"[6] Mary, of course, is the "ma femme" of Cather's text, the offstage goddess who commands the devotion of the two priests who are so devoted to each other and whose love consoles Latour after Vaillant's departure for Colorado (253–5). As he calmly waits for death to come for him, however, the Archbishop's tranquility seems to stem less from a religious man's anticipation of a reunion with God or the Mother of God than from the confidence that death will reunite him with his beloved friend. "*Since your brother was called to his reward,*" Latour writes to Joseph's sister just months before his own death, "*I feel nearer to him than before. For many years Duty separated us, but death has brought us together. The time is not far distant when I shall join him*" (263). For Whitman, too, death is welcomed as a passage to a place where manly love is not deviant but triumphant: ". . .how calm, how solemn it grows to ascend to the atmosphere of lovers,/Death or life I am then indifferent, my soul declines to prefer,/(I am not sure but the high soul of lovers welcomes death most)" ("Scented Herbage of My Breast").

For Willa Cather, lesbian/American/writer, there would be no Miss Furr and Miss Skeene being openly and "regularly gay," nor even a Clarissa Dalloway feeling that Sally Seton's single kiss was "the most exquisite moment of her whole life."[7] Instead, there would be two celibate priests who trot across the desert together on matching sterile mules in their battle to cleanse the "Augean stable" of the Catholic church in the territory of New Mexico and thus protect "the interests of the Church in the whole of North America" (6–7). Their intimacy may be safely idealized because it is predicated upon the explicit renunciation of sex. In Latour's case that renunciation is accompanied by a horror of the feminine so intense that he is "annoyed . . . exceedingly" when he realizes that a dark shadow rolling across his bedroom in the night is "a bunch of woman's hair that had been indolently tossed into a corner when some slovenly female toilet was made in this room" (149). Thus, it would seem that the order imagined in *Death Comes for the Archbishop*, though homo-erotic, is virulently anti-queer and misogynistic, making it more like than unlike the "Platonism without sodomy, . . . marriage without copulation" (375) that Fiedler sees in the male-male love stories told over and over again in American fiction. On some level that is obviously true, though I would argue that the book's insistent tenderness, its utopian aims, and its quietly lavish displays of male bodies and male intimacies argue against its being read in the phobic, terroristic terms in which I earlier read *O Pioneers!*

Some of the best evidence that *Archbishop* is not merely or chiefly eroto- or homophobic lies in the fact that, like *Leaves of Grass*, it is rich in the pleasures of an eroticized looking that is not subjected to punishment or prohibition.[8] Indeed, such pleasures are literally divine, if one accepts Latour's definition of miracles as instances of "human vision corrected by divine love." Latour, it seems, is always on the lookout for miracles. The relationship between the sometimes "alien" Latour and the "queer lad" Vaillant (224) is initiated in a moment of scopic pleasure, as the older Jean notices Joseph in a group of new students at the seminary, and the younger man, "seem[ing] to feel his glance, . . . came up at once, as if he had been called" (223–4). Intimacy is intensely ocular, even for the narra-tor, who asserts in an early description that Latour is "a priest in a thou-sand, one knew at a glance" (18). Though he loves only the "lively, ugly" Vaillant (225), time and again Latour's eyes are drawn to men who, like himself, look remarkable in their buckskin clothes. He feels, for example, "a quick glow of pleasure in looking at [Kit Carson]" (75), while the imperious, desirous Padre Martinez makes such a strong impression that Latour, having met him only once, "could see him as if that were only yes-terday" (140). At a party, he is wont to take advantage of the opportunity to observe men "in repose" and see the ways in which each one "seemed to have become his story. . . . [O]ne had only to see [Don Manuel Chavez] cross the room, or sit next him at dinner, to feel the electric quality under his cold reserve; the fierceness of some embitterment, the passion for danger" (182–3). Friends recognize and try to satisfy Latour's eye-hunger. Don Antonio Olivares, a prosperous rancher, gives him gifts of hammered silver, and his wife, Dona Isabella, remarks "that her husband always gave Father Vaillant something good for the palate, and Father Latour something good for the eye" (178).

The fantasy that compels Cather's *Archbishop* is the fantasy that what Michael Moon calls "the circuit of the loving gaze" can be "successfully completed or resolved" ("Disseminating Whitman" 109). Thus, as death approaches, Latour goes back over "the great *picture* of his life" (288, emphasis added) and winds up back at that moment on the verge of their departure from France when his beloved Joseph "was being torn in two *before his eyes* by the desire to go and the necessity to stay" (297, emphasis added). In life, a glance is sufficient for Jean to choose Joseph "for his friend" and for Joseph to realize he has been chosen (225). The death of the desiring subject restores rather than ruptures the circuitry of mutual gazing, as Jean sees again Joseph choosing "their life together" (281) rather than the comfort of life near his family in France. *Archbishop* lingers over the look—these scenes of desirous glancing, of repeated re-cognition—not phobically, but lovingly. Only Padre Martinez, with his "full lips thrust out and taut, like the flesh of animals distended by fear or desire" (141), turns the narrative's specular economy into an economy of threat, and Latour's desire to view him as an "impotent" (141) relic of an "old order" betrays his need to contain that threat, perhaps to maintain the boundary between his own homoerotic gazing and the possibility of active, "thrust out" homosexuality. (In the plot, of course, Martinez represents the threat of active *het-erosexuality* in violation of his vows of celibacy. What's interesting is that Latour, for political reasons, decides to do nothing to "discipline" Martinez, which Vaillant exhorts him to do. He counts on age to prevent Martinez from "play[ing] the part of Don Juan much longer" [156], which turns out to be a shrewd move. Martinez dies in the next chapter [162].)

Death Comes for the Archbishop, with its phantasmatic investment in the erotics of the male gaze, offers a good opportunity for returning to the questions about "gay and lesbian literary history" and "queer literary history" with which I began this interrogation of Cather's fictional and critical projects of the 1920s. One way to situate the text more or less comfortably in "gay and lesbian literary history" is to read it as a carryover of the gender-bending masquerades of Cather's youth, to argue, in other words, that William Cather, M.D., grew up to be William Cather, S.J., and that Latour and Vaillant are "really" lesbians trapped in men's bodies. This is essentially the move Lillian Faderman makes in including Cather's 1896 story, "Tommy, the Unsentimental," in *Chloe Plus Olivia* as an example of "the literature of sexual inversion" (234–5). Conversely, one might read *Archbishop* as a continuation of the project begun in "Paul's Case" and see it, as Claude Summers sees that earlier story, as a "contribution to gay male literature" ("A Losing Game" 103). Both strategies strike me as problematic, for they install Cather in "gay and lesbian literary history" by assuming she writes from the closet—i.e., by assuming that some operation of conceal-ment or disguise is always in play. Both strategies beg important questions about authorial intention and the movement from life to art.[9] Let me be clear: "Gay and lesbian literary history" is a history worth having, and Willa Cather ought to be included in it, if for no other reason than that she was a lesbian and she wrote literature. My goal here is to speculate on how a "queer literary history" might usefully *supplement*—without displacing or devaluing—the crucial recovery of writers, themes, motifs, and traditions that has gone into the making of "gay and lesbian literary history."

The priest-in-the-closet model is less productive than a queers-in-the-desert model as a way of reading *Death Comes for the Archbishop* because it obscures how fully and frankly the narrative is given over to telling the story of Latour's love for Vaillant, how completely it is driven by the rhythms of "their life together." To suggest that the male couple merely camouflages the story's "true" lesbian content (or, worse, to view it as a sign of Cather's misogyny or "masculine" identification) is to miss how far the text goes to destabilize the connection between sex and gen-der through a complex process of mingling, switching, and redistributing of attributes and energies that achieves a particular intensity within the unit of the couple. Latour and Vaillant's is a "queer love" because they are same-sex partners who float between the rigid binaries of gender and collaborate in the production of a shared and powerful subjectivity simi-lar to—if not quite as campy and audacious as—what Sue-Ellen Case sees in the dynamic duo of the butch-femme couple: "These are not split sub-jects, suffering the torments of dominant ideology. They are coupled ones that do not impale themselves on the poles of sexual difference or meta-physical values, but constantly seduce the sign system, through flirtation and inconstancy into the light fondle of artifice, replacing the Lacanian slash with a lesbian bar" ("Toward a Butch-Femme Aesthetic" 295).

Latour himself acknowledges the collaborative nature of their enter-prise. "You must realize that I have need of you here, Father Joseph," he says at one point in a bid to keep his vicar in Santa Fe. "My duties are too many for one man" (207). Despite their roles as enforcers of Catholic sexual discipline—a role that, as we saw in the example of Padre Martinez, Latour is reluctant to perform—their relationship stands outside the regime of compulsory heterosexuality in a utopian space that is expanded and reproduced not through the technology of sex but through the voluntary affiliations of religious devotion and conversion.[10] For Vaillant in particular, the separation from the biological family for the nonbiological holy/queer family is painful, a "betrayal" made possible only because of Latour's stronger will: "It was because of what Father Latour had been to him in that hour [of decision], indeed, that Father Joseph was here in a garden in Santa Fe" (204). The secure future of the "family" is thematized in the text in the figure of Bernard Ducrot, the young seminarian who becomes "like a son to Father Latour" (265) in his last years. He is like Latour in being "handsome in person and of unusual mentality" (266) and even serves as his amanuensis, as the Archbishop "dictate[s] to his young disciple certain facts about the old missions in the diocese; facts which he had come upon by chance and feared would be forgotten" (274). Ducrot guarantees that the "family" and, equally important, its history will survive.

Finally, if we "queer" *Archbishop* rather than try to "lesbianize" it, we can more fully attend to the ways in which the text draws from a Jewettian rhetoric of romantic friendship and a Whitmanian rhetoric of adhesiveness to construct a queer counterdiscourse of "natural"/"unnatural" love. This is so, I would argue, because queer theorizations of same-sex desire have focused on this particular binary with a relentlessness that neither feminist nor gay and lesbian approaches to the issue have so far matched. Sue-Ellen Case's work is again relevant. *Archbishop* isn't exactly a "queer revel [that] constitute[s] a kind of activism that attacks the dominant notion of the natural," but its more low-key approach and its fascination with Father Vaillant's ugliness seem accounted for in Case's analysis of queer subversiveness: "Like the Phantom of the Opera, the queer dwells underground, below the operatic overtones of the dominant; frightening to look at, desiring, as it plays its own organ, producing its own music" ("Tracking the Vampire" 3). The "underground" of Latour's insistence that it is "natural enough" that he should have "felt the need of [Vaillant's] companionship" (251) and so summoned him back to Santa Fe is Whitman's more explicit and emphatic declaration that the intensely physical love of comrades is also "natural":

> *comes one a Manhattanese and ever at parting kisses me*
> *lightly on the lips with robust love,*
> *And I on crossing of the street or on the ship's deck give a kiss in return,*
> *We observe that salute of American comrades land and sea,*
> *We are those two natural and nonchalant persons.*

("Behold This Swarthy Face")

Where Whitman's comrades kiss, Cather's merely bless, but, in the final image she offers of her two priests together, the potent yet "natural" eroticism of "Calamus" is apparent in the far from nonchalant embrace of two manly/womanly/motherly "fathers," and it stands as the most eloquent defense of same-sex affection her pen would ever issue:

> [Latour] knelt, and Father Vaillant, having blessed him, knelt and was blessed in turn. They embraced each other for the past—for the future.   (260)

With that embrace, as exquisite in its way as Sally Seton's kiss, we may move to considering how the literal love story played out quietly in the plot of *Archbishop* relates to another love story developed in more figurative fashion and to how the two together clarify the cultural work of this deceptively ambitious text. In a reciprocal exchange of blessings and a simple embrace, Cather unites her bishop and his vicar—Jean and Joseph, the (self-described) pedant and the wily pragmatist, the builder of a cathedral and the "great harvester of souls" (259–60)—and in so doing she makes her answer to "classic American literature" all that she wanted it to be: both a revisionary mending together of prior texts and the making of a "new" text inflected but not infected by its encounter with the past, nourished, as it were, in the soil of what was, by 1927, a far from "empty country." The ease of that embrace "for the past—for the future" suggests that a crucial sense of balance had also been restored in *Archbishop*, making its narrative collage of contrasting cultures and histories not a "dangerous crossing" of rhetorics and perspectives but a careful layering that seems as full of motion and power as the desert sand-storm with its "moving walls and tapestries of sand" or the great clouds that were "forming and moving all day long" and so "powerfully affected the world beneath them" that "the whole country seemed fluid to the eye" (222, 95–6).

The creative instability that permeates the narrative of *Archbishop* and the landscape it so lyrically describes establishes a significant distance between its point of view and Latour's, providing a critique of both his rage for personal and political order and his relentless Europeanism. As his deep but mostly unspoken devotion to Vaillant indicates, Latour is in many respects a sympathetic figure, and he stands in Cather's narrative as the "culture hero"—"introducer of agriculture, of irrigation, and of improved house-building"—Mary Austin identified as the leading actor in Native American epic (*CHAL* IV: 619). Further, Latour himself undergoes a "conversion" from the naive and dangerous assimilationism he espouses when he first settles in Santa Fe, vowing in a letter home to "help the [American military] officers at their task here" because "the Church can do more than the Fort to make these poor Mexicans 'good Americans.' And it is for the people's good; there is no other way in which they can better their condition" (35–6), to a somewhat resigned pluralism, evident in his acknowledgment near the end of his life that "his diocese changed little except in boundaries. The Mexicans were always Mexicans, the Indians were always Indians" (284). He comes to recognize, too, the brutality of American efforts to expropriate Indian lands and resettle the tribes away from their ancient homes, describing as "misguided" Kit Carson's slaughter of the Navajos at Canyon de Chelly (1864) and comparing the restoration of their territorial rights (1868) to the end of slavery (290–1). Still, though Latour describes himself as "a lover of justice," he insists he can do nothing to assist the Indians because "in a Protestant country the one thing a Roman priest could not do was to interfere in matters of Government" (292, 294)—despite his early eagerness to get involved in helping that same government "make these poor Mexicans 'good Americans.' " Equally problematic is that Latour's pluralism rests on the assumption that race and ethnicity are clear and static components of identity: "The Mexicans were always Mexicans, the Indians were always Indians"—and the Europeans, he fails to mention, were always Europeans. That this last point is true of Latour is demonstrated by the fact that his most significant act of culture-building was, as Mary Austin put it, "to build a French cathedral in a Spanish town," which she described as "a calamity to the local culture."[11]

As a cultural "tapestr[y] of sand," Cather's narrative goes beyond the sensibility of her Archbishop in order to expose the limitations of both assimilationism and pluralism, a move accompanied by far less ambivalence than that which marked a similar critique in *My Ántonia*. The cultural and ideological boundaries Latour battles constantly to maintain[12] (in, for example, something as simple as sitting down to Vaillant's French onion soup for Christmas dinner, a soup that he savors as "the result of a constantly refined tradition" [38], or in something as complex as his struggle against the rebellious Padre Martinez, who warns Latour not to interfere with the native traditions of Mexican and Indian Catholics by trying to impose "European civilization" and "French fashions" upon him and his followers [147]) prove to be lines drawn in the constantly shifting desert sand. He may ultimately consolidate his power and command the respect of seemingly everyone in his diverse and vast diocese, but the narrative tests and undercuts his certainty at every turn: his Indian guide, Jacinto, kneels with Latour to say the "Our Father" before the two men go to sleep, but there is no sign that he abandons his belief that the stars are not, as the Padre insists, "worlds, like ours," but "leaders—great spirits" (92–3); the battle with Martinez ends, as has already been noted, not in a clear victory but only when the priest dies after Latour has excommunicated him for organizing the schismatic Holy Catholic Church of Mexico; Vaillant responds to his plan to build a grand Midi Romanesque cathedral with wonder and uneasiness, telling his bishop, "I had no idea you were going in for fine building, when everything about us is so poor—and we ourselves are so poor" (241).

Such qualifications undermine the authority of Latour's vision and suggest that Cather, too, despite her Gallic sympathies, perhaps recognized the absurdity of putting a French cathedral in a Spanish town. More important, though, the narrative's critique of Latour's initial, implicitly violent assimilationism and his later, rigid pluralism exposes the cultural "love story" that comprises the dreamwork of *Death Comes for the Archbishop*: the fantasy of a dynamic, syncretic culture that is neither blandly "American" nor narrowly "ethnic," neither a melting pot nor a multicultural cafeteria line of proximate but unrelated options. In this respect the New Mexico figured in *Archbishop* resembles the "mongrel Manhattan" analyzed in Ann Douglas's *Terrible Honesty*. Douglas argues that the cultural proximity of black and white artists in New York in the 1920s resulted in cross-race influences so profound that a complexly mixed (i.e., "mongrel") culture developed and moved into the mainstream of American art and entertainment (73–82). Cather's New Mexico is a similarly mixed-up space—a "queered" culture, perhaps, rather than a "mongrel" one—in which the kind of racial and ethnic categories that form the boundaries of Latour's mental diocese are so destabilized that the grounds for making a statement such as "the Mexicans were always Mexicans, the Indians were always Indians" disappear.[13] Cather's narrative rejects the essentializing tendencies of pluralism's racial/cultural pigeonholes as well as the insider–outsider dichotomies that her Bishop experiences as a translation problem. Just before his dialogue with Jacinto about the stars, Latour sits with his guide, "each thinking his own thoughts as the night closed in about them," and reflects upon what he sees as the enormous differences between them:

> The Bishop seldom questioned Jacinto about his thoughts or beliefs. He didn't think it polite, and he believed it to be useless. There was no way in which he could transfer his own memories of European civilization into the Indian mind, and he was quite willing to believe that behind Jacinto there was a long tradition, a story of experience which no language could translate to him. (92)

Latour seems disappointed that he cannot, like a physician giving some beneficent injection, "transfer . . . European civilization into the Indian mind," but the narrative seeks to negotiate without denying the cultural differences and distances that his emphasis on untranslatability and each man's confinement in the cell of "his own thoughts" maximizes. Just as Cather had throughout her life and her fiction resisted making "hateful distinction[s]" based on gender, her most confident attempt to reground the American "classics" avoids being overwhelmed by similar distinctions on the basis of race or ethnicity by insisting upon the interconnectedness and interpenetrativeness of the many "different" cultures situated in the *Archbishop*'s New Mexico. Thus, for example, in contrast to *O Pioneers!* and *My Ántonia*, *Archbishop* is untroubled by marriages across ethnic lines—the Anglo scout, Kit Carson, is married to a Mexican woman and brings his "gentle half-breed daughter" (180) to the party at the Olivares's; Dona Isabella is "a Kentucky girl" with "a delicate blonde complexion" (176) married to a large, heavy Mexican man with a taste for lavish living.[14] Further, the narrative displays the kinds of cultural dexterity that develop in multicultural environments—Dona Isabella sings in three languages, and "My Nelly Was A Lady" is among her husband's favorites, because, the narrator explains, "The Negro melodies of Stephen Foster had already travelled to the frontier, going along the river highways, not in print, but passed on from one humble singer to another" (177). The narrator, it seems, is familiar with Louise Pound's work on oral literatures, but Latour looks away when Pablo the banjo-player begins to play, because he lacks Dona Isabella's dexterity: "The banjo always remained a foreign instrument to Father Latour; he found it more than a little savage" (182).

The narrative's refusal to authorize Latour's perspective so levels the playing field that Cather's contest of cultures looks more like a game of Earth Ball—a noncompetitive sport in which the object is for players to play with rather than against each other—but that is the utopian dream of *Archbishop*. Crucial, too, is that in this syncretic "tapestr[y] of sand," instead of the long vanished Indians who haunt *The Professor's House*, indigenous cultures are represented by figures who are as sympathetic and fully idealized as Latour and who, indeed, in some respects resemble him. Eusabio, for example, the Navajo chief he befriends, is, like Latour, "respected for his intelligence and authority, and admired for his fine presence." He also has something of Latour's aristocratic bearing, "with a face like a Roman general's of Republican times." His elegant dress and heavy jewelry contrast with the priest's simple vestments, but the underlying similarity between the two men is apparent in the greeting they exchange when Latour comes to visit his friend shortly after the death of Eusabio's son:

> At first [Eusabio] did not open his lips, merely stood holding Father Latour's very fine white hand in his very fine dark one, and looked into his face with a message of sorrow and resignation in his deep-set, eagle eyes. A wave of feeling passed over his bronze features as he said slowly:
>
> "My friend has come."
>
> That was all, but it was everything; welcome, confidence, appreciation. (220)

As important as the equally "fine" white and dark hands that are here locked together is that, despite Latour's earlier frustrations, language can and does "translate to him" the Indian's "story of experience." Having come to Eusabio's to resolve the crisis of his longing for Vaillant, the "message" of the grieving father's "sorrow" is not lost on him, and the Navajo's simple, "My friend has come," though an emotional and linguistic understatement ("That was all"), is, by its very compactness, both efficient and sufficient ("but it was everything") and available for immediate translation into the European's "civilized" frame of reference ("welcome, confidence, appreciation").[15] Their mutual regard and their shared experience as "fathers" do not erase the cultural differences between the European priest and the Indian chief, but they do significantly diminish the power of such differences to foster isolation and miscommunication, suggesting as they do that any man's "own thoughts" are as much alike as unlike another's. When cultures come into contact, *Archbishop* repeatedly demonstrates, such acts of translation are both possible and necessary. As Padre Martinez points out, "the secret dances of the Indians" and "the bloody rites of the Penitentes" (147) are New World "translations" of Catholicism that Latour will have to understand and accept if he is to survive. Similarly, the priest constantly translates his experiences in New Mexico into terms that break down the defamiliarization he undergoes there: thus, when, in the "geometrical nightmare" of his first journey in the desert, he encounters a juniper tree with a twisted trunk, he sees in it "the form of the Cross" and kneels down before it in prayer (17–18); the Indian settlements on top of rocky, almost inacessible mesas like Acoma remind Latour that, "The rock, when one came to think of it, was the utmost expression of human need . . . . Christ Himself had used that comparison for the disciple to whom He gave the keys of His Church" (97); when he visits Canyon de Chelly after the Navajos have reestablished their settlement there and sees crops growing and sheep grazing "at the bottom of the world between the towering sandstone walls," Latour remarks that, "it was like an Indian Garden of Eden" (295).

Translation is as important to the project of *Archbishop* as history is to that of *The Professor's House*, and though it, too, is slippery, though there is always something lost in translation, Cather's faith in the process and the project seems in the later text as solid as the rock of Acoma. In the story of Jean and Joseph, she translates into muted but deeply subversive terms the tale of same-sex love that had preoccupied her since she anxiously inscribed herself within the passion play of Willie and Willwese during those scorching prairie summers in the 1890s. In the story of multicultural interconnectedness and convergence, she translates Mary Austin's reading of Native American epics—with culture heroes instead of warriors and the goal of "making the world work well together" (*CHAL* 4:625)—into a novel that presents the making of America as a benign, somewhat fantastic process in which even the government is endowed with enough kindness and good sense to restore the Navajos to the paradise they lost not through a fall but a massacre. Cather's translation of historical reality into literary utopia is undeniably a partial and glossy view,[16] but she was searching in *Archbishop* for an alternative to the fragmented, hostile worlds of men and women, Jews and gentiles, orphan Anglo boys and dead

Indian mothers she had mapped out in *The Professor's House*. Translation made possible the cultural syncretism—the blending, blurring, and borrowing of groups too close to one another for the "comfort" of "purity"—she saw as the most effective reply to her own doubts and to D. H. Lawrence's "diabolism."

When translation fails, one is left, like Latour with his ear to the ground of Jacinto's cave, listening with inexplicable terror to "one of the oldest voices on earth," "the sound of a great underground river, flowing through a resounding cavern," "a flood moving in utter blackness under ribs of antediluvian rock." Told by Jacinto that "this place is used by my people for ceremonies and is known only to us," Latour cannot shake the feelings of vertigo and repugnance that overwhelm him in the cavern formed by "two great stone lips," and afterward he begins to suspect that the stories he has heard about Jacinto's Pecos tribe worshiping snakes and guarding "somewhere in the mountain . . . an enormous serpent which they brought to the pueblo for certain feasts" (122) are true. Unable to translate the voice or the experience into familiar terms, Latour is left with the unsatisfactory conclusion that "neither the white men nor the Mexicans in Santa Fe understood anything about Indian beliefs or the workings of the Indian mind" (127–35). He is left, in other words, sounding a good deal like D. H. Lawrence at a Hopi snake dance.

Lawrence's essay of 1924, "The Hopi Snake Dance," which Cather would likely have seen in *Theatre Arts Monthly*, is his own Lawrentian/American fantasy of opposed and mutually untranslatable cultures locked in combat. An uneasy witness to what he describes as "this circus-performance of men handling live rattlesnakes that may bite them any minute," Lawrence finds the spectacle "uncouth in its touch of horror."[17] Significantly, the author of *Studies in Classic American Literature* hears in the chants of the snake dancers a voice similar to the one that so unnerves Cather's Archbishop, a voice that also presses up from a remote underground world of snakes and rivers:

> It is a strange low sound, such as we never hear, and reveals how deep, how deep the men are in the mystery they are practising, how sunk deep below our world to the world of snakes, and dark ways in the earth, where the roots of corn, and where the little rivers of unchannelled, uncreated life-passion run like dark, trickling lightning, to the roots of the corn and to the feet and loins of men, from the earth's innermost dark sun. (68)

When the dance is over, the spectators depart, and Lawrence seems as overwhelmed and mystified by difference as Latour is in Jacinto's cave:

> We say they look wild. But they have the remoteness of their religion, their animistic vision, in their eyes, they can't see what we see. And they cannot accept us. They stare at us as the coyotes stare at us: the gulf of mutual negation between us.   (72)

In the simple gestures of handshakes and embraces and the pared-down language of understated affections that bring together people of different temperaments and cultures, Cather translates Lawrence's drama of "mutual negation" and racial hatred into a story in which love is powerful enough to make "our perceptions . . . finer," so that instead of the cold stare of the coyote, "our eyes can see and our ears can hear what is there about us always." She may eschew his desire to become "the whole caboodle" (1), as Rebecca West put it in a review of *Archbishop* that imagined how Lawrence would have executed the Stone Lips scene,[18] but the "daring" of Cather's encounter with Lawrence's reading of American culture was nonetheless substantial and utterly unsentimental. To Lawrence, "classic American literature" was the allegorization of the destructiveness he saw as the underside of the New World dream. For Cather, who probably agreed but crafted in *Archbishop* a hopeful alternative, the "classic" could be, simply yet stubbornly, a discourse of miracles.

Conclusion

Queer (R)Age
Notes on the Late Fiction and the Queering of the World

> The only guarantees I can give of my work . . . are the subjective character
> of my speculations, the uncertainty of my footing in something as delusive
> as my own passion, and the bewildering mobility of my desire.
> —Teresa de Lauretis, *The Practice of Love*

No More Masks!, or How Do You Solve a Problem Like *Sapphira*?

At the Seventh International Willa Cather Seminar, held in June 1997 in
Winchester, Virginia, the talk was all of *Sapphira and the Slave Girl*, Cather's
last novel, published in 1940 and set in the Shenandoah Valley where the
author was born and the scholars were gathered. Well more than half of the
papers presented at the week-long seminar focused on the book that Toni
Morrison describes in *Playing in the Dark* as "this troublesome, quietly
dismissed novel" (19). So compulsively did conversation keep returning to
the tale of the dropsical, vindictive slave mistress that I was reminded of the
scene early in Rodgers and Hammerstein's *The Sound of Music* in which a
group of concerned nuns gather to sing out their contradictory feelings
for an ebullient but unpredictable young novice. "How do you solve a
problem like Maria?" the sisters muse as they struggle to reckon with a figure of such vast energy that she might "throw a whirling dervish out of
whirl" and such ambiguity that she strikes one sister as a demon, another
as a darling, and a third as a Christlike lamb. While Sapphira Colbert
is nobody's darling, she is like Maria in being vexing, unsettling. And
Cather's critics, trying to take up Morrison's challenge to move beyond
merely dismissing the novel as signaling "the failure of Cather's gifts" (18),
are not unlike the bemused nuns whose sweet voices run together in a
frantic effort to "solve a problem like [Sapphira]."

As I add my voice to the chorus, let me say from the outset that I'm not sure the problem of *Sapphira* can or should be "solved," because, as Morrison's eloquent and generous critique suggests, the text is profoundly enigmatic, a "fugitive" in terms of its place in Cather's career and in that it "describes and inscribes its narrative's own fugitive flight from itself" (19). In Morrison's reading, that fugitive status is the result of the novel's doomed but brave effort to "address an almost completely buried subject: the inter-dependent working of power, race, and sexuality in a white woman's battle for coherence" (20). Of one thing I am certain, however: The problem of *Sapphira* cannot be solved by deploying the masquerade model that has been used elsewhere to explain how Cather negotiated "the dilemma of the lesbian writer" (Fetterley). Such an approach, though useful in figuring out the comparatively modest enigmas of a text such as *My Ántonia*, is grossly reductive when applied to the structural and affective complexities of *Sapphira and the Slave Girl*.[1] To suggest that "the lesbian writer" is so compelled to tell and yet to camouflage the story of her sexual desires that she would stage a vicious drama of heterosexual miscegenous rape/seduction is, in my judgment, to turn her into the pathetic, erotically obsessed creature of turn-of-the-century inversion theory. She has only one story to tell, and the shamefulness of it makes the novel a nightmarish per-version of the "truth" of her desires.

Desire probably makes liars of us all, but a "queering" of *Sapphira* aims at elucidating not the author's secret motive but the text's (sometimes vicious, not always controlled) display of the "bewildering mobility" of desires, as de Lauretis puts it in the passage I have used as an epigraph. As I have tried to suggest throughout this study, the origin of desires matters less than their movement along and across the multiple vectors of sex, gender, race, and nation. Bewildering as *Sapphira* is, it is important to charting the course of Cather's "queering" of "America," her imaging of the nation in supercharged corporeal figures and her interventions into the cultural politics of the early twentieth century. It is also typical of Cather's work from the 1930s (the period of the novel's composition)[2] in seeming to be a dystopian un-writing of earlier utopian works or moments. Thus, for example, in her novel of 1935, *Lucy Gayheart*, Cather deconstructs the tale of female artistic triumph she had written in *The Song of the Lark*. Then, in 1936, in the revised preface to *The Best Stories of Sarah Orne Jewett*, published in *Not Under Forty* as "Miss Jewett," Cather writes herself and her precursor out of American literary history by reimagining the scene of "the young student of American literature in far distant years to come" taking up the edition and proclaiming it a masterpiece as a scene of failed connection and miscommunication. In the revised version, the student is "a young man, or woman, born in New York City, educated at a New York university, violently inoculated with Freud," and "perhaps of foreign descent: German, Jewish, Scandinavian" (92–3). For this "hypothetical young man" (and that the "young man, or woman" so quickly becomes merely a man is telling), who speaks "American English" correctly but without any connection to its "emotional roots," Jewett's text is written in an "old Yankee" language that is foreign to the "new American." "When he tries to put himself in the Yankee's place," Cather gloomily asserts, "he attempts an impossible substitution" (93–4). The "rich discovery" of the earlier preface is refigured as a linguistic and even a biological impossibility, as the language of "substitution" suggests. Jewett's "gift of sympathy" remains, but the reader's capacity for empathy seems to have disappeared. Gone, too, is the confident prediction that *The Country of the Pointed Firs* has, along with *The Scarlet Letter* and *Huckleberry Finn*, "the possibility of a long, long life." In its place is a much diminished compliment to the "vivid and intensely personal experience of life" that accounts for Jewett, Twain, and Hawthorne's distinctive "style[s]" (95).

Finally, in *Sapphira and the Slave Girl*, Cather un-writes the utopian fantasy of queer love in/as "America" that impelled *Death Comes for the Archbishop*. Her last novel is appropriately described as a tale of "queer (r)age" because it depicts the body as a battleground where competing desires and possibilities circulate with a terrifying mobility, even as the protagonist sinks more deeply into the physical immobility created by her illness. In Sapphira's white, female, aging, disabled body—which, significantly, is drained of its color as the illness progresses and yet seems whiter ("she was always pale now," reflects Sapphira's daughter Rachel, as she looks at her mother in her wheelchair [15])—Cather figures the paranoid subjectivity of a nation of free and equal people that had systematically denied the freedom, equality, and personhood of women and African Americans. As owner of the "Dodderidge niggers" (8) she brought into her marriage to Henry Colbert, Sapphira is economically powerful, but as a married woman she is politically in-valid and cannot sell her "property" without her husband's signature. A composed but conniving "mistress of the situation" (268), Sapphira is nevertheless dependent upon the labor of slaves whose very names—i.e., Washington and Jefferson (33)—recall the founding ideals as well as the founding contradictions of the nation. She bears "her disablement with courage," according to Rachel

(15), yet her disability is also the mark of monstrous corporeality, of a body out of control of its size and shape and unable to tend to its own most intimate needs: "She regarded her feet and ankles with droll contempt while Till drew on the stockings and tied a ribbon garter below each of her wax-white, swollen knees" (32).

Disability in *Sapphira and the Slave Girl* serves multiple and contradictory functions. It signifies the queerness of the relation a person has with a body she regards "with droll contempt" as well as the corruption of a social and economic system that idealizes the immobile white woman and takes for granted the infinite expropriability of black labor, for Sapphira's sick but carefully ornamented "wax-white" body is merely an exaggerated version of the Southern lady who presided over so many plantation households, as Elizabeth Fox-Genovese has demonstrated in her study of black and white women of the slaveholding South.[3] Like the nineteenth-century sentimental texts to which it is complexly indebted—most notably, of course, *Uncle Tom's Cabin*—*Sapphira* uses disability to activate both readerly sympathy and readerly repudiation.[4] Sapphira's incapacity is invoked on the one hand to justify her suspicions about her husband and the young, beautiful, able-bodied Nancy, for in her mind "the meaning of illness" is marginality and the denial of personhood: "To be crippled and incapacitated, not to come and go at will, to be left out of things as if one were in one's dotage" (105). On the night after Jezebel's funeral, left alone in the dark room of her disability, Sapphira is tormented by the sight of candles burning in her husband's room down at the mill, which figures in her "dream of disaster" (107) as a site of illicit activity that excludes and makes a fool of her. On the other hand, Sapphira's disability is the mark of a menacing subjectivity, an excessive and unregulated selfhood that is simultaneously violable (because of her physical vulnerability) and violating (because of her willingness to place others at risk in pursuit of her own desires). Her representation in Cather's narrative conforms to Rosemarie Thomson's reading of the threat posed by the disabled figure to American ideals of self and society:

> Disability's indisputably random and unpredictable character translates
> as appalling disorder and persistent menace in a social order predicated
> on self-government. Furthermore, physical instability is the bodily
> manifestation of political anarchy, of the antinomian impulse that is
> the threatening, but logical, extension of egalitarian democracy. The
> disabled body stands for the self gone out of control, individualism run

rampant: it mocks the notion of the body as compliant instrument of the limitless will and appears in the cultural imagination as ungovernable, recalcitrant, flaunting its difference as if to refute the fantasy of sameness implicit in the notion of equality. (43)

Sapphira and the Slave Girl may be said to demolish "the fantasy of sameness" enshrined in the notion of equality on several levels, but one of the great problems posed by the text is the difficulty of assessing the judgments it makes of the "real" world of differences it calls into being. Sapphira's disability foregrounds and literalizes the dependency and the instability of the master-slave relationship, but she is not the Diva Citizen of *The Song of the Lark* who celebrates difference and revels in contradiction. Sapphira experiences the illness that transforms her body as an ontic wound that exacerbates her already prodigious narcissism and fuels a rage to preserve her authority. Her story is in some respects a gothic rewriting of *O Pioneers!*, for she is endowed with Ivar's self-loathing and his foot fetish as well as Alexandra's determination to eliminate threat and to stabilize hierarchies. What is most troubling, however, is the text's strenuous effort to redeem the character in the end and, indeed, to establish identification with her by seeming to validate her most pernicious actions. That effort is evident in the plot in, for example, Rachel's doubts, expressed after the fact, about having helped Nancy escape: "Maybe I ought to a-thought about how much [Sapphira] suffers, and her poor feet. . . . Maybe I ought to have thought and waited" (247). Sapphira seems interested in redeeming herself when, several months later, she suggests to Henry that Rachel and her surviving child come spend the winter at the Mill House after her other daughter has died of diphtheria (266–7). Such "kindness" provokes Henry to reassess his wife's behavior and think admiringly of "that composure which he had sometimes called heartlessness, but which now seemed to him strength." Despite his abolitionist sympathies and his fondness for the young woman whom his wife had plotted to sell or hurt, Henry seems finally to share her views and even to approve of her actions: "There are different ways of being good to folks," he tells Sapphira. "Sometimes keeping people in their place is being good to them" (268).

Still more insidious are the efforts to redeem Sapphira on the deeper levels of narrative, which are evident in the epilogue.[5] In the first chapter of the epilogue a still distant voice narrates the twenty-five years that have passed since Nancy's escape in 1856, a period that includes the Civil War, Reconstruction, the emergence of "a different world," and the rise of a "new generation," as the narrator puts it. The voice is clearly nostalgic for Sapphira's world of "old distinctions" (277). In the second chapter of the epilogue, however, the task of telling the story of Nancy's return to Back Creek is abruptly taken over by a first-person narrator who is, like Sapphira, ill and manipulative and committed to the preservation of racial hierarchy, and who names herself in a postscript "Willa Cather." The five-year-old child waits in her mother's bed with a cold for the reunion of Nancy and Till, which is, for her benefit and at Till's suggestion, staged in the bedroom rather than outside, when Nancy alights from the stagecoach. Such spectacle-making and the white child's unself-conscious reinscription of racial stereotypes—in describing Till as a "little old darky" (283) and noting approvingly "the shade of deference in [Nancy's] voice when she spoke to my mother" (284)—indicate that the post-Civil War world is not so "different" from Sapphira's world after all. The white child feels entitled to intrude upon the scene of intimacy between the black mother and daughter, to eavesdrop upon their stories, and, presumably, to appropriate and repackage them in a novel called *Sapphira and the Slave Girl.* The child perpetuates Sapphira's denial of black women's subjectivity, and "Willa Cather" seems untroubled by that denial, as she identifies the genesis of the story as chiefly linguistic, rooted in the "lively fascination" that certain "Frederick County surnames" had for her in childhood (295).

Perhaps the transparency of the child's racism—right down to her casual deployment of slaveowner's discourse in referring to the long-free black woman whom she has never met as "our Nancy" (281)—suggests that it is being aggressively displayed so that it might be dislodged rather than merely perpetuated. Perhaps, too, the incursion of the first person and the authorial signature serve purposely to fracture the narrative, thereby exposing its duplicitous character, its violent and radical incoherences. Perhaps. Willa Cather's last novel is, though, like most of her works, easy to read but hard to figure out. It is written in the mode she had seemed to reject in *Death Comes for the Archbishop*—that of the Lawrentian "earthly story with a hellish meaning," which allegorizes the making of America as inherently and inevitably terroristic, a process in which the bodily differences I have called "queer," whether they are differences of race, sex, gender, or physical ability, provoke fear and loathing rather than cultural dynamism and a creative instability successfully negotiated through love and translation.

If, in *Archbishop*, Cather writes in a discourse of miracles, in *Sapphira*, she concludes her career as a novelist in a discourse of nightmares.

The (R)Aging of Queer Critique

What is now called queer theory and/or critique emerged out of a context that might also be called *queer (r)age*—i.e., out of the anger and activism triggered by the epidemic of premature *a*ging and death caused by HIV and AIDS, an epidemic that in its early years in the U.S. dispro-portionately affected gay men.[6] AIDS was never the exclusive focus of queer activism, though, and the word "queer" has been intended by those who embraced it and operated under it to signify a broad-based assault on social constructions of the "normal." Much like the fiction of Willa Cather (or the fiction of Willa Cather as I have read it here), queer activism is fueled by "the operant dream . . . of a community united in diversity, queerly ourselves" (Chee 17) and by the determination to attack—angrily, sorrowfully—the betrayals of that dream in a culture hostile to whatever calls itself or is called "queer." As the 1990s draw to a close, queer activism seems to have had its moment, and the Human Rights Campaign, with its more conventional lobbying style and its support for such assimilationist goals as gay marriage, has replaced Queer Nation as the most visible advocate for sexual minorities in the U.S. In the academy, however, the (r)aging of queer critique proceeds apace, though the "rage" at this point refers as much to its trendiness as to its feisty, fractious demeanor, and the "aging" may mean it's getting prematurely old in the rush toward institutionalization, as the prolifera-tion of journals, conferences, anthologies, and the articles that map out without quite systematizing the field (such an un-queer gesture, that) attest. To those of us who recall that Elaine Showalter's essay "Feminist Criticism in the Wilderness," when it was first published in *Critical Inquiry* in 1981, proved that the field was no longer young nor particularly wild, such developments induce ambivalence and a sense of déja vu.[7] What happens when the assault on normativity becomes just another line on the *vita*? another academic program? another day at the office? What happens when Lauren Berlant and Michael Warner are only half-kidding when they wonder, in the pages of *PMLA*, "What does Queer Theory teach us about *X*?" (343).

Part of what happens when a field reaches such milestones is undeni-ably good. They assure legitimacy not just in the cynical, careerist sense, but in a deeper—and deeply necessary—structural sense as well. They assure visibility, continuity, access to the means of what Berlant and Warner call "culture building" and thus to the possibility of "making the world queerer" (347–8). Queer people have suffered much from being constructed as the objects rather than the agents or subjects of knowledge, so such opportunities are not to be taken lightly. In these pages, my intervention into the project of making the world and our knowledge of it queerer has been undertaken at a practical level. My goals have been experimental—i.e., to test the efficacy of queer critique as an interpretive procedure, to see what it can teach us about "*X*" when "*X*" equals "the fiction of Willa Cather" or "figures of the body" or "the formations of literary history in the U.S. in the 1920s." Queering Cather seemed worthwhile on a local level because within Cather studies her lesbianism is now generally accepted but seldom interrogated. Since the spate of articles on the author's sexual/textual masquerades that followed O'Brien's *The Emerging Voice*, sexuality has been relegated to the background (or the cutting-room floor) of such major contributions to the field as Deborah Carlin's *Cather, Canon, and the Politics of Reading*, Guy Reynolds's *Willa Cather in Context*, and Joseph Urgo's *Willa Cather and the Myth of American Migration*. On a broader level, Cather is a useful test case for exploring the kinds of questions outlined above because she lived through the pathologization of women's romantic friendships, the turn into the twentieth century—with all its attendant social transformations—and the period of intense cultural nationalism that occurred in the U.S. after World War I. Each of these discursive or historical shifts contributed to the "queering" of "America"—i.e., to the development of a modern, urban, industrial nation with a sexually and racially heterogeneous population anxious about its diversity and engaged in a fierce contest to authorize a politics and a semiotics of American bodies.

Willa Cather stepped into this contest at least as early as 1892, when, at the age of eighteen, she wrote to a woman she loved that she wouldn't have attended a party at her house if she had known how queer she would feel when she realized she was seeing Louise for the last time before a lengthy separation. I did feel queer, she admits. I didn't know it had gotten such a hold on me. But queerness did indeed have a hold on Cather, and the radical sense of alienation and otherness she experienced as a pioneer in the newly discovered/invented world of "unnatural" love would inflect her relationships to the discourses of normativity and nationality throughout her long, productive career. In the nation built in Cather's fiction, the "queer" may on the one hand be a utopian agent of challenge and change—may be curative, salvific, or at least, like Tillie Kronborg, entertaining—and "America" may be tolerant or even proud of queers who make money or die heroically. The "queer" may on the other hand be a source of profound menace—contagion, threat, disorder—that must be expelled from the body politic or, in the grimmest moments (as in *Sapphira and the Slave Girl*), seems to image the irredeemable corruption of the body politic. Cather's queering of America by no means proceeds on a straight or always happy course. Under the circumstances, how could it? Why on earth would we need or expect it to? Her track is devious, painful, and strange at least as often as it is smooth and easy to navigate. But sometimes, like Eden Bower in "Coming, Aphrodite!" floating in her balloon above Coney Island—in black tights and silver slippers that catch the light and leave the spectators on the beach "all shading their eyes and gazing upward at the slowly falling silver star" (*CS* 85–6)—Cather's feet lift off the ground and the tracks of the queer are written in the sky. With a little daring and the right accessories, Eden demonstrates, as Thea Kronborg and *The Wizard of Oz*'s Dorothy Gale had before her, a girl can take herself anywhere. Hang on, Toto—I have a feeling we're not in [Nebraska] anymore.[8]

Notes

Introduction. The Novelist, the Critic, and the Queer

1. For discussion of the liabilities of "Queer theory" by some of its most astute promoters and practitioners, see Halperin 64–5; Sedgwick, "Queer Performativity" 4, 13–15; Butler, "Critically Queer" 18–20; Edelman, "Queer Theory"; and Duggan, "Making It Perfectly Queer." Lesbian feminism has been the location from which some of the strongest critiques of the queer critical/political turn have arisen. See O'Driscoll, Stein, and Walters. Walters's essay is the most skeptical, raising troubling questions about the theory and the politics called "queer": "it often (and once again) erases lesbian specificity and the enormous difference that gender makes, evacuates the importance of feminism, and rewrites the history of lesbian feminism and feminism generally" (843). My goal in this study is to avoid some of those potential pitfalls by using "queer" as a way of keeping multiple marginalities and histories in play without simply lumping them together or denying the specificity of any one.

2. The *OED* indicates that the origins of "queer" are obsolete but that its first recorded usage as an adjective was in 1508. The meanings cited are: "1. Strange, odd, peculiar, eccentric, in appearance or character. Also, of questionable character, suspicious, dubious. . . . 2. Not in a normal condition; out of sorts; giddy, faint, or ill; *esp.* in phrase *to feel queer*. Also *slang*: Drunk. 1800. 3. *Queer Street*: an imaginary street where people in difficulties reside; hence any difficulty, fix, or trouble, bad circumstances, debt, illness, etc. 1837." As a verb, "queer" was first used in 1790 and meant "1. a. To quiz or ridicule; to puzzle. b. To impose upon; to cheat. 2. To spoil, put out of order. 1812. 3. To put (one) out; to make (one) feel queer. 1845."

3. Chauncey bases this claim on Gershon Legman's study "The Language of Homosexuality: An American Glossary," in George W. Henry, *Sex Variants* (New York: Paul B. Hoeber, 1941), vol. 2, appendix 7, 1174–5. See *Gay New York* 15–16.

4. In an earlier essay, though, Chauncey reports that in the seaport community of Newport, Rhode Island, where navy investigators conducted an inquiry into "immoral conditions" at the Naval Training Station in 1919–1920, "queer" designated men who "assumed the sexual and other cultural roles ascribed to women." See "Christian Brotherhood or Sexual Perversion?" (297–9). I see this

not as a contradiction but as evidence for the slipperiness of the term and the high degree of subjectivity involved in its usage.

5. The headline appeared originally in *Broadway Brevities*, 14 March, 1932: 1, according to Chauncey (*Gay New York* 447). He reproduces it in *Gay New York* 300.

6. Parts of Barney's autobiography are printed in Jean Chalon's *Portrait of a Seductress: The World of Natalie Barney*. Faderman in *Odd Girls* and Shari Benstock in *Women of the Left Bank: Paris, 1900–1940* both cite this passage (on 58 and 289, respectively), but neither considers the implications of Barney's "queer" self-identification.

7. My use of the term "disobedience" here owes something to Nancy Walker's useful *The Disobedient Writer: Women and Narrative Tradition*, which calls "disobedient" those texts that resist and overturn the assumptions and "narrative necessities" of the prior texts with which they are engaged (3).

8. The tradition of biographically inflected criticism includes the work of the pioneers of Cather criticism, Mildred Bennett and Bernice Slote. See Bennett's *The World of Willa Cather* and Slote's long introductory essay in *The Kingdom of Art: Willa Cather's First Principles and Critical Statements, 1893–1896*. See also Lee and Skaggs.

9. Readings that attend to Paul's probable homosexuality include Rubin, Summers ("'A Losing Game in the End'"; and Sedgwick, "Across Gender, Across Sexuality."

10. The phrase "political quietism" is from Edward Said's *The World, the Text, and the Critic* (Cambridge: Harvard UP, 1983) 245. It is quoted in Halperin 21. For a good summary of similar critiques of Foucault's work, see Halperin 21–4.

11. The 1915 edition of the novel makes a little more of Thea's marriage to Fred Ottenburg, but not much. In detailing Aunt Tillie's pride in her niece's international success as an opera singer, the narrator remarks, "When the Denver papers announced that Thea Kronborg had married Frederick Ottenburg, the head of the Brewers' Trust, Moonstone people expected that Tillie's vain-gloriousness would take another form. But Tillie had hoped that Thea would marry a title, and she did not boast much about Ottenburg" (*SL* 1915, 484–5). These lines are excised from the 1932 edition.

My reading of Thea Kronborg as queer triumphant owes much to Elizabeth Wood's deft analysis of the place of Cather's diva in a narrative tradition "of opera and the female voice as these are represented by women writers" (28). Under the rubric of "Sapphonics"—"a mode of articulation, a way of describing a space of lesbian possibility, . . . a range of erotic and emotional relationships among women who sing and women who listen" (27)—Wood reads *The Song of the Lark* as a lesbian *Kunstlerroman* in which the singer's boundary-crossing contralto voice acts as "a destabilizing agent of fantasy and desire" (32).

12. For an analysis of Cather's decanonization, see Sharon O'Brien, "Becoming Noncanonical: The Case against Willa Cather."

13. *O Pioneers!* was a Hallmark Hall of Fame production, directed by Glenn Jordan and written for television by Robert W. Lenski, 1992. *My Ántonia* was a

USA Pictures production, directed by Joseph Sargent, written for television and produced by Victoria Riskin, 1995. My thanks to Deb Price for helping me track down this information.

14. There is by now a substantial body of work that situates Cather within gay/lesbian traditions, examines her "masquerades," or offers up a case study of individual characters. In addition to those mentioned in the text and in n. 9, see Adams, Cramer, Flannigan, Irving, Petry, Russ, and Shaw.

15. I offer this critique in regard to readings of *My Ántonia* in my essay, "'It Ain't My Prairie': Gender, Power, and Narrative in *My Ántonia.*" Blanche Gelfant describes Ántonia as an "ultimately strange bisexual" in her important essay on sex in *My Ántonia*, "The Forgotten Reaping-Hook" (107).

16. On the importance of the Romer decision and the 1993 revisions to the military's policies on homosexuals for gay litigation strategies, see Janet Halley's brilliant "legal archaeology" of the status/conduct distinction and Butler's "Status, Conduct, Word, and Deed."

17. On the Cather-Fitzgerald connection, see Matthew Bruccoli's discussion of Fitzgerald's letter to Cather expressing concern that he had unintentionally plagiarized from *A Lost Lady* in *The Great Gatsby.* See also Quirk.

Part 1: Fear of a Queer Prairie: Figures of the Body and/as the Nation in Letters and Early Novels

1. My understanding of desire, gender, and epistolarity has been shaped by Linda S. Kauffman's vital work in this area, including *Discourses of Desire: Gender, Genre, and Epistolary Fictions* and *Special Delivery.*

2. Wald's study, *Constituting Americans: Cultural Anxiety and Narrative Form* considers not only novels but also autobiographies and a range of cultural and historical narratives, but the model she develops of narratives anxiously participating in the imagining of a community has important implications for thinking about Cather.

1. Driving One-Handed: The Law, the Letter, and the Unsanctioned Voice

1. Louise Pound is notable for much more than having been the object of Willa Cather's passionate affection when she was a college student. Her subsequent professional achievements as a scholar of oral literatures will come up again in part 2 of this study, because she made a significant contribution on the subject to the *Cambridge History of American Literature.* Throughout her long career Pound broke paths for educated women and for the profession of literature in the U.S. She was, among other things, the first woman elected president of the Modern Language Association (in 1955—at the age of eighty-two) and a founding editor of the journal *American Speech.* For more on Pound, see *EV* 117–46 as well as the list of "Professional Activities and *Vita*" compiled by Mamie Meredith and Ruth Odell in Louise Pound, *Selected Writings of Louise Pound* (1949; Westport, CT: Greenwood Press, 1971) 362–5.

2. James Woodress discusses Cather's will in *LL* 505. Some late letters to her old friend Carrie Miner Sherwood speak to Cather's sense of having been wounded by life and her increasingly suspicious attitudes toward people. In one, Cather talks about how hard things have always hit her, so hard that the inside of her is full of dents and scars; another refers to her having bitter enemies in Red Cloud, some of whom have pretended to be friendly. Willa Cather to Carrie Miner Sherwood, 29 April 1945 and 26 January 1947, Willa Cather Historical Center, Red Cloud, Nebraska.

3. According to Pat Phillips, executive director of the Willa Cather Pioneer Memorial and Educational Foundation, Red Cloud, Nebraska, personal communication, 22 October 1996, Cather's nephew, Charles Cather, is executor of the estate, and all of the restrictions in Cather's will are still in force. Scholars working with the archives at the Willa Cather Historical Center in Red Cloud have to read a copy of the will and sign a statement indicating they agree to abide by its stipulations regarding direct quotation. However, as I discovered in the course of my Cather research, different repositories have different policies regarding photocopying. Of the archives I have visited, the Willa Cather Historical Center, Indiana University's Lilly Library, and the University of Virginia's Barrett Library will not make photocopies. Harvard's Houghton Library and Duke's Perkins Library will make copies, but at Duke researchers still have to sign a statement about the stipulations in the will.

4. Cather mentions Wilcox, disparagingly, in a couple of columns from 1899 and 1903. See *WP* 2:694–5 and 963.

5. Reverse in that most of the legal disputes over quotation marks have been, according to de Grazia, over lax usage—i.e., inaccuracy in quotation, violating the guarantee that quotation marks signal verbatim reproduction of another's words (284, 286). The prohibitions in Cather's will prevent me from offering my reader precisely that guarantee. Alas.

6. Other readers of the letters have, of course, come to different conclusions about what they reveal. Woodress avers, for example, that Cather fell in love with Pound, but he insists that "to call this a lesbian relationship . . . is to give it undue importance," apparently because he believes Pound's feelings were not as intense as Cather's (85). In the course of Joan Acocella's vicious attack, published in the *New Yorker*, on feminist and lesbian critics of Cather, who, in her conspiratorial view, essentially kidnaped Cather into their camp by using lesbianism as a way to prove "Cather's feminist credentials" (69), she reads the Pound letters to support the claim that "Cather was homosexual in her feelings and celibate in her actions" (68–9).

On the conceptual, historical line between "romantic friendship" and "lesbianism," see Lillian Faderman, who draws the line most sharply, in *Surpassing the Love of Men, Odd Girls and Twilight Lovers*, and "The Morbidification of Love Between Women by 19th-Century Sexologists," *Journal of Homosexuality* 4 (1978): 73–90. Other important work in this area includes Carroll Smith-Rosenberg, "The New Woman as Androgyne: Social Disorder and Gender Crisis,

1870–1936," *Disorderly Conduct: Visions of Gender in Victorian America* (New York: Knopf, 1985) 245–96; Nancy Sahli, "Smashing: Women's Relationships Before the Fall," *Chrysalis* 8 (Summer 1979): 17–27; Martha Vicinus, "Distance and Desire: English Boarding-School Friendships," *Signs* 9.4 (1984): 600–22; Esther Newton, "The Mythic Mannish Lesbian: Radclyffe Hall and the New Woman," *Signs* 9.4 (1984): 557–75. Newton's essay, which, along with those by Smith-Rosenberg and Vicinus, is reprinted in Martin Duberman, Martha Vicinus, and George Chauncey, Jr., eds., *Hidden From History: Reclaiming the Gay and Lesbian Past* (New York: NAL, 1989), has some interesting implications for thinking about Cather's sexual identity because she was, like Radclyffe Hall, of the second generation of New Women, who were born in the 1870s and had to reckon in one way or another with modernist sexual freedom. Lisa Duggan offers some new possibilities for thinking about discursive shifts in the field of sexuality, proposing in "The Trials of Alice Mitchell," *Signs* 18.4 (Summer 1993): 791–814 that we "look at the project of constructing identities as a historical process of contested narration, a process in which contrasting 'stories' of the self and others—stories of difference—are told, appropriated, and retold as stories of location in the social world of structured inequalities" (793).

7. The phrase "female world of love and ritual" is from Smith-Rosenberg's famous article of that name, which first appeared in *Signs* 1.1 (1975): 1–29 and is reprinted in *Disorderly Conduct* 53–76. I describe that world as "supposedly idyllic," because recent work has argued for a more subtle and gradual paradigm shift in the movement from romantic friendship to lesbianism, as some evidence suggests elements of deviance or sexual threat apparent earlier in the nineteenth century and some scholars are now less willing to give the turn-of-the-century sexologists all the credit for "inventing" lesbianism and homosexuality. See George Chauncey Jr. "From Sexual Inversion to Homosexuality: Medicine and the Changing Conceptualization of Female Deviance," *Salmagundi* nos. 58–9 (Fall/Winter 1983): 114–46 and "Christian Brotherhood or Sexual Perversion? Homosexual Identities and the Construction of Sexual Boundaries in the World War I Era," *Journal of Social History* 19 (1985): 189–212; rpt. in *Hidden From History* 294–317.

The letter referred to here is Cather to Louise Pound, 15 June 1892, Louise Pound Papers, Manuscript Department, Duke University Library.

8. My reading of this particular line in Cather's letter is different from O'Brien's. She sees Miss De Pue as the source of the view that "feminine friendship" is "unnatural" and reads Cather as agreeing with her that it was. I see Miss De Pue and Cather as agreeing on the unfairness of that view, but O'Brien and I both read the line as evidence of Cather's acute awareness of the stigma her culture attached to her feelings for Louise. See *EV* 131–4.

9. For a detailed discussion of Cather's prolonged and public episode of cross-dressing, see *EV* 96–113.

10. I use the masculine proper name with the feminine pronoun throughout this discussion to mark the disjuncture that was always apparent in Cather's drag

show. A note from Louise's sister Olivia, for example, which is appended to the letter I am discussing here, indicates that because of Willa's masculine dress the Pound family always called *her* "William." People played along, but they seemed to have always known that they were playing.

11. The illustrations to which Cather refers here are by the nineteenth-century painter and illustrator Elihu Vedder. Bernice Slote reports that the Cather family library included a copy of FitzGerald's translation of *The Rubaiyat* with illustrations by Vedder, published by Houghton Mifflin in 1886 (*KA* 385). I examined an 1884 printing of the same edition at the Library of Congress, and the illustrations are, as Cather suggests, dramatic. Vedder made enough of an impression on her that she favorably mentioned him in an 1895 address to the University of Nebraska literary societies. Her topic was Edgar Allan Poe, and she marveled that, "Without encouragement or appreciation of any sort, without models or precedents he built up that pure style of his that is without peer in the language, that style of which every sentence is a drawing by Vedder" (*KA* 385).

12. A recent translation of *The Rubaiyat* by Peter Avery and John Heath-Stubbs is less literary and more faithful to the language of the original than is FitzGerald's, and it refers in several places to the lover as male. See *The Ruba'aiyat of Omar Khayyam*, trans. Peter Avery and John Heath-Stubbs (New York: Penguin, 1979). On the place of FitzGerald's *Rubaiyat* in fin de siècle aestheticism and homosexual subcultures, see *EV* 135 and Joseph Cady's entry on nineteenth-century English literature in Claude J. Summers, ed., *The Gay and Lesbian Literary Heritage* (New York: Henry Holt, 1995), 244.

13. For more on this vast subject, see Edward Said's masterful *Orientalism* (New York: Vintage, 1979).

14. By "theatrical," I don't mean that queer desires are merely a matter of self-display or self-creation (though they are certainly partly that). I refer also to the definition of "theatrical" that Judith Butler offers in "Critically Queer." Arguing that the performative character of gender is "not a radical fabrication of a gendered self [but] a compulsory repetition of prior and subjectivating norms, ones which cannot be thrown off at will, but which work, animate, and constrain the gendered subject, and which are also the resources from which resistance, subversion, displacement are to be forged," Butler posits that "theatricality" (evident in Cather's cross-dressing and the many traditions of drag performance and queer activism Butler notes on 23) is a powerful resignifying practice, a means of miming and exposing "both the binding power of the heterosexualizing law *and its expropriability*" (22–3). Butler's point is to object to the tendency to oppose the theatrical to the political within contemporary queer politics, insisting that "the increasing politicization *of* theatricality" has served to "proliferate[] sites of politicization and AIDS awareness throughout the public realm" (23).

15. Cather to Louise Pound, 29 June 1893, Louise Pound Papers, Manuscript Department, Duke University Library.

16. See Willa Cather to Mariel Gere, 1 June 1893, Willa Cather Historical Center, Red Cloud, Nebraska.

17. Note, too, that de Lauretis borrows from the psychoanalysts Jean Laplanche and J.-B. Pontalis's *The Language of Psychoanalysis* in arguing for a broader definition of sexuality and the sexual that is germane to the argument I am making about Cather's lesbianism and those that others have made vis-à-vis individuals whose sexual self-identifications were supposedly unclear. "Sexuality," according to Laplanche and Pontalis, "does not mean only the activities and pleasure which depend on the functioning of the genital apparatus: it also embraces a whole range of excitations and activities which may be observed from infancy onwards and which procure a pleasure that cannot be adequately explained in terms of the satisfaction of a basic physiological need (respiration, hunger, excretory function, etc.)" (quoted in de Lauretis's *The Practice of Love* 284). The notion that the "sexual" encompasses a range of "excitations and activities" and that lesbianism is defined by a specifically sexual desire, whether or not that desire is ever acted upon, can be useful in resolving the definitional and evidentiary problems that have plagued studies in lesbian history, because it offers a way to distinguish lesbianism from mere woman-identification without simply conflating it with a sexual act. Cather's letters to and about Pound are full of the signifiers of desire, which is in my mind incontrovertible proof that the structuration of her desires was lesbian. As will soon become clear, however, I also think the letters offer some evidence that Cather in fact acted upon her desire for Pound.

18. One sign that Wilcox's influence was perhaps a lingering one is that in "Paul's Case" the protagonist, suffering his own crisis of desire, hears "The Blue Danube" as he steps into the dining room at the Waldorf. The music is part of the "bewildering radiance" that "flood[s] Paul's dream" as he tries to become "exactly the kind of boy he had always wanted to be" (*CS* 184–5).

19. Willa Cather to Mariel Gere, 1 August 1893, Willa Cather Historical Center, Red Cloud, Nebraska. O'Brien for some reason overlooks this letter and thus mistakenly surmises that Pound's failure to come to Red Cloud "may have signfied the cooling of her feelings" (131). The epistolary record of Cather's other intimate relationships offers nothing to compare to the letters to and about Pound. Nothing remains, for example, of the early correspondence to Isabelle McClung, the Pittsburgh socialite with a fondness for artists whom Cather met in 1899 and who was, some claim, the great passion of her life. *The Song of the Lark* is dedicated to McClung, who married in 1916, obviously altering relations between the two women. Woodress reports that three letters have survived, but they were all written by McClung late in her life (141). Similarly, from her four decades with Edith Lewis, we have but a single letter, written by Cather in the early 1930s, which does not speak to the nature of their relationship.

20. The text of Cather's send-up of Roscoe Pound is reprinted in a piece by Mildred Bennett in the *Willa Cather Pioneer Memorial Newsletter* 41.1 (Spring 1997): 5–7. In the essay, "Friends of Willa Cather," Bennett reports that Pound's bitterness toward Cather over the incident persisted for nearly sixty years. When the two had lunch together in 1957, Pound brought out a copy of the article and read it "with a voice trembling with emotion—probably rage." When asked about

rumors of Cather's lesbianism, Pound replied, "But who was her partner?" Bennett continues:"I said I didn't know but thought perhaps she could help me. 'No,' she said,'I can't.' "Apparently Pound and Bennett agree with de Lauretis that it takes two women to make a lesbian, yet each for some reason ignores the obvious answer to the question: Edith Lewis.

21. The letters discussed here are Cather to Mariel Gere, 16 June 1894; 4 August 1896; and 25 April 1897, Willa Cather Historical Center, Red Cloud, Nebraska.

22. On Cather's usage of the name "Willa Sibert Cather," see Lewis 19, Bennett 235, and O'Brien 107. Editors of her early journalism note that Cather published several reviews under the name "Sibert" in the late 1890s (*WP* 1:384–5), but she didn't use it as part of her full name for publication until 1900 (*KA* 29). She continued to use it until she moved from Houghton Mifflin to Alfred Knopf in 1920. All of her books from *Youth and the Bright Medusa* (1920) onward are published under the name "Willa Cather."

2. "Filling Out Nice": Body-Building and Nation-Building in the Early Novels

1. For the concept of the "extraordinary" body, I am indebted to Rosemarie Garland Thomson's recent ground-breaking work in the field of disability studies. See *Extraordinary Bodies: Figuring Physical Disability in American Culture and Literature.* My discussion here also draws upon studies of the politics of the body in the U.S. and turn-of-the-century discourses of race, gender, and sexuality. See especially Bederman, D'Emilio and Freedman, and Sanchez-Eppler.

2. For a provocative discussion of contemporary contestations of national identity and national sexuality, see Berlant and Freeman (esp. 193–9). They argue that Queer Nation's parodic tactics of crossing borders and occupying spaces in order to "simulate 'the national' with a camp inflection" operate "precisely in the American mode" (196). Though Cather is by no means a Queer Nationalist in the contemporary sense and not a parodist in the literary sense, she does in her contestations of identity operate in what strikes me as a specifically, though probably not uniquely, "American mode."

3. Cather worked on the magazine on a full-time basis only through October 1911, when she gave up her position as managing editor and took a leave of absence to work on *Alexander's Bridge*. She returned on a half-time basis in 1913 to fulfill a number of commitments to her mentor, founding editor S. S. McClure, including ghostwriting his autobiography. See *LL* 248–59.

4. Deborah Carlin provides a useful overview of how Cather's perceived celebration of the national myth has earned her a place in "some versions of an American literary canon" but skewed Cather studies toward the first half of her oeuvre (7). I would add that that already narrow focus also privileges the so-called "pioneer novels" (*O Pioneers!*, *The Song of the Lark*, and *My Ántonia*) and devalues the crucial body of short fiction from this period as well as the novels (*Alexander's Bridge* and *One of Ours*) with male protagonists whose stories involve leaving the

prairie rather than "taming" it.

5. Such a pattern of reading Cather's early fiction is apparent, for example, in O'Brien (*EV* 74, 387–93) and "Combat Envy and Survivor Guilt." The latter essay doesn't simply see Claude Wheeler as a "bad guy," noting Cather's partial identification with her hero and her fascination with "the transformation in identity solders experienced in battle" [189], but it ultimately sees feminine and maternal powers of survival ascending in the end); Maureen Ryan, "No Woman's Land: Gender in Willa Cather's *One of Ours*," argues that the novel exposes Claude's conventional attitudes about gender and American culture and also valorizes women's endurance; Fetterley, "Willa Cather and the Fiction of Female Development," reads *The Song of the Lark* as "an exceptional text in its uncompromising portrayal of a woman who grows up to get what she wants" (222) and says nothing about the rest of Cather's early fiction; Ammons, "The Engineer as Cultural Hero," reads *Alexander's Bridge* as "a negative judgment of Progressive Era America and of the social construction of masculinity in the United States at the time" (756).

6. Paul, of course, had no defender to argue for the value of his difference from the majority. His hairy-legged father enforces the bourgeois order of Cordelia Street—regular hours, work, thrift, suspicion of the world of theater and actors— and is in New York to take his son back to that order when Paul decides to kill himself.

7. Cather's "corporeal utopianism" was probably inherited directly and self-consciously from Whitman, an inheritance she acknowledges in the title of her novel, borrowed from his poem, "Pioneers! O Pioneers!" Cather's relationship to Whitman will be discussed in greater detail in part 2 of this study. I'm less convinced than O'Brien (*EV* 440) that Cather really critiques the manly pioneer ethos declaimed in this thumping marching song, which calls upon "Western youths" and the "youthful sinewy races" to "take up the task eternal" of conquest, expansion, and settlement (ll. 9, 7, 15). As will soon become clear, the logic of my reading suggests that the novel in important ways endorses that ethos.

8. On the issue of landscape in *O Pioneers!*, see those readings that emphasize Cather's revision of American pastoral myths: O'Brien sees Cather criticizing "the power relationship between a male protagonist and a feminine landscape that informs the traditional American pastoral, in which nature is an object—either the virgin land to be raped or the bountiful mother to be sought—against which the male self is defined." For Cather, "both the female hero and the maternal land are subjects, and Alexandra defines herself in relation to—instead of against—the natural world" (*EV* 434). Gilbert and Gubar argue that in *O Pioneers!* and *My Ántonia*, Cather "creates a mythic America which is girlhood, for she tells the story of the gender dislocation fostered by immigration into the wilderness, a dislocation that results in the death of the father, the diminution of the son, and the empowerment of the daughter with the concomitant centrality of female work" (*Sexchanges* 184). Judith Fryer reads *O Pioneers!* as the "authentic story" of "an ordinary woman working in a particular place and time" in which "the great fact

is the land" (259). See also Neil Gustafson's critique of feminist readings of *O Pioneers!*, including Carol Fairbanks (*Prairie Women: Images in American and Canadian Fiction.* New Haven: Yale UP, 1986), Donovan, and Elizabeth Jane Harrison (*Female Pastorals: Women Writers Revisioning the American South.* Knoxville: U of Tennessee P, 1991). Though I take issue with Gustafson's snide remarks about feminist critics trying to "recruit" Cather's novel "in support of a larger assumption" (153) about the relationship between gender and landscape or nature, I concur generally with his reading of Alexandra, particularly with the point that she shares and fulfills her father's dreams rather than repudiating them and that her mystical, artistic, and "feminine" qualities are matched by the "masculine" attributes of "a skilled land speculator, an ambitious entrepreneur, and a capable capitalist" (159). In my judgment, though, it is still a mistake to read Alexandra as if she were a real person and not a force-field, a space upon which and across which a range of differences play.

9. Annette Kolodny's work remains crucial to any discussion of landscapes in American literature and culture. In addition to *The Lay of the Land* and *The Land Before Her*, see a recent essay proposing a new literary history of the frontiers. She would include Cather in that history, noting that in her fiction the physical terrain is what ecohistorian Carolyn Merchant describes as an active partner, "acquiesc[ing] to human interventions through resilience and adaptation or 'resist[ing]' human actions through mutation and evolution" ("Letting Go Our Grand Obsessions" 12).

10. My discussion here has benefited from Brooks's discussion of the "talking bodies" that emerged with the rise of the positivist sciences and popular pseudosciences derived from them in the nineteenth century. See *Body Work* 221–56. For a global survey of how visual artists of the twentieth century have figured the body from the age of positivism to the moment of postmodernism, see la Biennale di Venezia. Of especial interest are Jean Clair, "Impossible Anatomy 1895–1995: Notes on the Iconography of a World of Technologies" (xxv–xxi); Maurizio Bettini, "Loving Statues" (19–25); Paolo Fabbri, "Deformities of the Face" (27–31); Gunter Metken, "Behind the Mirror: Notes from the Portrait in the Twentieth Century" (33–7); Philippe Comar, "The Body Beside Itself" (39–43) and "A Made-to-measure Identity" (45–7).

11. For explorations of Cather's relationship to such traditions in *O Pioneers!*, see Donovan 104–9, Woodress 242–8, and Rosowski, *The Voyage Perilous* 45–61.

12. I borrow from Haraway's delightful essay fully aware that the analogy I am making between Akeley's dioramas and Cather's novel will strike some readers as strained, if not willfully perverse. I risk taxing the reader's patience in order to call attention to the importance of realism, naturalism, and natural history to the project of *O Pioneers!*. Ultimately, this move will serve to complicate the text's and Cather's supposed "nostalgia." Also, I follow Haraway in referring to the dioramas as "Akeley's," though African Hall was not constructed until after his death. Haraway reports that Akeley went to New York to work for the American Museum of Natural History in 1908 and that "his plan for the African Hall took

shape by 1911 and ruled his behavior thereafter" (252). He is appropriately described as "author" of the exhibition because his was the mind that governed and unified its composition (256–7).

13. I refer here to Julie Abraham's brief but provocative reading of *O Pioneers!* in *Are Girls Necessary? Lesbian Writing and Modern Histories* 41–4.

14. Cather's subplot of adultery gestures toward *Madame Bovary* in a number of ways, but it does so particularly in its lingering over the body of the dead woman. For marvelous readings of Flaubert's lingering, see Brooks 89–96 and Bronfen 157–65.

15. We know that Emil is buried in the Norwegian graveyard because Alexandra goes there the day she gets caught in the rain. We can assume that Marie is buried in the Catholic graveyard, though no mention is made of it in the text. Much earlier in the story, Emil and Marie discuss the ethnic and religious politics of the local graveyards while he is mowing the Bergson family plot. See 79–80.

16. For a wide-ranging discussion of the ways in which immune system discourse has figured into bodily and global politics throughout the twentieth century, see Donna Haraway, "The Biopolitics of Postmodern Bodies," esp. 204–9 and 217–21. Haraway notes that the marked bodies of "woman, the colonized or enslaved, and the worker" have been deployed to generate "accounts of rational citizenship, bourgeois family life, and prophylaxis against sexual pollution and inefficiency, such as prostitution, criminality, or race suicide" (207), which, I am arguing, is precisely what happens in *O Pioneers!* in the marking of queer bodies as impure.

17. See especially the introduction and first chapter of *Constituting Americans*. My discussion here is also influenced by a range of feminist work in legal and social theory which, in the wake of Butler's *Gender Trouble*, has reckoned with liberal individualism's construction of the juridical subject as bodiless. Within the context of U.S. cultural history, see Sanchez-Eppler and Thomson. Within the context of debates about feminist legal strategy, see Poovey and Cornell. For a discussion of how anxieties about titles and ownership have figured into U.S. fiction and particularly Hawthorne's *The House of the Seven Gables*, see Michaels, "Romance and Real Estate."

18. Butler's discussion of the "trouble" with the term "queer," given its discursive history, is worth keeping in mind in the current rush to reclaim the name, for she raises serious questions about the limits of resignification and insists that the term can never be "fully owned, but always and only redeployed, twisted, queered from a prior usage and in the direction of urgent and expanding political purposes." Her suggestion that such a "queering" "might signal an inquiry into (a) the *formation* of homosexualities (a historical inquiry which cannot take the stability of the term for granted, despite the political pressure to do so) and (b) the *deformative* and *misappropriative* power that the term currently enjoys" informs the project of this study on every level. See *Bodies* 226–30.

19. On the issue of homosexuality and homosociality in *One of Ours*, see Cramer, Abraham 44–6, Woodress 332–3, and Lee 180–2.

20. I am by no means the first reader to declare that Willa Cather was not in the final analysis a realist. As previously noted, Woodress and Rosowski see her as a Romantic. Jo Ann Middleton sees her as a modernist. Others call her a pastoralist.

21. I should point out that realist strategies of representation served Cather very well in her short stories and that the "queer" often fares better there—perhaps because so many of the stories are written in the "revolt from the village" tradition ("Paul's Case," "The Sculptor's Funeral"). Even though the queers are dead, they look better than the grotesques who survive in these stultifying bourgeois communities. Compare, for example, Harvey Merrick's hideous mother to Harvey Merrick's beautiful corpse. There is much more to be said on the subject of Cather's short fiction, certainly.

22. A crucial resource for reading the turn-of-the-century American body is John S. Haller and Robin M. Haller, *The Physician and Sexuality in Victorian America* (1974; New York: Norton, 1977). See especially chapters 1 and 5. Bederman also discusses the signifying force of the white male body in discourses of American civilization during this period. See especially chapters 1 and 3.

23. Roosevelt had been out of office for four years, but as the 1912 election approached, "The World We Live In" column in *McClure's* 38 (1912): 60 mused upon the former president's sudden reappearance in the public eye through his newspaper columns. Noting that "there is in the air the unusual public sentiment for recalling a man for the third time to the presidential chair," the column concludes that it would be curious but "thoroughly American" if Republicans would choose Roosevelt as a compromise candidate. As it turned out, Roosevelt ran against the incumbent William Howard Taft on a third-party Progressive ticket, opening the door for Democrat Woodrow Wilson to win the election.

For a more detailed discussion of *Alexander's Bridge* as it originally appeared in *McClure's* see my introduction, *Alexander's Bridge*, by Willa Cather (Oxford and New York: Oxford UP, 1997) vii–xxxiii.

24. See also George Kibbe Turner, "The Daughters of the Poor; a Plain Story of the Development of New York City as a Leading Center of the White Slave Trade of the World, under Tammany Hall," *McClure's* 34 (1909): 45–61. Harold S. Wilson in *McClure's Magazine and the Muckrakers* (Princeton: Princeton UP, 1970) cites a number of other *McClure's* articles on the subject and credits the magazine with "stimulat[ing] a national panic and, finally, national action" on the issue of prostitution: "Soon President Roosevelt proclaimed adherence to the international white slave treaty, excluded prostitutes by the immigration act of 1908, and helped create a public sentiment favorable to the Mann Act of 1910" (221–2).

Cather discusses the magazine's interest in the issue of prostitution in a 1911 letter to Elizabeth Shepley Sergeant. She tells Sergeant about a visit she received at the office from a Hull House woman, who tells her about a Miss Wyatt, who has given herself over wholly to the cause of the white slave. (Wyatt had published a series in *McClure's* in 1910, according to Wilson 222, n. 56.) Cather remarks that the woman seemed to her to be maddened by having lived too long in the company of a horrible idea. She ends the letter by saying she'd like Sergeant to meet Isabelle McClung, who is so fond of lovely things and so full of them, and so frightened of reformers. See Cather to Elizabeth Shepley Sergeant, 4 June 1911, Barrett Library, University of Virginia. Despite Cather's oft declared skepticism about philanthropy and women reformers in particular, I should also point out that she had spoken admiringly and at length of Jane Addams in a column in the Lincoln *Courier* in March, 1900, insisting that she was neither an extremist nor a fanatic but "a candid, large-minded student of men and measures, a fearless critic of life" (*WP* 2:744).

25. Thea's lesbian fan club includes, in addition to yours truly, Fetterley, "Willa Cather and the Fiction of Female Development"; Wood, "Sapphonics", Castle, *The Apparitional Lesbian* 212–13; and Leonardi and Pope, *The Diva's Mouth* 89–106. Wayne Koestenbaum is not a lesbian, but he does mention Thea in the course of his rhapsody on the diva, *The Queen's Throat* 87, 92.

26. I realize I'm compressing a great deal of literary history into a small space here, but my goal at this juncture is merely to establish a sense of the importance of "romance" in the first decade of Cather's career as a novelist. It helps to clarify the ambitions in her figuring of Thea. Hawthorne defines romance as "the truth of the human heart" in the preface to *The House of the Seven Gables*, while Norris says that "to Romance belongs the wide world for range, and the unplumbed depths of the human heart, and the mystery of sex, and the problems of life, and the black, unsearched penetralia of the soul of man" in his 1901 essay, "A Plea for Romantic Fiction." Though, as I noted earlier in this section, Cather praised *McTeague* for its "realism," I would propose that by the time of *The Song of the Lark* she was moving toward the antirealist aesthetic enunciated in "The Novel Démeublé" (1922).

"Romance" would subsequently prove to be one of the most powerful (and masculinist) terms in critical discourse about American fiction, for it is the primary organizing term in Carl Van Doren's discussion in the *Cambridge History of American Literature* and in Lawrence's *Studies in Classic American Literature*—and in much criticism up to the present. Lawrence's influence is felt, for example, throughout Harry Levin's *The Power of Blackness: Hawthorne, Poe, Melville* (1958; Athens: Ohio UP, 1980); Richard Chase's *The American Novel and Its Traditions* (Garden City, NY: Anchor, 1957); Leslie Fiedler's *Love and Death in the American Novel* (1960, rev. 1966; New York: Stein and Day, 1975); Joel Porte's *The Romance in America* (Middletown, CT: Wesleyan UP, 1969); Michael Davitt Bell's *The Rhetoric of American Romance* (Chicago: U of Chicago P, 1980); and Evan Carton's *The Rhetoric of American Romance* (Baltimore: Johns Hopkins UP, 1985).

27. Indeed, Cather never delivers her beautiful Swedish women to reproduction, ideally suited for the task as their "gleaming white" bodies would seem to be. See also Alexandra and *My Ántonia*'s Lena Lingard.

28. On the differences between the two editions, see Schwind's "The Benda Illustrations to *My Ántonia*" and "Textual Commentary" in the Willa Cather Scholarly Edition of *My Ántonia* (Mignon 481–521). I am using John Murphy's

Penguin edition of the novel because he reprints both introductions. I use "Cather" in quotation marks to distinguish the speaker in the introduction from the author of the book. It's important to make that distinction, since Cather doesn't sign this introduction, as, for example, she does the brief note at the end of *Sapphira and the Slave Girl*. Also, the following discussion summarizes and builds upon arguments I make in " 'It Ain't My Prairie.' " For a full unpacking of the textual evidence, see that essay.

29. For another take on *My Ántonia*'s relationship to the Americanization debates and the possibilities of pluralism, see Reynolds 73–98. On Stoddard, whose *The Rising Tide of Color* was first published in 1920, see Michaels, *Our America*. On the emergence of lesbian and gay enclaves in New York, see Faderman, *Odd Girls* 62–88 and Chauncey, *Gay New York* 226–67. Biographers generally insist that Cather was not a part of the Bohemian life of the Village, noting only that she was friends with Carl Van Vechten, who was gay and married and brought the Harlem Renaissance to the attention of the white reading public with his controversial novel, *Nigger Heaven* (1926), and that she may have attended Mable Dodge's famous salon. See Woodress 236. An interviewer for the *Cleveland Press* noted in 1925 that the prickly Cather, though reticent to speak on many subjects, was pleased to talk about "life in Greenwich Village before it became Bohemia, Inc." See Bohlke 87–8.

30. On Cather's private renunciation of "Bohemianism," see the discussion of her letters to Mariel Gere in chapter 1. For her public attack, in the course of a review of Clyde Fitch's play, *Bohemia* (based on Henri Murger's *Scènes de la vie de Bohème* [1848]), in the *Nebraska State Journal* of 5 April 1896, see *WP* 1:292–6. On the etymology of "Bohemianism," see Sedgwick, *Epistemology* 193 and Butler, *Bodies that Matter* 149.

31. In the text the phrase "of like nationality" refers not to Jim's marriage but to the marriages of the immigrant "hired girls." The principle clearly operates in a general fashion, however, as both Jim and Ántonia marry people of their own racial/ethnic group.

32. Cather made these remarks in an interview with Rose Caroline Feld originally published in the *New York Times Book Review*, 21 December 1924: 11. Reynolds discusses the same remarks in relation to *My Ántonia* in *Willa Cather in Context* 79. I am indebted to him for calling this interview to my attention.

33. Higham is careful to point out that "there were, in fact, several nativisms (xii)," some motivated by racial animus but others motivated by religious or political animus—specifically by anti-Catholic and antiradical hostilities. Michaels's definition of nativism seems to me monolithic and his application of it to literary texts reductive in overlooking irony and in conflating characters' points of view with those of texts and authors.

34. I hasten to acknowledge that I am overlooking the crude racial stereotyping that characterizes Jim's depiction of d'Arnault and that I realize Martha is not strictly speaking the product of miscegenation, since Ántonia and Larry Donovan would be accurately described as belonging to different ethnic groups

rather than different races, but *My Ántonia* is governed by the turn-of-the-century tendency to conflate the two.

35. I should clarify that "Americanism" actually names a range of early twentieth-century discourses, some of which were deployed by Progressives to advance the cause of assimilationism and some of which were deployed by nativists to advance the cause of Anglo-Saxon racial purity (and national power). See Bederman, Reynolds, Higham, and Michaels. Cather's remarks on the "deadly disease" of Americanization are clearly aimed at Progressive assimilationists, for she singles out social workers and missionaries as those who "devote their days and nights toward the great task of turning [immigrants] into stupid replicas of smug American citizens" (Bohlke 71).

36. Some readers have seen the claim as odd because Jim has said a sentence earlier, "I'd have liked to have you for a sweetheart, or a wife, or my mother or my sister—anything a woman can be to a man" (240), which has prompted speculation about why Jim has ruled out the available options of courtship and marriage with Ántonia in favor of merely incorporating her as memory and influence. See Fetterley, "*My Ántonia*" 155 and Adams 92.

37. Mencken's review originally appeared in his *Smart Set* (March 1919): 140–1. It is reprinted in John Murphy, ed., *Critical Essays on Willa Cather* (Boston: G. K. Hall, 1983) 145–6.

38. My reading of Cather here parallels Gardner's illuminating reading of Crane. On the Newport investigations, see Katz 398–9 and Chauncey, "Christian Brotherhood."

39. I by no means deny that "one of ours" participates to a troubling degree in all of these phenomena. The rhetoric of Cather's title anticipates the argument Lothrop Stoddard would make in his follow-up to *The Rising Tide of Color, Re-Forging America*, published in 1927. In the later volume Stoddard's white supremacism is less an issue, but his commitment to racial difference is articulated in language strikingly similar to Cather's: "No theoretical questions of 'superiority' or 'inferiority' need by raised. . . . The really important point is that even though America (abstractly considered) may not be nearly as good as we think it is, nevertheless it is *ours*" (quoted in Michaels, *Our America* 65).

For a summary of the negative critical reactions to *One of Ours*, see LL 333–4.

40. Many feminist readings of *One of Ours* have emphasized the gap between Claude's view and the narrator's (or Cather's) view of the war. Among them are Schwind, "The 'Beautiful' War"; O'Brien, "Combat Envy and Survivor Guilt"; and Ryan.

41. O'Brien makes this point in relation to *One of Ours* in "Combat Envy and Survivor Guilt," though she also notes that, despite such critique, "the novel still offers plentiful support for the view that Claude Wheeler creates a new, and in Cather's opinion an enriched, self in World War I" (191). For a more general discussion of masculinity, femininity, and the Great War, see Sandra M. Gilbert and Susan Gubar's monumental *No Man's Land: The Place of the Woman Writer in the Twentieth Century*, 3 vols. See especially the first two chapters of vol. 1, *The War of*

the Words, and chapter 6 of vol. 2, *Sexchanges*.

42. I am indebted to discussions with Geoffrey Saunders Schramm for helping me to see this crucial problem in *One of Ours*'s construction of homosociality and homosexuality.

43. For readings of the sniper scene, see Cramer 147–8, Abraham 45–6, Lee
181, and Woodress 332–3.

44. In her reading of Wilde's *The Importance of Being Earnest* in *Tendencies*, Eve
Kosofsky Sedgwick notes the importance of "the word and notion 'German' " as a
signifier of homosexuality in turn-of-the-century cultural systems. According to
Sedgwick, "Virtually all of the competing, conflicting figures for understanding
same-sex desire—archaic ones and modern ones, medicalized and politicizing,
those emphasizing pederastic relations, gender inversion, or 'homo-' homosexuality—were coined and circulated in this period in the first place in German, and
through German culture, medicine, and politics" (65–6). Sedgwick also discusses the
especial signifying force of Wagner in this discursive field, arguing that in the urbane
world of Wilde "the very name 'Wagner' is a node of gay recognition and attribu-
tion" (66). The sniper scene, which so obviously associates Germany and homosexuality, thus establishes another crucial connection between Claude Wheeler and
Cather's most flagrantly Wagnerian heroine, Thea Kronborg.

See also James Steakley's "Iconography of a Scandal: Political Cartoons and the
Eulenburg Affair in Wilhelmin Germany" in *Hidden From History*, 233–63. Steakley
argues that in the aftermath of a series of trials charging prominent members of
Kaiser Wilhelm II's entourage and cabinet with homosexuality the German army
in World War I was portrayed in French and Italian cartoons as "perversely effeminate" and the French referred to homosexuality as "*le vice allemand*" (247).

45. The most exhaustive study of "homosexual panic" as a literary phenom-
enon is, of course, the work of Eve Kosofsky Sedgwick. See both *Between Men:
English Literature and Male Homosocial Desire*, esp. chapter 5, and *Epistemology of the
Closet*.

46. On board ship Claude thinks about why he waited for the U.S. to enter
the war before enlisting when he might have gotten into the action earlier by
joining the Canadian army or the French Foreign Legion, but he realizes that was
not " 'the Wheelers' way.' " The Wheelers, Claude thinks, were "afraid of doing
anything that might look affected or 'romantic.' They couldn't let themselves
adopt a conspicuous, much less a picturesque course of action, unless it was all in
the day's work" (265–6).

47. Van Leer's concept of "the queening of America" has been useful to my
thinking about Cather's "queering of America," but they are not exactly the same
thing. He uses theories of minority discourse to analyze "a group of processes by
which rhetorics and situations specific to homosexual culture are presented to a
general readership as culturally neutral. The crossover affords power and perhaps
sly revenge, as straight culture takes for its own a humor it only incompletely
understands" (65). His is basically a model of camp appropriation and reappropri-
ation. My reading of Cather's "queering of America" does not see her as speak-

ing from a clearly defined lesbian subcommunity, though I think the marginality she experienced as a lesbian inflects her relationship to dominant discourses. She was not a camper, though, despite Claude's diva dance on the parapet, unless by "camper" we imply the moral seriousness of a Girl Scout.

Part 2: Queering the "Classics": Willa Cather and the Literary History of the United States

1. Woodress paraphrases this letter on 422 and notes the source on 554 (Willa Cather, letter to Mr. Bain, 14 January 1931, University of Michigan). That Woolf was on Cather's mind during the crucial period of the mid-twenties under consideration here is apparent from a letter she wrote to Blanche Knopf asking to be sent a copy of Woolf's *The Voyage Out* (1915). I'm in an awful plight for something to read, she tells Knopf, and don't know what to order, but I want to try that. See Willa Cather, letter to Blanche Knopf, rec'd. 7 October 1926, Box 689, Folder 1, Alfred A. Knopf, Inc. Archives, Harry Ransom Humanities Research Center, University of Texas.

3. "In a Prohibition Country": The Culture Wars of the 1920s

1. For the reader's convenience, I cite the version of this and all of Cather's essays from the 1920s published in *Not Under Forty*, but everything I discuss was also contained in the original versions unless otherwise indicated. O'Brien discusses "148 Charles Street" and the importance to Cather of her relationship with Annie Fields in *The Emerging Voice* 314–22.

2. On the formation of "American literature" as an academic discipline and its tendencies to narrow the canon, see Lauter, Vanderbilt, and Shumway. Shumway claims "there was no organized opposition to white male hegemony" during this process, even from outside the academy, and that the work of such oppositional thinkers as Gertrude Stein, Amy Lowell, and Mary Austin "had no impact on the discipline" (9–10). Whether or not the opposition was organized or "significant" (10)—though one wonders how "significance" is to be measured—I think it is important to attend to the dissenting voices that, had they more effectively intervened in these debates, would have constituted a radically different object of study. Shumway seems to acknowledge this point in his discussion of Mary Austin's chapter on Native American literature in the *Cambridge History of American Literature*. Its inclusion suggests that "When the *Cambridge History* appeared [1917–1921] it was still possible for the academy to have constituted American literature in many different ways. . . . American literature could have been conceived as multilingual and multiethnic as early as 1920" (92–3).

3. Cather has Fields "slyly" inject an allusion to New York into her reading of Milton (64), which is important in view of Fields's connection to Boston's great publishing houses of the nineteenth century. The allusion recognizes the rising cultural power of New York, which was where Cather was living and working when she met Fields. By the time the essay was written, Cather had also left Houghton Mifflin, the publishing house descended from the one founded by

Fields's husband, a move discussed in detail below.

4. Carafiol offers this observation in the course of a trenchant analysis of how a rigorous historicity "ought to shake the ground from under the field" (539) of American literary studies, forcing it to abandon at last "the ahistorical idea of America" (540) that has served as a disciplinary metanarrative. For other examples of New Americanist and post-Americanist self-critique, see Kaplan and Pease, eds., *Cultures of U.S. Imperialism*; Kolodny, "Letting Go"; Kutzinski; Pease, ed., *National Identities and Post-Americanist Narratives*; and Sundquist, ed., "American Literary History: The Next Century."

5. The story of the dramatic changes in American publishing during this period is told in John Tebbell's three-volume *A History of Book Publishing in the United States*. See especially 2:130–1 and 3:52–5. On the evolution of the company that became Houghton Mifflin, see 2:246–56. On Knopf, see 3:113–16.

6. Willa Cather, letter to Ferris Greenslet, 19 May 1919, Willa Cather Letters, Houghton Library, Harvard University.

7. Willa Cather, letter to Ferris Greenslet, 28 March 1915, Willa Cather Letters, Houghton Library, Harvard University.

8. Willa Cather, letter to Mr. [Roger Livingston] Scaife, 30 October 1915, Willa Cather Letters, Houghton Library, Harvard University.

9. Willa Cather, letter to Ferris Greenslet, 19 May 1919, Willa Cather Letters, Houghton Library, Harvard University.

10. Willa Cather, letter to Ferris Greenslet, 12 January 1921, Willa Cather Letters, Houghton Library, Harvard University.

11. Willa Cather, letter to Ferris Greenslet, 12 January 1921, Willa Cather Letters, Houghton Library, Harvard University.

12. Willa Cather, letter to Ferris Greenslet, 30 May 1919, Willa Cather Letters, Houghton Library, Harvard University.

13. Cather's language and the sexual implications of her metaphors cannot, I hasten to say, be attributed to the fact that she was a woman, though her gender likely heightened her concerns about seeming disloyal or overly ambitious. However, the nature writer John Burroughs (1837–1921), who also published with Houghton, suggests that such language was a company policy that applied to writers of both genders, sometimes with comic results. John Tebbel reports that Burroughs once told an interviewer: "At times I thought of taking a book manuscript to some other firm but always was persuaded not to. Mr. Houghton said a publisher and an author were like man and wife and shouldn't be separated. I couldn't quite see the analogy. If he was the man, I had only one husband, but he had a whole harem of authors" (3:52). Tebbell also notes that Burroughs subsequently switched publishers.

14. For a thorough discussion of the childbirth metaphor and its resonance throughout Western literary history, see Friedman.

15. Willa Cather, letter to Ferris Greenslet, 17 February 1924, Willa Cather Letters, Houghton Library, Harvard University.

16. Sharon O'Brien takes up some of these questions, particularly of Cather's

relationship to a male-dominated publishing and critical establishment during the 1920s and 1930s, in her study of the shifts in Cather's literary reputation, "Becoming Noncanonical: The Case against Willa Cather." I probe more deeply into the ways in which these issues figure into Cather's editing of Jewett.

17. As O'Brien notes in "Becoming Noncanonical," Van Doren was in fact a fan of Cather's, including a positive assessment of her in a subsequent literary history, *Contemporary American Novelists: 1900–1920* (1922) (243). Woodress includes Van Doren among the friends who came to visit Cather at her Friday afternoons on Bank Street (281). For my purposes, though, Van Doren's work in the *Cambridge History*, particularly his use of "romance" as a way of organizing and hierarchizing American fiction, is most important.

18. The line quoted is from Austin's essay of 1932, "Regionalism in American Fiction," but her other major work in the field of Native American literature is her volume of commentary and (loose) translations of Native American poetry, *The American Rhythm*, published, like Lawrence's *Studies*, in 1923. Also worth noting is that Austin had an essay, "The American Form of the Novel," in the same number of the *New Republic* (12 April 1922)· as Cather's "The Novel Démeublé." Some of Austin's remarks on the democratic, participatory structure of the American novel—she insists, for example, that the democratic novelist must be "inside his novel rather than outside in the Victorian fashion" (4)—overlap in interesting ways with Cather's comments on the open, evanescent quality of the art of things felt rather than named.

Austin's biographer, Esther Lanigan Stineman, discusses the ups and downs of the Cather-Austin friendship in *Mary Austin: Song of a Maverick*. See especially 127–9.

19. The phrase quoted is from Kurt L. Daniels's review of *Studies in Classic American Literature* in the *New Republic* 24 October 1923: n. p. Much could be said, certainly, on the contemporary reception and the long-range influence of Lawrence's *Studies*, but that would be a digression from my point about Cather's engagement with Lawrence and the literary history he helped to promulgate. For other reviews see John Macy, "The American Spirit," *Nation* 10 October 1923: 398–9; Stuart P. Sherman, "America Is Discovered," *The Literary Review* of the *New York Evening Post* 20 October 1923: 143–4; Alyse Gregory, "Artist Turned Prophet," *Dial* January 1924: 66–72; "D. H. Lawrence Bombs Our Literary Shrines," *Current Opinion* September 1923: 305–7; H. I. Brock, "D. H. Lawrence Strings Some American Literary Pearls," *New York Times Book Review* 16 September 1923: 9+; Maurice Francis Egan, "On the Sin of Being an American," *The Literary Digest International Book Review* September 1923: 28–9; Raymond M. Weaver, "Narcissus and Echo," *The Bookman* November 1923: 327–8.

20. Lewis puts the date of Lawrence's visit to her and Cather's apartment in the spring of 1925, which would have been after the Jewett project was completed, but Woodress, based on the dating of a letter Cather wrote about the visit, puts it in 1924 (353–4 and 546).

21. Willa Cather, letter to Ferris Greenslet, 10 May 1924, Willa Cather

Letters, Houghton Library, Harvard University.

22. I realize I am not being entirely fair to Lawrence here in placing so much emphasis on his all-male canon and on his misogynist construction of female creativity in his reading of *The Scarlet Letter*. One could, as Robert Levine has suggested to me (personal correspondence), argue that *SCAL* itself "queered" American literary history by calling attention to a number of (male) writers who were not at the time canonical and by celebrating comradely relationships over heterosexual ones. I concede the point, but in the Jewett volume and *The Professor's House*, Cather contends most directly with Lawrence's gendering of literary history.

23. Willa Cather, letter to Ferris Greenslet, 17 February 1924, Willa Cather Letters, Houghton Library, Harvard University.

24. Willa Cather, letter to Ferris Greenslet, 19 May 1919, Willa Cather Letters, Houghton Library, Harvard University. As in the preface to *Jewett*, Cather here uses the masculine pronoun to refer to "the author."

25. Adrienne Rich, "The Spirit of Place," *A Wild Patience Has Taken Me This Far* (New York: Norton, 1981) 43.

26. Willa Cather, letter to Ferris Greenslet, 15 April 1924, Willa Cather Letters, Houghton Library, Harvard University.

27. When Jewett died in June 1909, Cather was in London and wrote a letter of condolence to Annie Fields in which the ghostly presence of her precursor is powerful indeed. She tells Fields she cannot bring herself to feel but that somehow Jewett is near her dear companion in Boston, and that if she herself could go to Fields there she would feel her presence even if she could not see her. When one is far away like this, she remarks, one cannot realize death. Other things become shadowy and unreal, but Miss Jewett herself remains so real that I cannot get past the vivid image of her to any other realization. Cather confesses, too, that everything she has done in England has been with a hope that it might interest Jewett—even to some clothes she was having made. Time may have tempered Cather's sense of awe toward Jewett, but the uncertainty that accompanied the editing and promoting of her predecessor indicates she remained an important and somewhat daunting figure. See Willa Cather, letter to Annie Fields, 27 June 1909, Willa Cather Letters, Houghton Library, Harvard University.

28. Willa Cather, letter to Ferris Greenslet, 17 February 1924, Willa Cather Letters, Houghton Library, Harvard University.

29. My argument here is intended to qualify feminist theories of influence that rely on the mother-daughter model without paying sufficient attention to daughterly acts of rebellion like Cather's. Sharon O'Brien argues, for example, that, "Cather's literary response to Jewett's fiction and friendship suggests a less competitive paradigm [than the Freudian pattern of struggle and competition that Harold Bloom sees characterizing male poets' relationships with their forebears]: the woman writer's willingness to define herself in connection with, rather than in opposition to, her female precursor" (*EV* 364–5). Clearly, Jewett and Cather are no Laius and Oedipus at the crossroads, but Cather's need to assert a physical, editorial power over her predecessor suggests they aren't exactly or always Demeter

and Persephone either. Perhaps Aunt Em (a surrogate or stepmother) and Dorothy from Victor Fleming's 1939 film version of *The Wizard of Oz* supply a model of the mother-daughter bond that more accurately reflects its tensions as well as its persistence as the daughter matures. Dorothy's dream of a place "over the rainbow" is, after all, set into motion by her preoccupied aunt's peremptory, "Now, Dorothy dear, stop imagining things. You always get yourself into a fret over nothing. Now, you just help us out today and find yourself a place where you won't get into trouble." Both a rebel and an artist, Dorothy obviously does not "stop imagining things," and she runs away with Toto in defiance of Aunt Em's decision to surrender the dog to Miss Gulch. A quick dose of guilt brings the "daughter's" rebellion to an end, however, as Professor Marvel tells Dorothy that Aunt Em, whose tearful face in his crystal ball suggests that "Someone has hurt her, someone has just about broken her heart," appears to be ill. "You don't suppose she could really be sick, do you?" Dorothy exclaims. "Oh, oh, I've got to go home right away!" Cather's apparently contradictory desires both to please Jewett and to cut "her" up and bind "her" into a new form conform to a similar pattern of loyalty to and rebellion against the mother figure—a pattern evident as well in Rich's need to impose an emphatic closure upon her relationship with Dickinson: "this is my third and last address to you."

Gilbert and Gubar's examination of what they term the "female affiliation complex" comes closer to the dynamics I see in the Jewett-Cather relationship, though they don't devote much attention to that particular connection and their reading of Cather is generally darker than my own. Still, their description of the psychocultural situation of the women writers of Cather's generation may help to account for some of the marks of stress on her *Jewett*: "Turn-of-the-century and twentieth-century women writers, finding themselves for the first time in possession of a uniquely female literary history, have frequently sought to ensure the viability of their own literary future by paradoxically sending love 'forward' into the past, 'forward' into the arms of powerful aesthetic foremothers. At the same time, though, such writers have at last begun to experience an anxiety about the binds and burdens of the past that can be understood in terms comparable to (if different from) those Harold Bloom extrapolates from Freud's writings about psychosexual development." See *The War of the Words* 165–224, esp. 167.

30. Indeed, Cather's choices have arguably defined the parameters of the Jewett canon from 1925 to present. Of the eleven stories she included in the volume of short stories that accompanied *The Country of the Pointed Firs*, "A White Heron," which she placed in the lead-off position, has been the most frequently anthologized and studied of Jewett's works. Recently, "Martha's Lady," "Miss Tempy's Watchers," "The Town Poor," and "The Dulham Ladies" have earned attention as studies of women's relationships and communities, while "The Flight of Betsey Lane" has been celebrated as a portrait of an elderly female rebel. Cather's remaining selections, including "Going to Shrewsbury," "The Only Rose," "The Guests of Mrs. Timms," "Aunt Cynthy Dallett," and "The Hiltons'

Holiday," which she included because it was one of Jewett's personal favorites, have drawn less popular and critical attention, but what is also striking is all that Cather's effort to determine "the best" of Jewett has pushed out of literary history. She offers nothing Jewett published before 1886, which omits the excursion narratives from *Country By-Ways*, and she ignores all of her forays into the gothic. These biases have generally persisted, though feminist critics have begun to consider Jewett's interest in the supernatural. See, for example, Elizabeth Ammons, "Jewett's Witches," in Gwen L. Nagel, ed., *Critical Essays on Sarah Orne Jewett* (Boston: G. K. Hall, 1984) 165–84. To my mind, though, Cather's decision to exclude "The Passing of Sister Barsett" from the ranks of Jewett's "best" stories is an oversight history has yet to rectify. Its slyly comic treatment of women's rituals, relationships, and duties as caretakers suggests that Jewett was far less sentimental than many of her critics have proven to be—and it is also a decidedly "better" story than "The Hiltons' Holiday."

31. See Marco A. Portales, "The History of a Text: Jewett's *The Country of the Pointed Firs*," *New England Quarterly* 55.4 (December 1982): 586–92, for a good summary of the textual problems with *Pointed Firs*. I should point out that the fault here isn't entirely Cather's, because she was in part going along with a precedent established in a posthumous edition (1910) of Jewett's works, which had inserted "William's Wedding" and "A Dunnet Shepherdess" into *Pointed Firs*. Still, instead of correcting what was clearly a mistake (though a mistake authorized by Jewett's sister Mary), Cather's remaking of Jewett's text perpetuated it and complicated matters further by adding "The Queen's Twin" into the mix.

32. Charles Miner Thompson, "The Art of Miss Jewett," *Atlantic Monthly* 94 (October 1904): 491. Cather would likely have connected Jewett to Hawthorne even without Thompson's precedent, but she was familiar with his essay. An excerpt from it serves as the epigraph to *The Best Stories of Sarah Orne Jewett*. Thus, instead of the piece of "old-lady-poetry" that Cather so reviled, the volumes are preceded by Thompson's paean to "the trailing arbutus," because this "fragrant, retiring, exquisite flower, which I think [Miss Jewett] would say is the symbol of New England virtue, is the symbol also of her own modest and delightful art."

33. Absent from the family photograph I have snapped in this analysis is, I realize, a grandmother figure. From Jewett's letters and from her fiction, we may suppose that Harriet Beecher Stowe would be the most serious contender for this spot, but Cather would never have ranked *Uncle Tom's Cabin* up with *Pointed Firs*, *The Scarlet Letter*, or *Huckleberry Finn* because she would have found both its politics and its religion too heavy-handed for her taste. Indeed, in the only commentary on Stowe I have located, Cather disparages *Uncle Tom's Cabin* as "the work of a woman who sat up under cold skies of the north and tried to write of one of the warmest, richest and most highly-colored civilizations the world has ever known, a Puritan blue-stocking who tried to blend the savage blood of the jungle and the romance of Creole civilization." See *KA* 269–70. In Cather's eyes,

Stowe is both an inauthentic regionalist and a failed romancer—and a "blue-stocking" to boot. In Cather's literary family of high achievers, Stowe would clearly have been out of place, though, as I note in the conclusion to this study, her novel of slavery, *Sapphira and the Slave Girl*, clearly draws upon *Uncle Tom's Cabin*, most notably in the story of Nancy's escape along the underground railroad.

34. Pound's essay, "The History of English Literature: What It Is and What It Is Not," originally appeared in the *English Journal* 7 (September 1918): 413–18. It is reprinted in *Selected Writings of Louise Pound* (1949; Westport, CT: Greenwood, 1971) 269–74.

35. Obviously I refer to the 1925 version of the preface to *Jewett* and not the essay version printed in *Not Under Forty* (76–95), in which she omits the yoking together of *Pointed Firs*, *The Scarlet Letter*, and *Huckleberry Finn* and, instead of the optimistic image of a future student discovering Jewett's text, she offers a sardonic, xenophobic, and anti-Semitic view of contemporary students rejecting it. Those troubling revisions are discussed in my conclusion, which looks at Cather's work in the 1930s.

36. Tompkins uses the phrase "Masterpiece Theater" to describe the politics of Hawthorne's reputation—i.e., the ways in which his "relation to the mechanisms that produced literary and cultural opinion" helped to create and sustain his place in the foreground of the culture of the nineteenth century (29)—which she analyzes in *Sensational Designs*.

37. This interesting essay of 1916 is reprinted in Rosowski and Slote. A later passage suggests that Walter Benn Michaels oversimplifies matters when he claims that the biological "vanishing" of the Native Americans made possible their birth as a pure and exemplary "culture" (*Our America* 38). Though it may be true that *The Professor's House* features only the artifacts of dead Indians, *Death Comes for the Archbishop* features a number of "living" Indians, and Cather's essay about visiting the Mesa Verde makes clear that she recognized the Anasazis of the region were not, as Tom's mentor Father Duchene theorizes, "utterly exterminated" (198), but that some of their descendants survived in the pueblo cultures of the early twentieth century:

> One has only to go down into Hopiland to find the same life going on today on other mesa tops; houses like these, kivas like these, ceremonial and religious implements like these—every detail preserved with the utmost fidelity. When you see those ancient, pyramidal pueblos once more brought nearer by the sunset light that beats on them like gold-beaters' hammers, when the aromatic pinion smoke begins to curl up in the still air and the boys bring in the cattle and the old Indians come out in their white burnouses and take their accustomed grave positions upon the housetops, you begin to feel that custom, ritual, integrity of tradition have a reality that goes deeper than the bustling business of the world.

Obviously, Cather is guilty here of a certain romantic racialism, but her development of the cliff-dwellers' world as an indigenous American cultural ideal is
rooted in her experiences among the living Indians of "Hopiland," who, though
vanish*ing*, for her were never really vanish*ed*.

38. Eve Sedgwick briefly discusses "Tom Outland's Story" as a "gorgeous
homosocial romance" that served to "refract and decompress the conditions of a
lesbian love and creativity" for Cather. See Sedgwick, "Across Gender, Across
Sexuality" 68–9.

39. Daniel Defoe, *Robinson Crusoe* (1719; New York: Norton Critical, 1975) 80.

40. In 1938 Cather did publicly acknowledge the parallels between Tom's
discovery of the ruins on Blue Mesa and Richard Wetherill's experiences at
Mesa Verde in a letter to Alfred Knopf's son, Pat, which was published in the
College English Association's newsletter (*LL* 370) and then in *On Writing*. In
explaining the experiment in form she was attempting in *The Professor's House*,
Cather writes that "Tom Outland's Story" was a window that opened upon St.
Peter's "overcrowded and stuffy" house to "let in the fresh air that blew off the
Blue Mesa, and the fine disregard of trivialities which was in Tom Outland's face
and in his behaviour." This, she says, "concerned me as a writer only, but *the Blue
Mesa (Mesa Verde)* actually was discovered by a young cowpuncher in just this
way" (*OW* 31–2, emphasis added). Cather's letter also indicates familiarity with
Gustaf Nordenskiold's *The Cliff Dwellers of the Mesa Verde* (1893; New York:
AMS, 1973), the most authoritative scientific account of the ruins and the arti-
facts on the mesa that would have been available when she was writing *The
Professor's House*.

41. One oft cited example of Cather's contempt for suffragists in particular is
her 1898 review of Elizabeth Cady Stanton's *The Woman's Bible*, which she
describes as a "valuable contribution to the humorous literature of the day" compiled by a group of "estimable ladies, who, without scholarship, without linguistic attainments, without theological training, not even able to read the Bible in
the original tongues, set themselves upon a task which has baffled the ripest scholarship and most profound learning" (*WP* 2:538–9). From the fiction, the
Prohibitionist Enid Royce Wheeler in *One of Ours* is the most detailed portrait of
the woman activist as neurotic extremist, though Wick Cutter's unpleasant wife
in *My Ántonia*, whom Jim describes as "a terrifying-looking person; almost a
giantess in height" (162), is found guilty of merely resembling hunger-striking
suffragists. "I have found Mrs. Cutters all over the world," Jim concludes, "sometimes founding new religions, sometimes being forcibly fed—easily recognizable,
even when superficially tamed" (164).

42. Such suspicion was widespread during the period of backlash and disappointment that followed the Great War and ratification of the Nineteenth
Amendment. See Flexner 306–24 on the difficult last stages of the fight for
women's suffrage and O'Neill 225–63 for the attacks on progressive politics and
women's organizations during the 1920s.

4. Comrades and Countrymen: Queer Love and a Dream of "America"

1. Woodress provides an overview of these attacks. See esp. 465, 469. Cather responded to her critics in a 1936 letter to *The Commonweal*, in which she sarcastically reflects upon "the Art of 'Escape' ":"Isn't the phrase tautological? What has art ever been but escape?" See *OW* 18–29. This letter shows Cather at her most defensive, though her point that the cause of social reform may be better served by serious political discussion and action than by writing or reading fiction seems not entirely unreasonable.

2. Sharon O'Brien,"Entering Jacinto's Cave:The Politics of Culture in *Death Comes for the Archbishop*," paper delivered at Willa Cather:The Fourth National Seminar, 1990.

3. See James Axtell, *The Invasion Within:The Contest of Cultures in Colonial North America* (New York: Oxford U P, 1985). Axtell's discussion focuses primarily on the contest among English, French, and Indian cultures of eastern North America, but the notion of competing and interacting cultures accurately describes the situation in the Southwest as well.

4. In a *Journal* column of 1896, Cather felt compelled to attack Whitman as "a poet without the exclusive sense of the poetic, a man without the finer discrimination, enjoying everything with the unreasoning enthusiasm of a boy," but she also acknowledged admiration for the "primitive elemental force" about "this optimistic vagabond." She seems, indeed, to have found his "enthusiasm" contagious:"His veneration for things physical and material, for all that is in water or air or land, is so real that as you read him you think for the moment that you would rather like to live so if you could. For the time you half believe that a sound body and a strong arm are the greatest things in the world." See *WP*1:279–82.

5. I refer, of course, to Fiedler's argument in *Love and Death in the American Novel* that a "homoerotic fable" (349) lies at the heart of much major American fiction, a fable in which "innocent" love between men is a flight from "respectability and belongingness" (362). Fiedler's insights into the operations of that "fable" are both dazzling and troubling, given his Freudian assumptions that such a tale is "juvenile,""regressive," and "narcissistic" (348). For some contemporary contestations of Fiedler's model, see Boone 226–77 and Looby.

6. Walt Whitman, "For You O Democracy," in Harold W. Blodgett and Sculley Bradley, eds., *Leaves of Grass* (New York: Norton, 1968) 117. Future references to poems in this edition will be made parenthetically within the text by title.

7. See Gertrude Stein,"Miss Furr and Miss Skeene," in Carl Van Vechten, ed., *Selected Writings of Gertrude Stein* (New York:Vintage, 1972) 564 and Virginia Woolf, *Mrs. Dalloway* (1925; New York and London: Harcourt Brace Jovanovich, 1953) 52.

8. For a discussion of the homoerotic, specular economy of *Leaves of Grass* and other Whitman texts, see Moon, *Disseminating Whitman* 62–87.

9. Julie Abraham comments insightfully on the limitations so far in critical discussions, including Sedgwick's reading of "Paul's Case," of lesbian writing about male homosociality/sexuality. She argues that such analyses have tended to "view the female couple as the privileged site of lesbian presence in a text" and assume that "If lesbians writers could do what they wanted or would do what they should, . . . they would write about lesbian couples" (32–5). I agree with Abraham's assessment of the limits as well as the implied prescriptivism of an interpretive practice dominated by the assumption that lesbian writers would or should write "lesbian novels"—i.e., realistic narratives of relationship constructed more or less out of the old plots of heterosexual desire.

Also, for a critique of Sedgwick's closet model as a way of theorizing homosexuality, see Van Leer 99–131.

10. Walter Benn Michaels also notes the importance of conversion in *Archbishop* as a way of solving "the problem of Americanization" (*Our America* 78).

11. The "calamity" to which Austin refers here is the one perpetrated by Archbishop Lamy, the historical figure upon whom Cather's Latour is based, who actually built the cathedral in Santa Fe. What so riles Austin is that she sees Cather as sympathetic to the Archbishop's imposition of French style upon the local culture. See *Earth Horizon* (Boston: Houghton Mifflin, 1932) 359. Austin's criticism got Cather so riled in turn that she subsequently denied having written any of *Archbishop* at Austin's home in Santa Fe and stopped corresponding with her altogether.

12. O'Brien makes a similar point about Latour in "Entering Jacinto's Cave." As I have already noted, she suggests that he is ideologically monolithic, while the text and Cather are less certain and more divided.

13. The notion of cultural "syncretism" is borrowed from Werner Sollors's *Beyond Ethnicity: Consent and Descent in American Culture* (New York: Oxford UP, 1986). Sollors argues that by placing an exclusive emphasis on a writer's descent—and placing her or him, for example, among Jewish-American or African-American or Italian-American writers—ethnic literary history so far has obscured "the pervasiveness and inventiveness of syncretism"—"the cultural interplays and contacts among writers of different backgrounds, the mergers and secessions that took place in America" (14–15). Cather's constant borrowings from history and ethnic cultures other than her "own" suggest that her vision of literary history was similarly syncretic.

14. The exception to this pattern of apparently successful marriages across ethnic lines is that of the murderous Buck Scales and his wife Magdalena. The narrative acknowledges the potential for danger in marrying outside one's own ethnic group: "All white men knew [Scales] for a dog and a degenerate—but to Mexican girls, marriage with an American meant coming up in the world" (71–2). That Scales has murdered three children produced in his marriage to Magdalena suggests that the "dog" stands for a hatred of racial intermixture which the text clearly condemns.

15. Another echo of Mary Austin's work on Native American literatures may

well enter into *Archbishop* here. In *American Rhythm*, Austin had written on the compactness of Native American expression: "No Indian ever says all his thought. Always there is some petal left furled, some secret untransfixed to be exhaled as a delicate perfume upon the inner sense" (60).

16. For a "de-glossying" of Cather's view of one important aspect of the history that lies behind *Archbishop*, see the essays in *Padre Martinez: New Perspectives from Taos* (Taos, NM: Millicent Rogers Museum, 1988).

17. Lawrence's essay originally appeared, with illustrations, in *Theatre Arts Monthly* 8:12 (December 1924): 836–60. The version I cite is the one reprinted, along with Lawrence's original shorter essay that incensed his hostess Mabel Dodge Luhan because of its lack of "vision," in Keith Sagar, ed., *D.H. Lawrence and New Mexico* (Salt Lake City: G. M. Smith, 1982) 63–72; quoted here from 65–6. Future references to this essay will be made parenthetically within the text by page number.

18. West's review is important because it is a contemporary assessment of Cather and Lawrence that reckons with their mutual attraction to the Southwestern landscape and is sympathetic to both writers. In considering the "difference in their daring," however, West seems concerned that Lawrence's "transcendental courage" and "ambition" will appeal more to modern readers than Cather's "grace." She imagines, for example, that Lawrence would have "been through the hole in the wall after the snake" had he written the scene in Jacinto's cave but says that Cather passes through the experience "responding sensitively and powerfully to its splendid portentousness, but [staying] with the Bishop the whole time" rather than trying, as Lawrence would, to respond to "an imperative call to further adventure" (6). West's praise for *Archbishop* is haunted by the same kinds of anxieties about gender and reception that haunted Cather during this period, as West worries that readers will conclude that Lawrence's desire "to extend consciousness beyond its present limits and elevate man above himself [will] entitle his art to be ranked as more important than that of Miss Cather" (6). She never identifies gender as a factor that might account for the "difference in their daring," but the terms she uses to spell out that difference—i.e., "ambition" versus "grace"—are clearly gender-marked. West was, of course, a very active and self-conscious feminist. Cather was familiar with West's work, offering an approving reference to her book, *The Strange Necessity* (1928), in a letter of 1943. See Willa Cather, letter to Mr. Phillipson, 15 March 1943, Willa Cather Historical Center, Red Cloud, Nebraska.

Conclusion. Queer (R)age: Notes on the Late Fiction and the Queering of the World

1. My argument here is in part a response to remarks made by Claudia Tate at the Cather Seminar. Tate suggested that the "real desires" of the text are same-sex desires and tied the enigmas of the novel back to Cather's history of cross-dressing and literary masquerading. Though I agree that desire in *Sapphira* is displaced onto the body of the black female (Nancy), I strongly object to the causal

reasoning that underlies Tate's claims, which seems to me homophobic in its implications, though not in its intentions.

2. Blanche Knopf expresses the hope that Cather is "seriously thinking about doing the Virginia book" in a letter of 1931, but Woodress reports that she actually wrote *Sapphira* between the spring of 1937 and the summer of 1940 (478–80). See Blanche Knopf, letter to Willa Cather, 28 April 1931, Box 689, Folder 1, Alfred A. Knopf, Inc. Archives, Harry Ransom Humanities Research Center, University of Texas.

3. See especially the first four chapters of *Within the Plantation Household*, particularly "The View from the Big House," which speaks both to Sapphira's skills as a manager and to her remoteness from the actual work of the household.

4. My discussion of disability in *Sapphira* has benefited from Rosemarie Thomson's analysis of "benevolent maternalism" in sentimental constructions of disability. See *Extraordinary Bodies* 81–102.

5. Deborah Carlin's discussion of the narrative puzzles of the novel and the way they dramatize the text's preoccupation with "the burden of the past" is much more detailed than what I offer here. See *Cather, Canon, and the Politics of Reading* 150–76.

6. The now defunct *OUT/LOOK: National Lesbian and Gay Quarterly* announced the "birth of a queer nation" in its winter 1991 issue. A number of articles in that issue, including Allan Bérubé and Jeffrey Escoffier's "Queer/Nation," trace the history and seek to define the goals and strategies of "a new generation of activists" (12). Bérubé and Escoffier articulate the purposeful amorphousness of the term "queer." One of the goals of the "new generation" is, they write, "to bring together people who have been made to feel perverse, queer, odd, outcast, different, and deviant" (12).

7. Jane Gallop discusses the role of Showalter's essay and others published in the same issue of *Critical Inquiry* in signaling the institutional establishment of feminist literary criticism in *Around 1981: Academic Feminist Literary Theory*. I single out Showalter's oft reprinted essay because it was an influential effort to map out the discipline of feminist criticism.

8. In L. Frank Baum's original version of *The Wizard of Oz*, which was published in 1900, Dorothy wore silver slippers like Eden Bower's and not the ruby slippers made famous in the film. Joseph Urgo, in the epilogue to *Willa Cather and the Myth of American Migration*, discusses *The Wizard of Oz* as an exemplary text of a culture of wanderers. I tuck in this allusion to the children's story and the film because I am struck by the similarity between Eden Bower and Baum's Dorothy and because the filmic Dorothy and her keen sense of fashion are also icons in gay/queer culture.

Works Cited

Abraham, Julie. *Are Girls Necessary? Lesbian Writing and Modern Histories*. New York and London: Routledge, 1996.

Acocella, Joan. "Cather and the Academy." *New Yorker* 27 November 1995: 56–71.

Adams, Timothy Dow. "My Gay Ántonia: The Politics of Willa Cather's Lesbianism." *Historical, Literary, and Erotic Aspects of Lesbianism*. Ed. Monika Kehoe. New York: Harrington Park Press, 1986. 89–98.

Addams, Jane. "Lack of Moral Education and Its Dangers." Ch. 3 of *A New Conscience and an Ancient Evil. McClure's* 38 (January 1912): 338–44.

Ammons, Elizabeth. "The Engineer as Cultural Hero and Willa Cather's First Novel, *Alexander's Bridge." American Quarterly* 38.5 (1986): 746–60.

Austin, Mary. *American Rhythm*. 1923; New York: Cooper Square Publishers, 1970.

———. "Regionalism in American Fiction." *English Journal* 21.2 (February 1932): 97–107.

Banta, Martha. *Imaging American Women: Idea and Ideals in Cultural History*. New York: Columbia UP, 1987.

Baym, Nina. "Melodramas of Beset Manhood: How Theories of American Fiction Exclude Women Authors." *The New Feminist Criticism: Essays on Women, Literature, and Theory*. Ed. Elaine Showalter. New York: Pantheon, 1985. 63–80.

Bederman, Gail. *Manliness & Civilization: A Cultural History of Gender and Race in the United States, 1880–1917*. Chicago and London: U of Chicago P, 1995.

Bennett, Mildred. *The World of Willa Cather*. 1951; Lincoln and London: U of Nebraska P, 1989.

Benstock, Shari. *Women of the Left Bank: Paris, 1900–1940*. Austin: U of Texas P, 1986.

Berlant, Lauren. "The Queen of America Goes to Washington City: Harriet Jacobs, Frances Harper, Anita Hill." *American Literature* 65.3 (1993): 549–74.

Berlant, Lauren, and Michael Warner. "What Does Queer Theory Teach Us about X?" *PMLA* 110.3 (May 1995): 343–9.

Berlant, Lauren, and Elizabeth Freeman. "Queer Nationality." Warner 193–229.

Bérubé, Allan, and Jeffrey Escoffier. "Queer/Nation." *OUT/LOOK: National Lesbian and Gay Quarterly* 11 (Winter 1991): 12–14.

Bohlke, L. Brent, ed. *Willa Cather in Person: Interviews, Speeches, and Letters*. Lincoln and London: U of Nebraska P, 1986.

Boone, Joseph A. *Tradition Counter Tradition: Love and the Form of Fiction*. Chicago: U of Chicago P, 1987.

Bronfen, Elisabeth. *Over Her Dead Body: Death, Femininity, and the Aesthetic*. New York: Routledge, 1992.

Brooks, Peter. *Body Work: Objects of Desire in Modern Narrative*. Cambridge: Harvard UP, 1993.

Bruccoli, Matthew J. " 'An Instance of Apparent Plagiarism': F. Scott Fitzgerald, Willa Cather, and the First *Gatsby* Manuscript." *The Princeton University Library Chronicle* 39 (1977–1978): 171–8.

Butler, Judith. *Bodies That Matter: On the Discursive Limits of "Sex"*. New York and London: Routledge, 1993.

———. "Critically Queer." *GLQ: A Journal of Lesbian and Gay Studies* 1.1 (1993): 17–32.

———. "Status, Conduct, Word, and Deed: A Response to Janet Halley." *GLQ: A Journal of Lesbian and Gay Studies* 3.2–3 (1996): 253–9.

Carafiol, Peter. "Commentary: After American Literature." *American Literary History* 4.3 (1992): 539–49.

Carlin, Deborah. *Cather, Canon, and the Politics of Reading*. Amherst: U of Massachusetts P, 1992.

Case, Sue-Ellen. "Toward a Butch-Femme Aesthetic." *The Lesbian and Gay Studies Reader*. Eds. Henry Abelove, Michèle Aina Barale, and David M. Halperin. New York and London: Routledge, 1993. 294–306.

———. "Tracking the Vampire." *differences* 3.2 (Summer 1991): 1–20.

Castle, Terry. *The Apparitional Lesbian: Female Homosexuality and Modern Culture*. New York: Columbia UP, 1993.

Chalon, Jean. *Portrait of a Seductress: The World of Natalie Barney*. Trans. Carol Barko. New York: Crown, 1979.

Chauncey, George. "Christian Brotherhood or Sexual Perversion? Homosexual Identities and the Construction of Sexual Boundaries in the World War I Era." Duberman 294–317.

———. *Gay New York: Gender, Urban Culture, and the Making of the Gay Male World, 1890–1940*. New York: Basic, 1994.

Chee, Alexander S. "A Queer Nationalism." *OUT/LOOK: National Lesbian and Gay Quarterly* 11 (Winter 1991): 15–19.

Chown, Linda. " 'It Came Closer than That': Willa Cather's *Lucy Gayheart*." *Cather Studies* 2 (1993): 118–39.

Cornell, Drucilla. "Gender, Sex, and Equivalent Rights." *Feminists Theorize the Political*. Eds. Judith Butler and Joan W. Scott. New York and London: Routledge, 1992. 280–96.

Cramer, Timothy R. "Claude's Case: A Study of the Homosexual Temperament in Willa Cather's *One of Ours.*" *South Dakota Review* 31.3 (Fall 1993): 147–60.

de Grazia, Margreta. "Sanctioning Voice: Quotation Marks, the Abolition of Torture, and the Fifth Amendment." *The Construction of Authorship: TextualAppropriation in Law and Literature.* Eds. Martha Woodmansee and Peter Jaszi. Durham and London: Duke UP, 1994. 281–302.

de Lauretis, Teresa. *The Practice of Love: Lesbian Sexuality and Perverse Desire.* Bloomington: Indiana UP, 1994.

——. "Sexual Indifference and Lesbian Representation." *The Lesbian and Gay Studies Reader.* Eds. Henry Abelove, Michèle Aina Barale, and David M. Halperin. New York and London: Routledge, 1993. 141–57.

D'Emilio, John, and Estelle B. Freedman. *Intimate Matters: A History of Sexuality in America.* New York: Harper and Row, 1988.

Donovan, Josephine. *After the Fall: The Demeter-Persephone Myth in Wharton, Cather, and Glasgow.* University Park and London: The Pennsylvania State UP, 1989.

Douglas, Ann. *Terrible Honesty: Mongrel Manhattan in the 1920s.* New York: Farrar, Straus and Giroux, 1995.

Duberman, Martin, Martha Vicinus, and George Chauncey, Jr., eds. *Hidden From History: Reclaiming the Gay and Lesbian Past.* New York: NAL, 1989.

Duggan, Lisa. "Making It Perfectly Queer." *Socialist Review* 22.1 (January/March 1992): 11–31.

——. "The Trials of Alice Mitchell: Sensationalism, Sexology, and the Lesbian Subject in Turn-of-the-Century America." *Signs* 18.4 (Summer 1993): 791–814.

Edelman, Lee. "Queer Theory: Unstating Desire." *GLQ: A Journal of Lesbian and Gay Studies* 2.4 (1995): 343–8.

Faderman, Lillian. *Chloe Plus Olivia: An Anthology of Lesbian Literature from the Seventeenth Century to the Present.* New York: Penguin, 1994.

——. *Odd Girls and Twilight Lovers: A History of Lesbian Life in Twentieth-Century America.* New York: Columbia UP, 1991.

——. *Surpassing the Love of Men: Romantic Friendship and Love Between Women from the Renaissance to the Present.* New York: Morrow, 1981.

Fetterley, Judith. "*My Ántonia*, Jim Burden, and the Dilemma of the Lesbian Writer." *Lesbian Texts and Contexts.* Eds. Karla Jay and Joanne Glasgow. New York: New York UP, 1990. 145–63.

——. "Willa Cather and the Fiction of Female Development." *Anxious Power: Reading, Writing, and Ambivalence in Narrative by Women.* Eds. Carol J. Singley and Susan Elizabeth Sweeney. Albany: State U of New York P, 1993. 221–34.

Fiedler, Leslie A. *Love and Death in the American Novel.* 1960, rev. 1966; New York: Stein and Day, 1975.

Fields, Annie, ed. *Letters of Sarah Orne Jewett.* Boston and New York: Houghton Mifflin, 1911.

FitzGerald, Edward. *The Rubaiyat of Omar Khayyam.* Illus. Elihu Vedder. Boston: Houghton Mifflin, 1884.

Flannigan, John H. "Thea Kronborg's Vocal Transvestism: Willa Cather and the 'Voz Contralto.' " *Modern Fiction Studies* 40.4 (Winter 1994): 737–63.

Flexner, Eleanor. *Century of Struggle: The Woman's Rights Movement in the United States.* Cambridge, MA: Belknap, 1959.

Foucault, Michel. *Madness and Civilization: A History of Insanity in the Age of Reason.* Trans. Richard Howard. 1965; New York: Vintage, 1988.

———. *The Use of Pleasure.* Trans. Robert Hurley. 1985; New York: Vintage, 1990.

Fox-Genovese, Elizabeth. *Within the Plantation Household: Black and White Women of the Old South.* Chapel Hill and London: U of North Carolina P, 1988.

Friedman, Susan Stanford. "Creativity and the Childbirth Metaphor: Gender Difference in Literary Discourse." *Feminisms: An Anthology of Literary Theory and Criticism.* Eds. Robyn R. Warhol and Diane Price Herndl. New Brunswick: Rutgers UP, 1991. 371–96.

Fryer, Judith. *Felicitous Space: The Imaginative Structures of Edith Wharton and Willa Cather.* Chapel Hill and London: U of North Carolina P, 1986.

Gardner, Jared. " 'Our Native Clay': Racial and Sexual Identity and the Making of Americans in *The Bridge.*" *American Quarterly* 44.1 (1992): 24–50.

Gelfant, Blanche. "The Forgotten Reaping-Hook: Sex in *My Ántonia.*" *Women Writing in America.* 1971; Hanover, NH: UP of New England, 1984. 94–116.

———. "Movement and Melody: The Disembodiment of *Lucy Gayheart.*" *Women Writing in America.* 119–43.

Gilbert, Sandra M., and Susan Gubar. *No Man's Land: The Place of the Woman Writer in the Twentieth Century.* 3 vols. (*The War of the Worlds, Sexchanges,* and *Letters from the Front*). New Haven: Yale UP, 1988–94.

Gustafson, Neil. "Getting Back to Cather's Text: The Shared Dream in *O Pioneers!*" *Western American Literature* 30.2 (1995): 151–62.

Haller, John S., and Robin M. Haller. *The Physician and Sexuality in Victorian America.* 1974; New York: Norton, 1977.

Halley, Janet E. "The Status/Conduct Distinction in the 1993 Revisions to Military Anti-Gay Policy: A Legal Archaeology." *GLQ: A Journal of Lesbian and Gay Studies* 3.2–3 (1996):159–252.

Halperin, David. *Saint Foucault: Towards a Gay Hagiography.* New York: Oxford UP, 1995.

Haraway, Donna. "The Biopolitics of Postmodern Bodies: Determination of Self in Immune System Discourse." *American Feminist Thought at Century's End: A Reader.* Ed. Linda S. Kauffman. Cambridge: Blackwell, 1993. 199–233.

———. "Teddy Bear Patriarchy: Taxidermy in the Garden of Eden, New York City, 1908–1936." *Cultures of United States Imperialism.* Eds. Amy Kaplan and Donald E. Pease. Durham and London: Duke UP, 1993. 237–91.

Hawthorne, Nathaniel. *The Scarlet Letter,* 1850; New York: Norton Critical, 1978.

Higham, John. *Strangers in the Land: Patterns of American Nativism, 1860–1925.* 1955; Westport, CT: Greenwood, 1981.

Irving, Katrina. "Displacing Homosexuality: The Use of Ethnicity in Willa Cather's *My Ántonia.*" *Modern Fiction Studies* 36.1 (Spring 1990): 91–102.

James, Henry. *The Portrait of a Lady.* 1881; New York: Norton Critical, 1975.

Jewett, Sarah Orne. *Country By-Ways.* Boston: Houghton Mifflin, 1881.

Kaplan, Amy, and Donald E. Pease, eds. *Cultures of United States Imperialism.* Durham and London: Duke UP, 1993.

Katz, Jonathan Ned. *Gay/Lesbian Almanac: A New Documentary.* New York: Harper, 1983.

Kauffman, Linda S. *Discourses of Desire: Gender, Genre, and Epistolary Fictions.* Ithaca and London: Cornell UP, 1986.

———. *Special Delivery: Epistolary Modes in Modern Fiction.* Chicago: U of Chicago P, 1992.

King, Katie. *Theory in Its Feminist Travels: Conversations in U.S. Women's Movements.* Bloomington and Indianapolis: Indiana UP, 1994.

Koestenbaum, Wayne. *The Queen's Throat: Opera, Homosexuality, and the Mystery of Desire.* New York: Poseidon Press, 1993.

Kolodny, Annette. *The Land Before Her: Fantasy and Experience of the American Frontiers, 1630–1860.* Chapel Hill and London: U of North Carolina P, 1984.

———. *The Lay of the Land: Metaphor as Experience and History in American Life and Letters.* Chapel Hill: U of North Carolina P, 1975.

———. "Letting Go Our Grand Obsessions: Notes Toward a New Literary History of the Frontiers." *Subjects and Citizens: Nation, Race, and Gender from Oroonoko to Anita Hill.* Eds. Michael Moon and Cathy N. Davidson. Durham: Duke UP, 1995. 9–26.

Kutzinski, Vera M. "Commentary: American Literary History as Spatial Practice." *American Literary History* 4.3 (Fall 1992): 550–7.

la Biennale di Venezia. *Identity and Alterity: Figures of the Body, 1895/1995.* Venice: Marsilio Editori, 1995.

Lauter, Paul. "Race and Gender in the Shaping of the American Literary Canon: A Case Study from the Twenties." *Feminist Studies* 9.3 (1983): 435–63.

Lawrence, D. H. *Studies in Classic American Literature.* 1923; New York: Penguin, 1981.

Lee, Hermione. *Willa Cather: Double Lives.* New York: Pantheon, 1989.

Leonardi, Susan, and Rebecca Pope. *The Diva's Mouth: Body, Voice, Prima Donna Politics.* New Brunswick: Rutgers UP, 1996.

Lewis, Edith. *Willa Cather Living.* New York: Knopf, 1953.

Lindemann, Marilee. Introduction. *Alexander's Bridge.* By Willa Cather. Oxford and New York: Oxford UP, 1997. vii–xxxiii.

———. " 'It Ain't My Prairie': Gender, Power, and Narrative in *My Ántonia.*" *New Essays on* My Ántonia. Ed. Sharon O'Brien. Cambridge: Cambridge UP, 1999. 111–35.

Looby, Christopher. " 'Innocent Homosexuality': The Fiedler Thesis in Retrospect." *Adventures of Huckleberry Finn: A Case Study in Critical*

Controversy. Eds. Gerald Graff and James Phelan. Boston and New York: Bedford, 1995. 535–50.

Michaels, Walter Benn. *Our America: Nativism, Modernism, and Pluralism*. Durham and London: Duke UP, 1995.

———. "Romance and Real Estate." *The American Renaissance Reconsidered*. Eds. Michaels and Donald E. Pease. Baltimore and London: Johns Hopkins UP, 1985. 156–82.

Middleton, Jo Ann. *Willa Cather's Modernism*. London and Toronto: Associated UP, 1990.

Mignon, Charles, with Kari Ronning, eds. *My Ántonia*. By Willa Cather. Lincoln and London: U of Nebraska P, 1994.

Miller, Harold T. "Houghton Mifflin Company." Princeton: Newcomen Society, 1984.

Moon, Michael. "Disseminating Whitman." *South Atlantic Quarterly* 88.1 (1989): 247–65.

———. *Disseminating Whitman: Revision and Corporeality in* Leaves of Grass. Cambridge and London: Harvard UP, 1991.

———. "Preface: Unnatural Formations." *American Literature* 69.1 (March 1997): 1–4.

Morrison, Toni. *Playing in the Dark: Whiteness and the Literary Imagination*. New York: Vintage, 1993.

Murphy, John, ed. *Critical Essays on Willa Cather*. Boston: G. K. Hall, 1983.

O'Brien, Sharon. "Becoming Noncanonical: The Case against Willa Cather." *Reading in America: Literature and Social History*. Ed. Cathy N. Davidson. Baltimore: Johns Hopkins UP, 1989. 240–58.

———. "Combat Envy and Survivor Guilt: Willa Cather's 'Manly Battle Yarn.' " *Arms and the Woman: War, Gender, and Literary Representation*. Eds. Helen Cooper, Adrienne Munich, and Susan Squier. Chapel Hill: U of North Carolina P, 1989. 184–204.

———. *Willa Cather: The Emerging Voice*. New York: Oxford UP, 1987.

———. *Willa Cather*. New York: Chelsea House Publishers, 1995.

O'Driscoll, Sally. "Outlaw Readings: Beyond Queer Theory." *Signs* 22.1 (Autumn 1996): 30–51.

O'Neill, William L. *Everyone Was Brave: A History of Feminism in America*. Chicago: Quadrangle, 1969.

Pease, Donald E., ed. *National Identities and Post-Americanist Narratives*. Durham and London: Duke UP, 1994.

Petry, Alice Hall. "Harvey's Case: Notes on Cather's 'The Sculptor's Funeral.' " *South Dakota Review* 24.3 (Fall 1986): 108–16.

Poovey, Mary. "The Abortion Question and the Death of Man." *Feminists Theorize the Political*. Eds. Judith Butler and Joan W. Scott. New York and London: Routledge, 1992. 239–79.

Quirk, Tom. "Fitzgerald and Cather: *The Great Gatsby*." *American Literature* 54.4 (December 1982): 576–91.

Reynolds, Guy. *Willa Cather in Context: Progress, Race, Empire*. New York: St. Martin's, 1996.

Romer v. Evans. 116 S. Ct. 1620 (1996).

Roof, Judith. *Come As You Are: Sexuality and Narrative*. New York: Columbia UP, 1996.

Rosowski, Susan, *The Voyage Perilous: Willa Cather's Romanticism*. Lincoln and London: U of Nebraska P, 1986.

Rosowski, Susan, and Bernice Slote. "Willa Cather's 1916 Mesa Verde Essay." *Prairie Schooner* 58.5 (Winter 1984): 81–92.

Rubin, Larry. "The Homosexual Motif in Willa Cather's 'Paul's Case.'" *Studies in Short Fiction* 12 (1975): 127–31.

Russ, Joanna. "To Write 'Like a Woman': Transformations of Identity in the Work of Willa Cather." *Historical, Literary, and Erotic Aspects of Lesbianism*. Ed. Monika Kehoe. New York: Harrington Park Press, 1986. 77–87.

Ryan, Maureen. "No Woman's Land: Gender in Willa Cather's *One of Ours*." *Studies in American Fiction* 18.1 (Spring 1990): 65–75.

Sahli, Nancy. "Smashing: Women's Relationships Before the Fall." *Chrysalis* 8 (Summer 1979): 17–27.

Said, Edward. *Orientalism*. New York: Vintage, 1979.

Sanchez-Eppler, Karen. *Touching Liberty: Abolition, Feminism, and the Politics of the Body*. Berkeley: U of California P, 1993.

Schwind, Jean. "The 'Beautiful' War in *One of Ours*." *Modern Fiction Studies*. 30.1 (Spring 1984): 53–71.

——. "The Benda Illustrations to *My Ántonia*: Cather's 'Silent' Supplement to Jim Burden's Narrative." *PMLA* 100.1 (January 1985): 51–67.

——. "This Is a Frame-Up: Mother Eve in *The Professor's House*." *Cather Studies* 2 (1993): 72–91.

Sedgwick, Eve Kosofsky. "Across Gender, Across Sexuality: Willa Cather and Others." *South Atlantic Quarterly* 88.1 (Winter 1989): 53–72.

——. *Between Men: English Literature and Male Homosocial Desire*. New York: Columbia UP, 1985.

——. *Epistemology of the Closet*. Berkeley: U of California P, 1990.

——. "Queer Peformativity: Henry James's *The Art of the Novel*." *GLQ: A Journal of Lesbian and Gay Studies* 1.1 (1993): 1–16.

——. *Tendencies*. Durham: Duke UP, 1993.

Shaw, Patrick W. "Victorian Rules and Left Bank Rebellion: Willa Cather and Gertrude Stein." *Willa Cather Pioneer Memorial Newsletter* 36.3 (Fall 1992): 23–7.

Shumway, David. *Creating American Civilization: A Genealogy of American Literature as an Academic Discipline*. Minneapolis: U of Minnesota P, 1994.

Skaggs, Merrill Maguire. *After the World Broke in Two: The Later Novels of Willa Cather*. Charlottesville and London: UP of Virginia, 1990.

Smith-Rosenberg, Carroll. *Disorderly Conduct: Visions of Gender in Victorian America*. New York: Knopf, 1985.

Sollors, Werner. *Beyond Ethnicity: Consent and Descent in American Culture.* New York and Oxford: Oxford UP, 1986.

Stein, Arlene. "Sisters and Queers: The Decentering of Lesbian Feminism." *Socialist Review* 22.1 (January–March 1992): 33–55.

Stineman, Esther Lanigan. *Mary Austin: Song of a Maverick.* New Haven and London: Yale UP, 1989.

Stoddard, Lothrop. *The Rising Tide of Color Against White World-Supremacy.* 1920; Westport, CT: Greenwood P, 1971.

Stone, Ruth. "Where I Came From." *Second-Hand Coat: Poems New and Selected.* Boston: Godine, 1987.

Summers, Claude J. " 'A Losing Game in the End': Aestheticism and Homosexuality in Cather's 'Paul's Case.' " *Modern Fiction Studies* 36.1 (Spring 1990): 103–19.

——, ed. *The Gay and Lesbian Literary Heritage.* New York: Henry Holt, 1995.

Sundquist, Eric, ed. "American Literary History: The Next Century." *American Literature* 67.4 (December 1995): 793–853.

Terry, Jennifer. "Theorizing Deviant Historiography." *differences: A Journal of Feminist Cultural Studies* 3.2 (1991): 55–74.

Thomson, Rosemarie Garland. *Extraordinary Bodies: Figuring Disability in American Culture and Literature.* New York: Columbia UP, 1996.

Tompkins, Jane. *Sensational Designs: The Cultural Work of American Fiction, 1790–1860.* New York and Oxford: Oxford UP, 1985.

Trachtenberg, Alan. *The Incorporation of America: Culture and Society in the Gilded Age.* New York: Hill & Wang, 1982.

Trent, William P., et al., eds. *The Cambridge History of American Literature.* 4 vols. New York: G. P. Putnam, 1917–21.

Urgo, Joseph R. *Willa Cather and the Myth of American Migration.* Urbana and Chicago: U of Illinois P, 1995.

Vanderbilt, Kermit. *American Literature and the Academy: The Roots, Growth, and Maturity of a Profession.* Philadelphia: U of Pennsylvania P, 1986.

Van Leer, David. *The Queening of America: Gay Culture in Straight Society.* New York: Routledge, 1995.

Wald, Priscilla. *Constituting Americans: Cultural Anxiety and Narrative Form.* Durham and London: Duke UP, 1995.

Walker, Nancy. *The Disobedient Writer: Women and Narrative Tradition.* Austin: U of Texas P, 1995.

Walters, Suzanna Danuta. "From Here to Queer: Radical Feminism, Postmodernism, and the Lesbian Menace (Or, Why Can't a Woman Be More Like a Fag?)" *Signs* 21.4 (Summer 1996): 830–69.

Warner, Michael, ed. "Introduction." *Fear of a Queer Planet: Queer Politics and Social Theory.* Minneapolis and London: U of Minnesota P, 1993. vii–xxxi.

West, Rebecca. "Miss Cather's Business as an Artist." Review of *Death Comes for the Archbishop,* by Willa Cather. *New York Herald Tribune Books* 11 September 1927: 1+.

Wharton, Edith. *The Age of Innocence*. 1920; New York: Collier, 1992.

——. *A Backward Glance*. 1933; New York: Scribner's, 1985.

——. *The House of Mirth*. 1905; New York: Norton, 1990.

——. *Summer*. 1918; New York: Perennial, 1979.

Wiesenthal, C. Susan. "Female Sexuality in Willa Cather's *O Pioneers!* and the Era of Scientific Sexology: A Dialogue Between Frontiers." *Ariel* 21.1 (1990): 41–63.

Wilcox, Ella Wheeler. *Poems of Passion*. Chicago: Belford, Clarke, 1883.

Wilson, Harold S. McClure's Magazine *and the Muckrakers*. Princeton: Princeton UP, 1970.

Wood, Elizabeth. "Sapphonics." *Queering the Pitch: The New Gay and Lesbian Musicology*. Eds. Philip Brett, Elizabeth Wood, and Gary C. Thomas. New York: Routledge, 1994. 27–66.

Woodress, James. *Willa Cather: A Literary Life*. Lincoln and London: U of Nebraska P, 1987.

Index

Abraham, Julie, 75, 153*n*13, 154*n*19, 158*n*43, 167–68*n*9

Acocella, Joan, 146*n*6

Adams, Timothy Dow, 145*n*14, 157*n*36

Addams, Jane, 50, 51, 53; Cather's comments on, 155*n*24

"America," as a term, 2–4, 77; images of, 34, 62, 78

American Girl, 34; in Cather's fiction, 39, 55, 61

Ammons, Elizabeth, 52, 151*n*5

Assimilationism/anti-assimilationism, in queer activism and critique, 10, 139–40; in Cather's fiction, 47, 55, 67–69, 71–72, 126–32

Austin, Mary: and "American litera-ture," 85, 91, 98, 102, 159*n*2; and Cather, 161*n*18, 168*n*11, 168–69*n*15; on Native American literature, 126, 130

Axtell, James, 116

Banta, Martha, 34

Barney, Natalie, 3

Baym, Nina, 91

Bederman, Gail, 8, 150*n*1, 154*n*22, 157*n*35

Bennett, Mildred, 144*n*8, 149–50*n*20, 150*n*22

Benstock, Shari, 144*n*6

Berlant, Lauren: on Diva Citizenship, 54–55, 59; on Queer Nationality (with Elizabeth Freeman), 150*n*2; on Queer Theory (with Michael Warner), 139

Bérubé, Allan, 170*n*6

Bohemianism, 8; in Cather's life, 30, 156*n*29, 156*n*30; in *MÁ*, 64–69, 78

Boone, Joseph A., 167*n*5

Bronfen, Elisabeth, 153*n*14

Brooks, Peter, 33, 152*n*10, 153*n*14

Bruccoli, Matthew J., 145*n*17

Burroughs, John, 160*n*13

Butler, Judith, 145*n*16, 153*n*17; on Cather, 8, 18, 62; on performativ-ity, 31, 148*n*14; on "queer," 47, 143*n*1, 153*n*18

Cambridge History of American Literature, 91, 98, 159*n*2

Carafiol, Peter, 85, 160*n*4

Carlin, Deborah, 35, 140, 150*n*4, 170*n*5

Case, Sue-Ellen, 123, 124

Castle, Terry, 155*n*25

Cather, Willa, *see also names of individ-ual writers and themes with important connections to Cather*; and Houghton Mifflin, 69, 86–90, 95; and Knopf, 69, 86–90, 95; and les-bianism, 19–20, 149*n*17, 149–50*n*20; and the queer, 1–4, 12–13, 20–24, 30, 35–36, 46–47, 54,

BETWEEN MEN ~ BETWEEN WOMEN
Lesbian and Gay Studies
Lillian Faderman and Larry Gross, Editors